DYNAMIC INSTRUCTIONAL LEADERSHIP

to Support
Student Learning
and Development

Comer Schools in Action
The 3-Volume Field Guide
Edward T. Joyner, James P. Comer, and Michael Ben-Avie, Editors

---

Six Pathways
to Healthy Child Development and Academic Success:
The Field Guide to Comer Schools in Action
James P. Comer, Edward T. Joyner, and Michael Ben-Avie, Editors

Transforming School Leadership and Management
to Support Student Learning and Development:
The Field Guide to Comer Schools in Action
Edward T. Joyner, Michael Ben-Avie, and James P. Comer, Editors

Dynamic Instructional Leadership
to Support Student Learning and Development:
The Field Guide to Comer Schools in Action
Edward T. Joyner, Michael Ben-Avie, and James P. Comer, Editors

Edward T. Joyner, Michael Ben-Avie, and James P. Comer, Editors

DYNAMIC INSTRUCTIONAL LEADERSHIP

to Support Student Learning and Development

The Field Guide to Comer Schools in Action

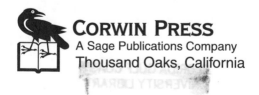

CORWIN PRESS
A Sage Publications Company
Thousand Oaks, California

For information:

Corwin Press, Inc.
A Sage Publications Company
2455 Teller Road
Thousand Oaks, California 91320
www.corwinpress.com

Sage Publications Ltd.
1 Oliver's Yard
55 City Road
London EC1Y 1SP
United Kingdom

Sage Publications India Pvt. Ltd.
B-42, Panchsheel Enclave
Post Box 4109
New Delhi 110 017 India

Printed in the United States of America

Library of Congress Cataloging-in-Publication Data

Dynamic instructional leadership to support student learning and development:The field guide to Comer schools in action / [edited] by Edward T. Joyner, Michael Ben-Avie, James P. Comer.
    p. cm.—(Comer schools in action)
Includes bibliographical references and index.
    ISBN 1-4129-0512-5 (cloth)—ISBN 1-4129-0513-3 (pbk.)
    1. Yale School Development Program. 2. Child development—United States.
3. Community and school—United States. I. Joyner, Edward T. II. Ben-Avie, Michael.
III. Comer, James P. IV. Series.
LB1117.D96 2004
305.231—dc22   2004007196

This book is printed on acid-free paper.

Acquisitions Editor:	Faye Zucker
Editorial Assistant:	Stacy Wagner
Production Editors:	Kate Peterson and Diana Axelsen
Copy Editor:	Carla Freeman
Typesetter:	C&M Digitals (P) Ltd.
Indexer:	David Luljak
Cover Designer:	Michael Dubowe
Figure Illustrator:	Mark Saba, Med Media Group, Yale University School of Medicine

For Donald J. Cohen, M.D.
Director, Yale Child Study Center, 1983–2001

Contents

Foreword

James Comer and colleagues at the Yale School Development Program (SDP) have made an enormous difference in schools and school districts across the country over the past three decades. There is a wealth of knowledge, insight, strategies, and lessons contained within the range of experiences of SDP parents, community members, students, teachers, staff, principals, districts, and other leaders. The beauty of the *Comer Schools in Action* set is that its three volumes have now given us access to this wealth of knowledge and ideas in one place. This collection is of inestimable value.

The first book lays the foundation: child development = education. *Six Pathways to Healthy Child Development and Academic Success* establishes the mission and vision. What we have here is a fundamental agenda for social reform.

Dynamic Instructional Leadership to Support Student Learning and Development then shows the Comer Process in action, making it clear that we are talking about systemic reform. The elements of reform are clearly set forth: the role of schools and districts, the need for integrated planning and curriculum, the careful focus on implementation, how teamwork drives and sustains change, how school-university partnerships can be developed, and how assertive achievement-oriented leadership at the school and district levels is a system responsibility.

The third book, *Transforming School Leadership and Management to Support Student Learning and Development*, represents a complete guide for how to introduce and carry out the Comer Process. It shows us what is involved in making initial decisions, how to proceed through six essential steps in the planning process, and how to start and continue assessment and monitoring. All the key relationships are addressed, both inside and outside the school. An important chapter sets out the SDP implementation cycle chronologically, taking us through timelines and activities for planning, foundation building, transformation, institutionalization, and renewal.

All in all, the *Comer Schools in Action* trilogy gives us the entire essence of Comer's success and the lessons learned along the way. It is theoretical, practical, and filled with ideas and guidelines for action that integrate theory and practice. The Comer trilogy is a landmark contribution to the field of educational change.

—Michael Fullan
University of Toronto

Preface

This field guide and its two companion books in the *Comer Schools in Action: The 3-Volume Field Guide* are reflective of the wisdom of Dr. James P. Comer, of the staff at the Yale School Development Program (SDP), and of all the people in the hundreds of schools in communities throughout the United States and abroad who have embraced the Comer Schools movement. This volume is the collective representation of what we have learned from parents, children, teachers, administrators, community leaders, politicians, college professors, clergy, and members of the helping professions.

Because we believe that the practitioner is an expert, we have included the voices of people in the field as well as those in the ivory tower. We are all scholar-activists, and when we combine our efforts, pool our knowledge, and achieve one accord on what we want for our children, we cannot be defeated. We can create schools and communities that foster the development of ethical behavior in young people and challenge them to high academic standards.

Enough data have been collected and analyzed by some of our best education researchers to demonstrate that SDP is tried, tested, and true and that its effectiveness as a comprehensive school reform model meets "the highest standard of evidence" (Borman, Hewes, Overman, & Brown, 2003). This field guide will help you see the program through the eyes of the people who have made it work, as well as the people who designed it and continue to refine it.

This field guide is based on and expanded from training materials that we have field tested for decades. It is the first commercially published field guide by our organization. Because we are constantly searching for more ways to help children and the people who serve them, it will not be the last.

—Edward T. Joyner, Ed.D.
Executive Director, School Development Program

REFERENCE

Borman, G. D., Hewes, G. M., Overman, L. T., & Brown, S. (2003). Comprehensive school reform and student achievement: A meta-analysis. *Review of Educational Research, 73*(2), 125–230.

Acknowledgments

The Yale School Development Program has been acknowledging instructional excellence since 1993 through its Patrick Francis Daly Memorial Award for Excellence in Educational Leadership. The Patrick Francis Daly Memorial Award is made annually to Comer school principals who have demonstrated outstanding leadership and commitment to children.

In his many years of service to the students of P.S. 15 in Brooklyn, New York, Patrick Francis Daly displayed the highest ideals of the school principalship. His commitment to the values inherent in the Comer Process earned him the admiration of his colleagues and the affection of the community of Red Hook that entrusted their children to his care.

On December 17, 1992, Patrick Francis Daly lost his life while going to the aid of a child. His legacy to his friends, fellow educators, and students includes the powerful idea that a school exists first and foremost to support the development of every child within it.

We wish to honor the 1993–2002 recipients of the Patrick Francis Daly Memorial Award for Excellence in Educational Leadership by listing their names here:

Malcolm Adler
Susan Allen
Dr. Lane S. Anderson III
Debra G. Barham
Gary Bartee
Dr. Ruth L. Baskerville
Antoinette L. Boissiere
Michael T. Bracy
Patricia Brandenberg
Alford Bridges
Alexander Brown
Jean Burwell
Marilee Bylsma
Richard Cansdale
Martha Carpenter
Dr. Julio Carrera
Dr. Herman D. Clark Jr.
John Cooke
Katherine Corbett
Joan Dameron Crisler

Rodger Cunningham
Patrick Francis Daly
Doris Davis
Patricia DeRenzo
Gloria Dingwall
Yvette Douglass
Brian Fitz-Harris
Lynn Foes
Jeffery F. German
Connie Gibb
Dr. Felicia D. Gil
Robert Golden
Elizabeth Goldiner
Carmen Gonzalez
Susan Greenberg
Dr. Carole A. Gupton
Gilbert Gutierrez
Marlene A. Guy
Dr. Gloria Hagopian
Catherine Hammond

Alan L. Harris

Maurice Harvey

Gandy A. Heaston

Dr. Fred Hernandez

Joyce Herron-Taylor

Doris Hicks

Edward Jefferson

Dr. Deborah Jones

Deborah Knight

Olga La Luz

Dr. Regina Lilly-Warner

Mary Manti

Carolyn McCalla

Dr. David McCalla

Richie Barber McDaneld

Sharon McElfish

Donna Cox Morrison

Lola Nathan

Dr. Grace Nebb

Edna Negron

William Ryan

Pamela Sanders-White

Dr. Nancy R. Shannon

Dr. Paul Stephenson

Verlene Tatum

Margie Thompson

Ann Van Sickle

Princess Dupont Whitfield

Dr. Lloyd G. Wimberley Jr.

Robyn Zgorski-Clifton

Beverly Crowther and Linda Brouard contributed to the clarity of the text of the three volumes in this collection. We only hope that they regain the clarity of their vision in time for the next book.

Publisher's Acknowledgments

Corwin Press extends its thanks to the following reviewers for their contributions to this work:

Michelle Barnea, Educational Consultant, Millburn, NJ

Dominic Belmonte, Golden Apple Foundation for Excellence in Teaching, Chicago, IL

Jo Ann Canales, Texas A & M University, Corpus Christi, TX

Robert Ricken, Educational Consultant, Lido Beach, NY

Mary M. Williams, University of San Diego, CA

About the Authors

Shontese Ash was a student member of the Comer Club of P.S. 138 in Brooklyn, New York, during the 2002–2003 school year.

Fatoumata Bah was a student member of the Comer Club of P.S. 138 in Brooklyn, New York, during the 2002–2003 school year.

Roma Begum was a student member of the Comer Club of P.S. 138 in Brooklyn, New York, during the 2002–2003 school year.

Michael Ben-Avie, Ph.D., directs the Impact Analysis and Strategies Group, which studies corporate, nonprofit, and government partnerships that promote youth development and student learning. He conducts national studies designed to evaluate the effectiveness of mentoring programs and psychological interventions on children's lifepaths. Dr. Ben-Avie has coedited books about the Yale School Development Program with James P. Comer, M.D., and colleagues and has published numerous book chapters, articles, and reports on educational change initiatives, high schools, parent involvement, and the relationship between youth development and student learning.

Kaleel Bethel was a student member of the Comer Club of P.S. 138 in Brooklyn, New York, during the 2002–2003 school year.

Fay E. Brown, Ph.D., is an associate research scientist at the Yale Child Study Center. She is the director of Child and Adolescent Development and the director of the Essentials of Literacy Process for the School Development Program. Her major focus is to help schools create and maintain developmentally appropriate conditions to ensure the holistic development of every child.

Aomi Castro was a student member of the Comer Club of P.S. 138 in Brooklyn, New York, during the 2002–2003 school year.

Marie Chauvet-Monchik is principal of P.S. 138, The Core Knowledge/Efficacy School, in Brooklyn, New York. She holds M.A. degrees in elementary education and in reading as well as a professional degree in administration. She began administering the Comer Process as an assistant principal at P.S. 138 in 1994. Her motto is "Educate to Elevate."

Constance R. Clark, Ed.D., educator and advocate for children, has served in the capacities of teacher, principal, associate superintendent, and deputy superintendent, District of Columbia Public Schools. Currently, she is superintendent of the Westbury School District, Westbury, Long Island. She has a B.A. degree from Spelman College in psychology and elementary education, an M.A. from Howard University in administration and supervision, and a Ph.D. in administration and higher education from George Washington University. She has received the

Outstanding Principal Award for Educational Leadership from the D.C. Public Schools; when she was principal of Smothers Elementary School the school received recognition as a U.S. Department of Education School of Excellence; and most recently, she was named Educator of the Year from Phi Delta Kappa International of Hofstra University and received the Superintendent's Award from the National Council of Negro Women.

James P. Comer, M.D., is the founder and chairman of the Yale School Development Program, Maurice Falk Professor of Child Psychiatry at the Yale Child Study Center, and Associate Dean of the Yale University School of Medicine. He has published seven books, more than 35 chapters, over 400 articles in popular journals, and more than 100 articles in professional journals. He has served as a consultant, committee member, advisory board member, and trustee to numerous local, national, and international organizations serving children and youth. Dr. Comer has been the recipient of the John and Mary Markle Scholar in Academic Medicine Award, the Rockefeller Public Service Award, the Harold W. McGraw, Jr. Prize in Education, the Charles A. Dana Award for Pioneering Achievement in Education, the Heinz Award for Service to Humanity, and many other awards and honors, including 41 honorary degrees.

Camille J. Cooper, former public school administrator, currently serves as director of the Teaching, Learning, and Development Unit of the School Development Program of the Child Study Center at the Yale University Medical School.

Christine L. Emmons, Ph.D., is director of program evaluation at the School Development Program. Her research focuses on the impact of the environment on the development of children.

Everol Ennis, M.Ed., is a School Development Program implementation coordinator with a background in counseling psychology. He serves as the intake coordinator for SDP and is the director of the Youth Development Unit, which oversees the Comer Kids' Leadership Academy. He is interested in issues relating to effective teaming and problem solving. In addition, he is involved in various community and civic organizations whose goals are to impact the lives of youths.

Kyosha Pierre Francois was a student member of the Comer Club of P.S. 138 in Brooklyn, New York, during the 2002–2003 school year.

Anthony Geathers was a student member of the Comer Club of P.S. 138 in Brooklyn, New York, during the 2002–2003 school year.

Alice Huff Hart, Ed.D., recently retired as associate superintendent for curriculum and instruction for Asheville City Schools. During her 37 years as an educator, she received numerous awards, including 1985 North Carolina Principal of the Year. She designed and edited a book, *Journeys in Education Leadership,* which contains essays on leadership by 17 North Carolina Principals of the Year. In 1997, she wrote *Seminar Teaching: Five Case Studies* for the Principals' Executive Program in Chapel Hill, North Carolina.

J. Patrick Howley, C.A.G.S., is the director of Teachers Helping Teachers and an implementation coordinator who specializes in human relations work such as team building, communication, and conflict resolution. He has been with the School Development Program for 13 years.

Garrick Jeffers was a student member of the Comer Club of P.S. 138 in Brooklyn, New York, during the 2002–2003 school year.

Edward T. Joyner, Ed.D., is the executive director of the Yale School Development Program. He served as SDP's first director of training, was the original designer of the SDP leadership development academies, and initiated university-public school partnerships to strengthen local school reform efforts. He is the architect of SDP's systemic initiative, which coordinates the work of the school board, central office, building staff, and the larger school community to create an optimal environment for teaching and learning throughout the school district. He currently oversees all of the operations of SDP and serves as the lead implementation coordinator for New York.

Dawn Kelley has been a Comer facilitator at Mott School in Trenton, New Jersey, for three years. In 1995, she was named Elementary Teacher of the Year by the New Jersey Education Association.

M. Ann Levett-Lowe, Ed.D., is deputy director of the School Development Program, responsible for program operations and professional development. She has served at every level in urban school districts, from special education teacher to superintendent, and has a special interest and extensive experience in leadership development.

April Lynch was a student member of the Comer Club of P.S. 138 in Brooklyn, New York, during the 2002–2003 school year.

Valerie Maholmes, Ph.D., has worked at the School Development Program for 10 years and is currently director of research and policy. Her areas of interest include examining the impact of school and classroom context on teachers' and students' sense of efficacy. She has served on the Board of Education for New Haven Public Schools and as chair of its Curriculum Committee.

Miriam McLaughlin is an implementation coordinator for the School Development Program in North Carolina and South Carolina. Her areas of specialization include resiliency, parent involvement, and working with groups. She is the coauthor of a number of books and articles on health and education processes.

Angelina Mezier was a student member of the Comer Club of P.S. 138 in Brooklyn, New York, during the 2002–2003 school year.

Tiki Morris was a student member of the Comer Club of P.S. 138 in Brooklyn, New York, during the 2002–2003 school year.

Keshia M. G. Pitt was a student member of the Comer Club of P.S. 138 in Brooklyn, New York, during the 2002–2003 school year.

Carol Pickett Ray is principal of Claxton Elementary School and former principal of Hall Fletcher Elementary School, both in Asheville, North Carolina. In 2002, she was selected as North Carolina's Western Regional Principal of the Year and was a recipient of ASCD's Lighthouse Award while she was principal of Hall Fletcher Elementary School.

Francis Roberts, Ed.D., is professor of education at C. W. Post Campus of Long Island University. He has been a schoolteacher, college professor, high school principal, superintendent of schools, and president of the Bank Street College of Education.

Christina Simpkins was a student member of the Comer Club of P.S. 138 in Brooklyn, New York, during the 2002–2003 school year.

William Steve Stone, Ed.D., is superintendent of the Edgecombe County public school system in Tarboro, North Carolina. He is actively involved in a variety of programs related to children and the communities that support them.

David A. Squires, Ph.D., is an associate professor in the Department of Educational Leadership at Southern Connecticut State University. His specialty areas are curriculum, school reform, learning organizations and organizational culture, and leadership. He is the author of *Aligning and Balancing the Standards-Based Curriculum* (Corwin Press, 2004).

Clint Thierens was a student member of the Comer Club of P.S. 138 in Brooklyn, New York, during the 2002–2003 school year.

Kenita Williams was a student member of the Comer Club of P.S. 138 in Brooklyn, New York, during the 2002–2003 school year.

Colin Wood was a student member of the Comer Club of P.S. 138 in Brooklyn, New York, during the 2002–2003 school year.

The Comer Process

Tried, Tested, and True

Edward T. Joyner

The Comer Process is both a structure and a process for K–12 education systems to support young people's academic learning and personal development. Recognizing that no child can perform well academically if he or she is hungry or has never been read to, the Comer Process trains and supports all stakeholders in taking care of the negative forces in each child's life, and in replacing those forces with positive ones to enable each child to develop well and, therefore, learn well. With more than 35 years of success behind us, we know our process is tried, tested, and true.

THE INFLUENCE OF ADULTS ON CHILDREN: A RECOLLECTION

I can remember very vividly my anticipation of the first day of school in the little rural, southern community where I was raised. It appeared to me that every adult in town knew that a fresh crop of children, or "chirrens" (to use my beloved Black southern dialect), were getting ready to go to school for the first time. This was an important event in Farmville, North Carolina, and I remember being so anxious the night before—wondering if I would be able to do the school work, as well as keep away from the dreaded paddle that was standard equipment in most of the elementary classrooms of my time. As I walked outside on that warm August morning in my mail-order dungarees, white T-shirt, and "tennis shoes," I knew that I was about to embark on a journey that had the potential to change my life forever.

We lived in a rented A-frame house with one bedroom, outdoor restroom facilities, and an outside faucet that was shared with two other families. Both my parents had said that they wanted all their children to have better lives than they, even as they were thankful for what little they were able to accumulate. They had 10 years of education between them but wanted all their children to get at least a high school diploma as well as aspire to go on to college.

It was unanimous in our community that education and good manners were the appropriate choice of weapons in a world that doubted the worth and potential of children who were poor and, in our case, Black. In a community like the one that shaped my values and aspirations, schools, communities, and religious institutions spoke from a common script.

My school's principal, Mr. Frances Howard Mebane, was an imposing figure in our community. He was built like a linebacker, dressed immaculately, spoke with great eloquence, and could recite, verbatim, verses from Paul Laurence Dunbar to William Shakespeare. He created a school that was an extension of our families, and I can never remember him using corporal punishment, even though it was permissible by law at that time. When we acted inappropriately, he would constantly remind us in his deep baritone voice: "You are better than that."

This phrase became a part of me, because I realized that we children were the hopes of our parents, teachers, and community. They believed that we were better than the dirt roads, outdoor plumbing, and unpainted houses in which we were born. They believed that a passion for learning and strong feelings of self-worth would see us through the most difficult times.

The adults in our little village made us believe that we could overcome. They told us that "nothing beats a failure but a try," and that "trouble don't last always." So even at a time of limited opportunity, we had a supply of unlimited hope. We realized that we were born behind in the race of life and had to run faster (according to the late and great Benjamin E. Mays, past president of Morehouse College). This story from my childhood is an example of the power of the public school. But it also speaks to the power of the community to work with the school to ensure that children are taught well and fully developed. This web of relationships among school and community created the safety net that protected my generation from the hostile forces around us.

THE INFLUENCE OF PUBLIC EDUCATION ON SOCIETY

The founders of our great nation recognized that universal, free public education was the cornerstone of democracy. Our early public schools were shaped by the collective wisdom that emerged from a powerful coalition of forces representing the family, the church, and the community. This coalition allowed schools to transform our nation's youth into fully contributing citizens, thereby enabling the United States to become the most powerful nation in human history. The American public school stands as one of the most accomplished social institutions created by our social democracy. It has contributed mightily to the democratic ideal of *E Pluribus Unum*—out of the many, one—by providing a common arena in which the sons and daughters of slaves, immigrants, and Native Americans could teach together, learn together, play together, and continue to build a society based on justice, fairness, and equality of opportunity. While it has never been a perfect institution, our public education system has paved the way for countless students who, under other circumstances, might have remained poor and uneducated. It also has unified this nation around a common core of ideas and has become the place where people who came to our shores willingly and unwillingly could contribute to the great mosaic known as American culture.

Our notion of education for the common good was conceived and carried out by schools and communities that spoke with a common tongue about what they wanted young people to learn and how they expected them to behave. There was near-unanimous agreement among adults regarding the values that they wanted to pass on to children and the content and skills that schools should deem necessary for work, play, and civic responsibility.

THE INFLUENCE OF JAMES COMER ON PUBLIC EDUCATION

Over the past three decades, Dr. James P. Comer has refused to let us forget that the work of schools is both the education and development of children. He has demonstrated that successful development requires good science and the best ideas from multiple disciplines. This is necessary to create a structure and a process to help schools prepare students to learn and prosper in a world that has become smaller and increasingly unpredictable. He has recognized, above all, that the American public school is the salvation for our nation and its youth. It is as vital to national security and world peace as our military because it is the central unifying and transformative institution in our culture. At its best, it has served countless children even when their families have failed them.

James Comer, who was born into a low-income family only two generations out of slavery, is a grateful beneficiary of this venerable institution. He has always made public his gratitude for the education that transformed his family's destiny and for his professional training as a child psychiatrist. He has dedicated his life to helping schools and communities develop the capacity to protect and widen the aspirations of children, especially those born into difficult circumstances. By virtue of his status as an academic and as one who has traveled the roads these children must travel, he knows the journey they must take to be successful in work and as citizens.

In all these years, Comer has not wavered in this magnificent obsession. Yet he recognizes that today's schools may face even more difficult challenges because of what he refers to as "troublesome changes in American culture and high technology devoid of high human contact." I agree with my mentor, and believe that the greatest threat to our culture is the social distance between children and adults at all socioeconomic levels. I grew up in a safer and more predictable world than did my own children. We must factor this into our thinking when we talk about what we want our schools to be.

CHILDREN AT RISK IN CONTEMPORARY AMERICA

We are faced today with a generation of young people of all racial and economic backgrounds who are growing up without the concerted support that many of the children in my generation received. Marian Wright Edelman (1992), the president of the Children's Defense Fund, captures the plight of contemporary youth when she states,

> Too many young people—of all colors, of all walks of life—are growing up today unable to handle life in hard places, without hope, without adequate attention, and without steady internal compasses to navigate the morally polluted seas they must face on the journey to adulthood. Millions of children are drowning in the meaninglessness of a culture that rewards greed and tells them that life is about getting rather than giving. (p. 15)

Many indicators clearly support Edelman's point. The increasingly violent nature of our society graphically illustrates that we are a nation in rapid moral decline. Growing up in a violent environment puts young people at risk. According to Mary Schwab-Stone, a pediatrician at the Yale Child Study Center, exposure to violence is associated with more antisocial activities, with alcohol use, with lower social achievement, with less perceived harm from engaging in risky behaviors, and with more willingness to fight. She further reports that more than 55 percent of the 8th and 10th graders surveyed in a midsize New England city reported that they had engaged in sexual intercourse. These students were 4.4 times more likely to drop out than students who reported no sexual activity. National figures indicate that there have been more than 1 million teenage pregnancies a year since 1983. The infection of approximately 2.5 million adolescents annually with sexually transmitted diseases is a by-product of such frequently unprotected sexual activity (Schwab-Stone, 1995).

The troubling statistics among our young are directly related to two factors: (1) the failure of adults to provide positive models worthy of emulation, and (2) a fragmented effort by the caregivers who share the responsibility for working together to create standards of behavior that encourage youth to behave in ways acceptable to the larger society of responsible citizens. Comer has not only been saying this for more than three decades but has also created a national and international organization that has shown hundreds of schools in communities across the United States and abroad how to repair the damage. He has taught us that schools working with families and communities can play a major role in changing the disturbing trends that presently characterize American society. We can teach our young people how to behave in constructive ways, and we can get them to perform at high levels within the classroom, but we must begin by providing better examples for our children and by supporting standards of behavior based on moral principles of justice, fairness, and a sense of responsibility for self and others. The African proverb "It takes a whole village to raise a child" effectively captures the breadth and depth of the work that has already been done and must continue to be done.

WHO ARE THE ROLE MODELS, AND WHAT EXAMPLES ARE THEY SETTING?

Implicit in the saying "It takes a whole village to raise a child" is our recognition that children learn well and develop well when all their adult guides demonstrate the highest shared values of the community. In the United States, that includes agreeing on the content and skills that children must learn in order to continue the work of American democracy. While this requires more effort today than in the past, Comer has taught us that teachers, parents, community members, policymakers, and college professors must continually engage in a conversation about mission. What kind of schools do we want for our children? What kind of behaviors—academic, social, and moral—do we want from our children? What examples must we set to guide them? This kind of conversation is fundamental to the development of what Ted Sizer (1992) refers to as "habits of heart and habits of mind."

We know that the quality of the relationships between children and the adults whom they deem to be significant can result in anything from building up to practically destroying a child's character. James (1890), Cooley (1902), and Mead (1934), agreed in principle that those with whom the individual identifies and who are important to him or her have the greatest potential for influencing that person's behavior. It follows that parents, teachers, and other school personnel significantly influence children's behavior. Children are socially anchored in their families and immediate communities. It is essential, therefore, that schools initiate structures and processes that enable them to collaborate with families and community groups to create a common set of values, principles, and expectations for students. Once critical stakeholders can agree on these, it becomes easier to create the programs and activities that provide the necessary experiences for students to develop their character and intellect.

Conflict or ambiguity among home, school, and community is likely to trigger inner conflict as children move back and forth among the social systems and attempt to assume the various roles required of them in each one. In contrast, when home, school, and community agree on the values and behaviors to be transmitted, children function better in all three contexts.

Comer has developed a structure and a process for all levels of our K–12 education system that supports young people's academic learning and personal development. He has developed a governance and planning process that uses systems theory and child development knowledge to create a "whole-village mentality" among stakeholders at the central office, school, family, and community levels.

DEVELOPMENTAL PATHWAYS AND THE WHOLE CHILD

Comer has identified six pathways that should serve (1) as a framework for analysis when assessing child and adolescent growth and development and (2) as focal points for activities and programs designed to facilitate that development. These pathways are physical, cognitive, psychological, language, social, and ethical. Taken together, they constitute what we refer to as the "whole child." Optimum development is a function of balance and synergy throughout a child's physical, cognitive, psychological, language, social, and ethical self (see Figure 1.1).

At the School Development Program (SDP), we train and support all our participating educators, parents, and community members so that they truly can have patience with development. An acorn does not become an oak tree overnight. Some children are born in very, very hard places, and that temporarily disrupts their development. It is the responsibility of the schools to engage in coalitions with parents

Figure 1.1 An acorn does not become an oak tree overnight

NOTE: A glossy color poster of this figure (11" × 17") for classroom use is available from www.comerprocess.org.

and community people to help these children. After all, the children do not have genetic deficits; they have *experience* deficits. No child will perform well academically if he or she is hungry or has never been read to. It's our responsibility as adults to work collectively to sweep away the negative forces in each child's life, to replace those forces with positive ones, and to be patient enough for the child to bloom.

REFERENCES

Borman, G. D., Hewes, G. M., Overman, L. T., & Brown, S. (2003). Comprehensive school reform and student achievement: A meta-analysis. *Review of Educational Research, 73*(2), 125–230.

Cooley, C. (1902). *Human nature and the social order.* New York: Scribner.

Edelman, M. W. (1992). *The measure of our success: A letter to my children and yours.* Boston: Beacon Press.

James, W. (1890). *The principles of psychology.* Cambridge, MA: Harvard University Press.

Mead, G. H. (1934). *Mind, self, and society.* Chicago: University of Chicago Press.

Schwab-Stone, M. (1995). No safe haven: A study of violence exposure in an urban community. *Journal of the American Academy of Child and Adolescent Psychiatry, 34*(10), 1343–1352.

Sizer, T. (1992). *Horace's school: Redesigning the American high school.* Boston: Houghton Mifflin.

2

Essential Understandings of the Yale School Development Program

Yale School Development Program Staff

The comprehensive school reform model known as the Comer Process, or Yale University School Development Program (SDP), was established in 1968 as a collaborative effort between New Haven Public Schools and the Yale Child Study Center, an academic research center dedicated to furthering the well-being of children through a clearer understanding of their psychology and growth. More than three decades of research demonstrate that full implementation of the Comer Process leads to high levels of student achievement and development, and that the Comer Process meets the highest standard of evidence of effectiveness. This chapter provides a brief reference guide to the Comer Process.

SDP AND THE COMER PROCESS

The Yale University School Development Program (SDP) is the forerunner of all modern school reform efforts in the United States. In 1968, a Yale Child Study

Center team that was led by James P. Comer, M.D., intervened in two public schools. The team consisted of a social worker, psychologist, special education teacher, and child psychiatrist. The operating system for schools that emerged during those early years in New Haven schools is today fondly known as the Comer Process.

The Comer Process is an educational change initiative based on the principles of child, adolescent, and adult development. It mobilizes teachers, administrators, parents, and other concerned adults to support students' personal, social, and academic growth. It also helps them make better programmatic and curriculum decisions based on students' needs and on developmental principles. The Comer Process is not a project or add-on, but rather an operating system—a way of managing, organizing, coordinating, and integrating activities. SDP practices considered highly controversial in 1969—whole-school change, school-based management, strong parental involvement in decision making, and teacher study groups—are now common in schools throughout the country.

Over the past three decades, our research and the research of others cited throughout this field guide have consistently found that schools that implement the Comer Process at high levels tend to experience high levels of student achievement and development. In general, schools that demonstrate high levels of implementation are those in which adults

- behave in a way that embodies the Comer Process and mind-set
- demonstrate flexibility and expertise in change management
- relate knowledge of child and youth development to student learning
- make decisions that are in the best interests of children

SIX DEVELOPMENTAL PATHWAYS

Of all the prominent educational reformers, only James P. Comer talks about healthy child development as the keystone to academic achievement and life success. Comer uses a metaphor of six developmental pathways to characterize the lines along which children and adolescents mature—physical, cognitive, psychological, language, social, and ethical (see Figure 2.1). In schools using the Comer Process, far more is expected from the students than just cognitive development.

SDP believes that development is the foundation for all learning:

- Child rearing, child development, and learning are inextricably linked.
- Development starts early and must be a continuous process.
- Children's most meaningful learning occurs through positive and supportive relationships with caring and nurturing adults.
- Parents are children's first teachers.
- All parents, staff, and community members, regardless of social or economic status, have an important contribution to make in improving students' education and their preparation for life; therefore, adults must interact collaboratively and sensitively with one another in order to bring out the best in children.

Figure 2.1 The developmental pathways panel

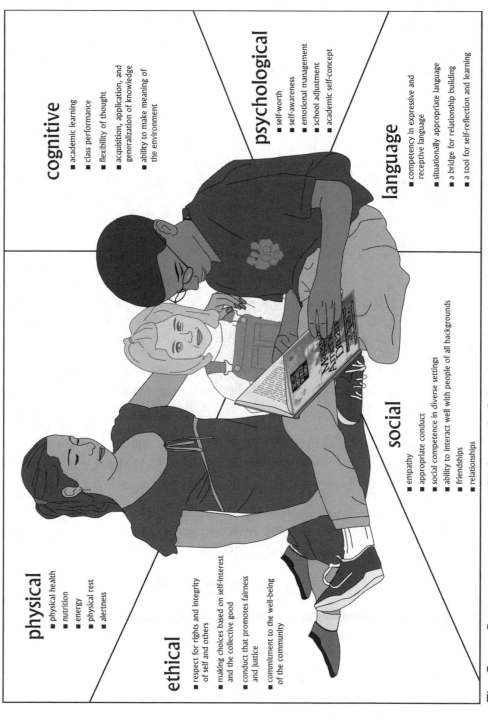

The Comer Process promotes growth along all of the six pathways critical to children's learning and development.

SDP is committed to the total development of children and adolescents by helping parents, educators, and policymakers create learning environments that support children's development along the critical pathways. Children who develop well, learn well. Our vision is to help create a just and fair society in which all children have the support for development that will allow them to become positive and successful contributors in family, work, and civic life.

AN OPERATING SYSTEM

The Comer Process provides a structure as well as a process for mobilizing adults to support students' learning and overall development. It is a different way of conceptualizing and working in schools, and it replaces traditional school organization and management with an operating system that works for schools and the students they serve. The schoolhouse graphic in Figures 2.2 and 2.3 displays the nine basic elements of the system.

The following three teams are the hallmark of the Comer Process:

- **School Planning and Management Team:** The SPMT develops a comprehensive school plan; sets academic, social, and community relations goals; and coordinates all school activities, including staff development programs. The team creates critical dialogue around teaching and learning and monitors progress to identify needed adjustments to the school plan as well as opportunities to support the plan. Members of the team include administrators, teachers, support staff, and parents.
- **Student and Staff Support Team:** The SSST promotes desirable social conditions and relationships. It connects all of the school's student services, facilitates the sharing of information and advice, addresses individual student needs, accesses resources outside the school, and develops prevention programs. Membership includes individuals in the school community who possess specialized knowledge, training, or expertise in mental health or child and adolescent development theory and practice.
- **Parent Team:** The PT involves parents in the school by developing activities through which the parents can support the school's social and academic programs. Composed of parents, this team also selects representatives to serve on the School Planning and Management Team.

All three teams operate under three Guiding Principles:

- **No-fault:** No-fault maintains the focus on problem solving rather than placing blame. No-fault does not mean no-accountability. It means *everyone* becomes accountable.
- **Consensus:** Through dialogue and understanding, this decision-making process builds consensus about what is good for children and adolescents. All go with what most think will work—understanding that if it doesn't work, other ideas will be tried.
- **Collaboration:** Collaboration encourages the principal and teams to work together. All agree not to "roadblock" the principal, who has legal responsibility; the principal agrees to be responsive to all members.

Figure 2.2 Schoolhouse model of the Comer Process

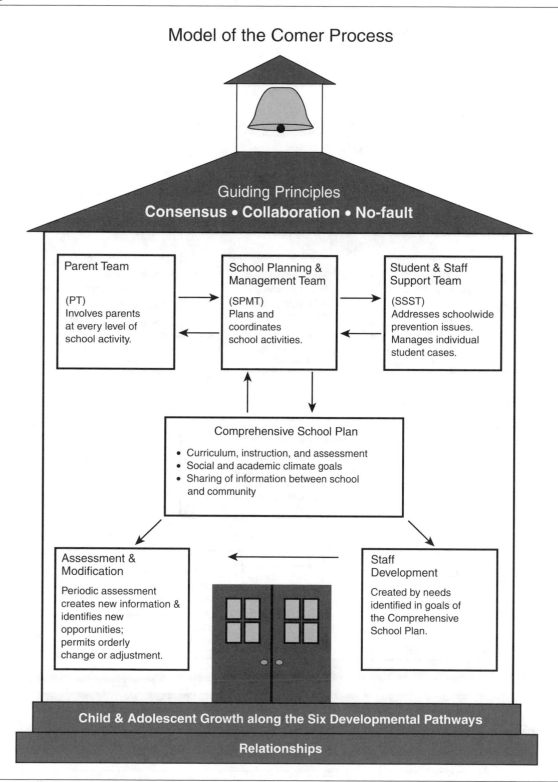

Figure 2.3 Programa de desarrollo escolar

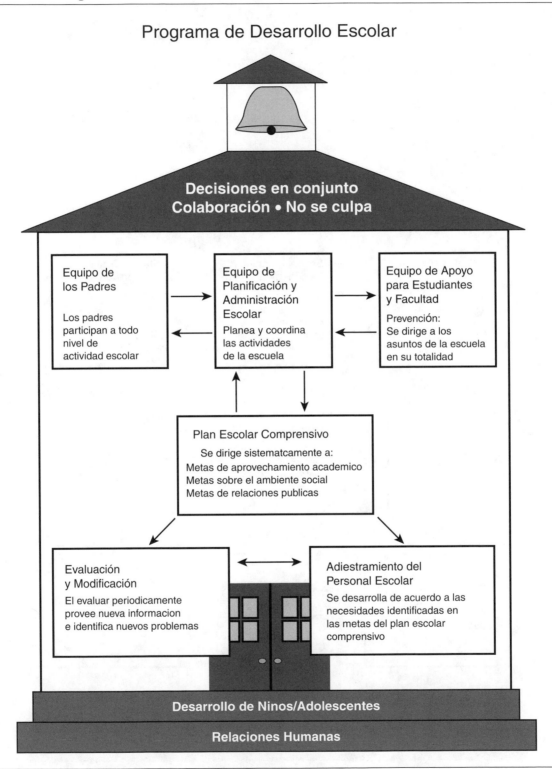

Programa de Desarrollo Escolar

Central to their work are the following three school operations, which are supervised by the School Planning and Management Team:

- **Comprehensive School Plan:** This planning process includes curriculum, instruction, and assessment, as well as social and academic climate goals based on a developmental understanding of students.
- **Staff Development:** Staff development is aligned with the goals of the Comprehensive School Plan; teachers become alert to their own professional development needs and take the lead in designing their own continuing education.
- **Assessment & Modification:** This operation provides new information and identifies new opportunities for support, based on the data of the school's population; data are used to modify the school plan as necessary, thus ensuring that the school is continuously improving its operations.

A school is permitted to call itself "a fully certified SDP school" only after it has completed the full five-year SDP Implementation Life Cycle (see Chapter 18 in *Transforming School Leadership and Management to Support Student Learning and Development*) and the administrators and major teams have met specific behavioral requirements as well as demonstrated excellent knowledge of SDP's approach. Before that time, other labels should be used, for example, "a school in the SDP training program" or "a school in the 1st year (at the 1st stage) of SDP training/implementation."

> For more information on how to become a member of the SDP network, please see our Web site, www.comerprocess.org.

Figure 2.4 School Development Program highlights

- Introduced in 1968 as a process for comprehensive school improvement
- Founded on principles of child development, social relationship theory, and public health
- Nine-element process that fosters positive school climate and creates optimal conditions for teaching and learning
- Not a project or add-on, but a way of managing, organizing, coordinating, and integrating activities
- Provides a strategy for data-driven decision making
- Emphasizes the alignment of curriculum, instruction, and assessment
- Provides schools, districts, and other partners with a framework for communicating and planning to improve conditions for children
- Provides continual support through facilitators and ongoing trainings for adult development as well as child and youth development
- When faithfully and fully implemented, produces extraordinary academic, social, and emotional benefits for the students

THIS FIELD GUIDE

Some members of the school community have a need to approach SDP through a deep understanding of its intellectual foundations. Others need to encounter powerful narratives of how schools improved. Some need to see detailed guidance on what, specifically, they need to do in the classroom. Others need to see how their specialized area fits under SDP's "umbrella." Thus, in our training academies and in this field guide, we provide three types of material:

- narratives that depict SDP in action
- SDP's philosophy
- SDP training materials, including practical exercises

The material in the field guide has been organized in three volumes, as follows:

- *Six Pathways to Healthy Child Development and Academic Success.* The theme of this volume is child and adult development, and the principles that underlie all of our work. To bring out the best in children, we must bring out the best in ourselves.
- *Transforming School Leadership and Management to Support Student Learning and Development.* This volume covers the nine core elements of the Comer Process as they have developed over time.
- *Dynamic Instructional Leadership to Support Student Learning and Development.* This volume continues with Comer Process practices in depth in the classroom, principal leadership, and evaluation of the process. It also describes SDP's approach to systemwide reform that makes the entire district the community of change.

The field guide is a critical resource, but not a replacement for SDP training. Participants in the leadership academies need ways to maintain and review their own experience of the academies once they are back home. They will be responsible for training their school communities in the Comer Process. This field guide will help establish a common language, mind-set, and behavior set within the community.

The take-home message is that *all* members of the school community need to engage in transforming the school—not only the principal or a few key individuals.

RESPONSIBILITIES OF THE SCHOOL COMMUNITY

We believe school communities should

- provide supportive work environments for teachers to maximize their ability to deliver instruction and provide developmental experiences to prepare students for life beyond school
- facilitate positive relationships among parents, students, and school staff to develop the bonds necessary for effective teaching and learning
- be structured to promote collaborative decision making and a culture of inclusion

- promote learning as a lifelong process
- value cultural, linguistic, and ethnic differences to enhance the educational process for all people
- use data from all levels of the system—student, school, and the district—to inform educational policies and practices
- view change as an ongoing process guided by continuous constructive feedback
- design curriculum, instruction, and assessment to align with national, state, and local standards and promote child and community development
- provide administrators with the support they need to lead and manage schools
- promote organizational coherence among school boards, educators, and parents
- provide a sound education with an emphasis on civic responsibility

An education system that fosters child and adolescent development will make it possible to maintain and improve our democratic society.

3

Systemic Reform

The School Development
Program's Answer to Fragmentation

Edward T. Joyner and Christine L. Emmons

Systemic SDP generates meaningful whole-district change that lasts beyond the tenure of any one principal or superintendent. It requires significant shifts in attitudes and behavior by all in the school community, as well as unwavering commitment to a curriculum in which development along all six developmental pathways is integral to academic learning. Stating that this global change process "is not for the faint of heart," SDP's executive director and director of program evaluation outline what is involved for those with the vision and will to embrace systemic reform.

WHY SYSTEMIC REFORM?

From its inception and for the first 27 years of its existence, the Yale School Development Program (SDP) focused on improving schools one at a time, and then clusters of schools within districts. Over time, a pattern of implementation and outcomes began to emerge. Given time, training, and financial support, schools would enthusiastically implement the Comer Process. School climate would improve, relationships between staff and parents would improve, and student behavior and academic achievement would improve. Within a few years, however, the principal would be reassigned or retire, a new principal with no training or knowledge about the Comer Process would be appointed, and implementation of reform would decline or cease altogether, generally resulting in the school going into a downward spiral. The lesson is that it is extremely difficult, if not impossible, for schools to sustain reform without the support of the district. Superintendents can abolish all reform efforts by decree and shift policy and focus as they see fit, whenever they see fit. School-by-school reform also results in the absurdity of one district having several reform models, possibly as many as there are schools in the district. This can be dizzying for both students and parents, who have to adjust to different models as students move up or across the system.

To address these and other problems arising from school-by-school reform, SDP decided to move in the direction of systemwide change. Four primary issues lay behind this decision. First, the very changes that bring about success in individual schools often lead to conflict with the district. This undermines the school's ability to implement and sustain change. Second, key systems such as curriculum guidelines, data collection, and analysis procedures need to be in place at the district level. This is necessary if schools are to manage reform and improvement in a coherent manner and monitor the gains that they make. Third, schools can sustain change only when a district has developed a plan of continuity and succession so that a critical mass of trained staff and parents can support the work as new leaders come in. Fourth, the collaboration of adults at all levels strengthens the network of district-school-classroom-home relationships, creating a safety net for children that greatly reduces the likelihood that any child will be left behind. The entire community is in constant communication about what needs to be done to ensure that the interests of children dictate decision making.

The SDP systemic reform initiative addresses the need to reduce the fragmentation, instability, and lack of focus that characterize too many school districts that serve low-income children. The work involves (a) creating inclusive structures for planning and decision making, (b) helping districts to establish and maintain focus on child and adolescent development, and (c) working with staff, parents, and policymakers to help them develop the skills and will to address the troublesome challenges that accompany any large-scale effort that requires collaboration, effective problem solving, and consensus decision making.

PHILOSOPHY OF SDP SYSTEMIC REFORM

"Systemic SDP" is a way to generate meaningful whole-district change. Essentially, it requires a major shift in adult behavior at all levels of the system to facilitate the intellectual and psychosocial development of students. Educators must adhere to the belief that first and foremost, the reason for all system activity is to meet the needs of students, and they must be willing to make the necessary changes in the school system to ensure that student development, rather than programs, is the primary factor in decision making.

Whole-district reform requires (a) an honest assessment of the current status of the system, (b) a statement of vision and mission that spells out the direction of change, and (c) a system of monitoring, supervision, and evaluation designed to help manage the change.

A journey of this magnitude—that is, SDP systemwide change—will not go forward or be sustained without the support and participation of the entire community. There can be no middle ground or neutrality in this endeavor. Each person, whether student, parent, teacher, other system employee, policymaker, politician, business person, or community representative, must be an active participant if meaningful system reform is to occur. Adult workers at every level within the school must be supported in their service to students.

NINE GOALS

SDP has developed nine specific goals for systemic change, along with a series of criteria that accompany each goal. Together, they form our vision of systemic change. These goals help to keep educators and change agents focused on the main areas for action.

Goal 1: To sustain a long-term, focused intervention for systemic change.

Goal 2: To transform the central office staff into an effective, collaborative planning and management team that engages in no-fault problem solving and consensus decision making. This group is responsible for the development of a comprehensive district plan that integrates and focuses the multiple directions of change. At the beginning, this plan outlines a strategy to support the implementation of SDP at each school. In a year or two, the plan will reflect the work of the local School Planning and Management Teams (SPMTs).

Goal 3: To devolve key management functions from the central office to school sites as local SPMTs become operational, especially in the areas of program planning and staff development.

Goal 4: To develop a strong base of individual school leadership supported by the central office.

Goal 5: To have every school operating as an effective SDP school.

Goal 6: To develop written curricula that are developmentally appropriate, are aligned with local, state, and national assessments, and reflect current research on teaching, learning, and development.

Goal 7: To maintain fully staffed and community-linked Student and Staff Support Teams (SSSTs) at every school.

Goal 8: To ensure a strong parent involvement program both at the building level and systemwide.

Goal 9: To have an ongoing, full-time staff position to facilitate the change process throughout the district.

PHASES AND STRUCTURES OF SYSTEMIC REFORM

Five Phases of the SDP Implementation Life Cycle

To achieve the nine goals outlined above, SDP proposes a change implementation sequence of five phases, which is referred to as the SDP Implementation Life Cycle:

1. Planning and Preparation

2. Foundation Building

3. Transformation

4. Institutionalization

5. Renewal

This is a systemic change model that requires parallel processes taking place at the district central office and in the schools, with the underlying support of the board of education (see Figure 3.1).

Board of Education

The board of education is engaged at the initial stages when the district is considering the adoption of SDP as the change model. Two actions by the school board mark the formal beginning of the systemic process in a district:

1. The school board designates SDP as the integrating intervention of the various district initiatives.

2. The board of education commits the district to at least five years of SDP implementation, irrespective of changes in the district superintendency or administration.

The board is also expected to approve funds for the implementation of SDP in the district and enact policies that support the SDP process, in other words, policies that ensure that the central focus of schooling is the healthy development of each child.

District Central Office

The District Planning Team shepherds the change process in the initial stages. Its members are representative of all critical stakeholders, and the superintendent plays a key role. Later, the team may be transformed into the District Steering Committee, the group that is responsible for managing the systemic reform process.

During the Planning and Preparation phase, the school district and SDP sign a memorandum of agreement, outlining the roles and responsibilities of each institution. This document serves as a guide for drafting detailed implementation plans. The central office is also expected to enact policies that support the systemic change process so that there will be coherence and not conflict.

Figure 3.1 Parallel processes for systemic change

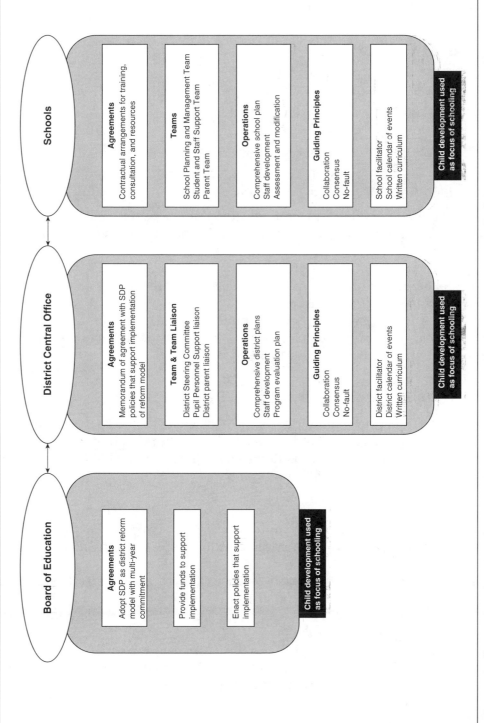

Board of Education

Agreements
Adopt SDP as district reform model with multi-year commitment

Provide funds to support implementation

Enact policies that support implementation

Child development used as focus of schooling

District Central Office

Agreements
Memorandum of agreement with SDP policies that support implementation of reform model

Team & Team Liaison
District Steering Committee
Pupil Personnel Support liaison
District parent liaison

Operations
Comprehensive district plans
Staff development
Program evaluation plan

Guiding Principles
Collaboration
Consensus
No-fault

District facilitator
District calendar of events
Written curriculum

Child development used as focus of schooling

Schools

Agreements
Contractual arrangements for training, consultation, and resources

Teams
School Planning and Management Team
Student and Staff Support Team
Parent Team

Operations
Comprehensive school plan
Staff development
Assessment and modification

Guiding Principles
Collaboration
Consensus
No-fault

School facilitator
School calendar of events
Written curriculum

Child development used as focus of schooling

SOURCE: Copyright © 2004 by The Yale School Development Program, Yale Child Study Center. All rights reserved. Reprinted from *Dynamic Instructional Leadership to Support Student Learning and Development: The Field Guide to Comer Schools in Action*, by Edward T. Joyner, Michael Ben-Avie, and James P. Comer. Reproduction authorized only for the local school site that has purchased this book. www.corwinpress.com.

PARALLEL STRUCTURES FOR SCHOOLS AND DISTRICTS

Schools are expected to implement nine elements: three teams, three operations, and three guiding principles. A parallel process should take place at the district level as well.

Teams and Operations

Three teams are based at each school:

- School Planning and Management Team (SPMT)
- Student and Staff Support Team (SSST)
- Parent Team (PT)

School Planning and Management Team

The SPMT, made up of representatives from the school staff, parents, other adult stakeholders, and students (in the case of middle and high schools), carries out the three operations:

- The development of a *comprehensive school plan* with specific goals in the social climate and academic areas
- *Staff development* activities based on building-level goals in these areas
- *Assessment and modification,* that is, periodic assessment that allows the staff to modify the program to meet identified needs

District Steering Committee

The District Steering Committee is a representative interdepartmental team of central office administrators and school staff that supports implementation. This committee, with input from its constituencies, will be responsible for the following operations, which parallel those of a school-based SPMT:

- The development of a multiyear *comprehensive district plan* that integrates all key school initiatives, and a multiyear *district strategic plan* that details the transformation process, with specific action steps for implementation at the school level
- *Staff development* activities based on district-level goals set forth in the comprehensive district plan and the district strategic plan
- *A program evaluation plan* that sets up procedures for measuring the degree of implementation and effectiveness of all programs and activities included in the comprehensive district plan and the district strategic plan. Periodic assessments will allow both district- and school-level management teams to assess progress and modify the program to meet identified needs.

Student and Staff Support Team

The SSST is composed of mental health, social service, and special education staff assigned to the school. The team addresses schoolwide climate and psychosocial issues that are likely to have an impact on the students' adjustment and life path choices. It also addresses individual student concerns. The SSST has representation on the SPMT.

Some issues raised by SSSTs need to be addressed at the district level. A representative from the Pupil Support Services (probably the psychologist or social worker) or one of the SSST chairs serves as a liaison with all the SSSTs, working with them to bring out these global cross-school issues. These concerns are brought to the District Steering Committee meeting for action.

The Parent Team

In each school, the PT works with staff to plan and support social and academic activities, and its members participate in various school events. The PT also helps to get parents involved in school activities. At the district level, a parent liaison on the District Steering Committee is responsible for working with PTs throughout the district to improve their effectiveness. PT concerns and needs are brought back to the District Steering Committee meetings, where they may be adequately addressed.

Guiding Principles

Successful implementation of the SDP model requires the acceptance of three guiding principles in the conduct of team meetings and in the general management of the school: collaboration, consensus, and no-fault problem solving.

- *Collaboration* occurs when each person on the team is free to express an opinion and everyone else listens and respects that opinion.
- *Consensus* means that to avoid "winner-loser" feelings, decisions are made by common agreement. Team members must transcend their own viewpoints so that they can not only live with the decisions that the team makes but also support them.
- *No-fault* is an approach to problem solving used by all teams working within the school. This means that the focus is placed on identifying, describing, and solving problems, rather than on assigning blame. The team accepts responsibility for problems that arise, but time and energy are not wasted on acts of blaming.

At the district level, these guiding principles are also practiced in the conduct of committee and department team meetings and in the general management of the district. Because of the legal responsibility of both the superintendent and the principal, areas of autonomy in which executive decisions need to be made must be clearly delineated.

Facilitators

In addition to the nine elements, there are other parallel operations going on at district and school levels. The Comer school facilitators guide the implementation of the Comer Process in each school building. The Comer district facilitator is responsible for guiding the systemic reform process districtwide, assisting school facilitators as needed with support such as staff development activities, leadership coordination, and problem solving.

CURRICULUM AND INTEGRATED PLANNING

The district should have a formal written curriculum that is aligned with local, state, and national assessment instruments, and should integrate the six developmental pathways (physical, social, cognitive, psychological, language, and ethical). The written school curriculum should flow from the district written curriculum.

The plans of the district and its schools should be integrated. For example, the schools develop their goals and comprehensive school plans based on the district goals, the comprehensive district plan, and the district strategic plan. The school calendar of events should be derived from and guided by the district calendar of events. Staff development planning should be a coordinated effort between the school and the district. Most important of all, the central focus of schooling at both district and school levels should be the development of the child along the six pathways mentioned above.

IMPLEMENTATION SITES OF SDP SYSTEMIC REFORM

The SDP systemic reform, funded by the Rockefeller Foundation, was piloted in three districts in the Northeast from 1994–1995 to 1996–1997. This approach, described by Gillette and Kranyik (1996), became the basis for the current systemic reform protocol. Lessons learned during the pilot were used to refine both the content and approach. The implementation of the refined SDP systemic reform process began in 1998 at the Westbury Union Free School District, with a partnership involving the C. W. Post School of Education at Long Island University, Westbury School District, and SDP.

In 1999, two school districts in North Carolina joined the systemic project: Asheville City Schools and Hertford County Public Schools. The City of Orange Public Schools, New Jersey, and Community School District 17, New York, became involved in 2001 (see Figure 3.2). Over a five-year period, the U.S. Department of Education has funded research into the systemic reform process.

NOT FOR THE FAINTHEARTED

In SDP systemic reform, the greatest in terms of position become the support system for those with less power: The school board supports the district and the schools to foster the development of all children in the district. The central office serves the schools, and the schools are organized around the service and well-being of the children. Those first five districts took a great risk to implement such comprehensive structural change. They have been pioneering a process that turns the educational enterprise on its head. It must be said that systemic reform is not for the faint of heart. And yet systemic reform increases the likelihood that the greatest number of students will learn and develop.

Figure 3.2 Participants initiating SDP systemic reform, 1998–2001

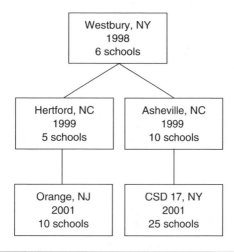

REFERENCE

Gillette, J. H., & Kranyik, R. D. (1996). Changing American schools: Insights from the School Development Program. In J. P. Comer, N. M. Haynes, E. T. Joyner, & M. Ben-Avie, *Rallying the whole village: The Comer Process for reforming education* (pp. 147–162). New York: Teachers College Press.

AUTHORS' NOTE: This research was funded by a grant from the United States Department of Education.

4

Systemic Reform

We Started With One School

Alice Huff Hart, Miriam McLaughlin, Everol Ennis, and William Steve Stone

Asheville City Schools in North Carolina is one of several school systems that have accepted the challenge of SDP's systemic reform process. Beginning with one pilot school, the district built capacity for change into its schools, its central office, and the community before introducing reform systemwide. The Asheville City Board of Education financed the pilot project, and consultation and training were supported through the SDP's systemic reform initiative sponsored by the U.S. Department of Education. A regional coalition of SDP schools also provided invaluable technical and moral support.

TEAMWORK DRIVES EDUCATIONAL CHANGE

Asheville, North Carolina, is a small city school district with 4,200 students. In the summer of 1998, the city's Student Achievement Task Force asked one of its subcommittees to address a serious achievement gap that was becoming evident between African American and White students based on school system data. The committee was as diverse in its membership as the task force itself and included educators, parents, and community representatives, thus ensuring that all members of the school community would be heard.

This special Task Force Subcommittee met for 18 months and became a close-knit team dedicated to the success of Asheville City students. They prepared a series of comprehensive recommendations and presented them to the board of education. Many discussions focused on the need for an improved management model for schools, and some members who were familiar with the School Development Program (SDP) recommended that the school system investigate SDP and its Comer Process.

At about the same time, Hall Fletcher Elementary School in Asheville was invited to a state conference for low-achieving schools. There, the school explored various models of school reform and settled on SDP as a nearly perfect fit with its needs. The emphasis on relationships, team organization, parent involvement, and the potential for addressing the developmental needs of students sparked the school's interest. Since Hall Fletcher's decision fit well with the recommendations of the Task Force Subcommittee, the central office administration recommended that the school be designated as a pilot site for implementing SDP in Asheville City Schools. The board of education agreed to fund the pilot project.

The decision to implement a pilot program allowed the system to thoroughly explore all aspects of SDP, including program costs. The small, manageable pilot could create a successful model that other schools could observe and replicate.

Piloting a program in one (or a few) schools is a great way to "learn by doing." The district focuses its support of change on one school. This support is empowering to the principal and the school management team that must implement the change. As small successes grow into larger ones, district and school administrators gain an understanding of what it takes to make these changes happen. In addition, a pilot school builds capacity in the district as its staff members gain experience in facilitating change.

Hall Fletcher's School Planning and Management Team (SPMT) did, in fact, emerge as a strong leadership force in the school. They promoted a common language throughout the school that focused on the guiding principles of collaboration, consensus, and no-fault. Efforts increased to nurture relationships within the school community.

Preparing the Ground for Systemwide Change

As Hall Fletcher began its first year of implementation, planning continued toward systemwide implementation. During their first leadership training with SDP at Yale, the Asheville team (consisting of selected staff from Hall Fletcher and the central office, including the associate superintendent) discussed their interest in implementing districtwide reform with the director of SDP. Subsequently, Asheville City Schools was offered the opportunity to become one of five districts nationwide implementing SDP through a grant from the U.S. Department of Education. The district applied for and received a grant that enabled other district personnel to attend SDP's developmental pathways training held at Yale.

In Asheville, an enthusiastic and knowledgeable principal and a supportive school district central office shared the progress of the pilot with the whole school community. Throughout the pilot year, members of the Hall Fletcher team and central office personnel shared progress reports on the pilot with all central office administrators and school principals, who, in turn, shared the information with their own school staff. This process laid the groundwork for systemwide change, preparing people by sharing information, involving them in early decision making, and preparing them for training. As school staffs heard about SDP, they became familiar with some of the language and gained some idea of the process.

Year 1 of the pilot was deemed a success based on several measures. The principal was committed and motivated, and she generated those same feelings in teachers, staff, parents, and students in her school. The work of the school reflected a good understanding of the components of the program. Changes were implemented appropriately and in manageable

> In Chapter 7, "A Demonstration of Comer-in-the-Classroom," Carol Pickett Ray, the principal of Hall Fletcher during this time period, tells the story of the school's transformation from her perspective.

stages. The school board and central administration provided resources and ongoing support for implementation. Most significant, however, was the overall achievement of Hall Fletcher students, which increased from 42 percent proficiency in the fall of 1999 to 66 percent proficiency in the spring of 1999.

Building Successful Teams for District Reform and School Management

With the initial success of the pilot accomplished, the next challenge was to build system capacity for successful teams in each of the other Asheville City schools. Central office staff along with the team from Hall Fletcher presented a modified version of SDP's leadership training to management team members from nine schools in the district. These team members, in turn, presented an overview of SDP and its Comer Process to their individual schools. In addition, the system began a gradual process of reorganizing the teams in each school.

Training in facilitation is critical for district personnel considering implementing SDP systemwide. Districts must know what to expect during the first, second, and third years of implementation. SDP is a process for change, and it takes time and training for schools to achieve full implementation. The goal of improved student achievement correlates positively with the level of implementation in the school. It is vital that districts and, ultimately, school boards understand this process and what must be accomplished to achieve positive outcomes for students.

In the spring of 1999, the school district central office established an Action Team (as distinct from the Task Force Subcommittee) to facilitate the systemic implementation of SDP. In this way, the central office took responsibility for training new educators, the school board, and community members in SDP's Comer Process. The Action Team is composed of representatives from each school, the associate superintendent, executive directors for elementary and secondary education, representatives from higher education, parents, and a school board member. Meetings provide a forum for schools to share and network with other schools and to gain the support they need for successful implementation of SDP. A subcommittee of this team, made up of the associate superintendent and executive directors for elementary and secondary education, steers the planning and implementation steps for the system.

A team that offers ongoing support for schools is essential to the success of any systemwide initiative. The team offers schools a way to connect with each other and a climate of support for their efforts. In addition, the team can address problems emerging systemically and put their collective expertise into problem solving. This team works cooperatively with the central office to facilitate implementation. In larger systems, teams of SDP principals or facilitators meet regularly for the same purpose.

In most schools, some form of the management team is in place. These teams are often less inclusive in their representation of the school community and less structured than the SPMT in the way they accomplish their meetings. In the past, the failure of some Asheville teams to be fully inclusive of parents had reinforced the belief that the teams were not effective in addressing students' needs. Also, the previous teams did not have principles to guide them in working effectively. In implementing the Comer Process, the school district facilitated a reorganization of school management teams so that they would reflect the whole school community, including parents and business partners.

Training teams to work within a structured time frame and with a shared leadership approach to decision making is another important step in implementation. In accordance with school board policy, the teams were elected to reflect the socioeconomic and racial makeup of their schools. The SPMTs were organized to meet monthly. Student and Staff Support Teams (SSSTs) were organized to meet as needed. All school personnel were involved at some level with the decision making of the teams.

Parent Teams (PTs) are a new concept in many schools. Asheville trained PT members to prepare them for active and visible roles in the life of the school. In the spring of 2001, training provided by a Yale consultant energized parents in the district and in the surrounding community. PT members from each school attended, and returned to their schools to initiate the development of a PT in their school. In 2002, PTs received additional training and coaching as part of the staff development plan.

Participation in SDP has energized Asheville City Schools. At every level, the school district reflects the nine elements of the Comer Process. The associate superintendent and executive directors for elementary and secondary education make sure that the Comer Process is visible in large and small ways in their own daily work. For example, they have created agenda forms for meetings that display the major components of the Comer Process, to remind everyone of the district's commitment to these philosophical and operational principles. Board of education members eat lunch each month in one of the schools. During their visit, they ask the principal for an update on the school's progress in implementing SDP. The leadership demonstrated by the board of education sets the tone for the system. The reform program is valued in a new way that engages the whole district, including the community, in meeting the needs of students. Commitment, planning, and enthusiasm have characterized district efforts thus far.

REGIONAL SUPPORT FOR SDP IMPLEMENTATION

A regional coalition of SDP-implementing schools and districts in North Carolina and South Carolina, known as the Carolina Comer Coalition, also provided important technical and moral support for the reform in Asheville. The coalition, which welcomes representatives from all interested SDP schools in the region, meets every two months to share ideas, solve problems, and discuss current state or regional issues. Districts take turns hosting the meetings. In 2001, members collaborated to provide training for all the districts involved in the coalition. Costs for participants were kept at a minimum by using an all-volunteer training staff. In addition, districts and schools in the coalition share local training opportunities. When one district offers training for its SDP schools, others are invited to attend at no charge.

For the North Carolina and South Carolina region, which is experiencing major budget constraints, this kind of collaboration has helped maintain the momentum of SDP and has also established some local self-sufficiency in training and follow-up coaching. Asheville participants claim that support from the coalition meetings has been invaluable to them. They have been able to share their problems and experiences and receive practical advice about implementation. Facilitators have been in regular contact with other SDP districts, have benefited from some of their training events, and have had opportunities to observe the Comer Process in action at other Carolina schools.

Box 4.1   Regional Training Centers Extend Support for SDP

To extend its capacity to serve an increasing number of schools and school districts, in the mid-1990s the Yale School Development Program (SDP) designated three sites with extensive experience as SDP Regional Training Centers (RTCs). The centers currently offer both introductory training and specialized workshops, and they consult with local schools, providing coaching and customized training in the Comer Process. Their work is closely coordinated with the national SDP office at Yale. A coalition of schools and districts that are implementing SDP in the Carolinas has become a fourth regional base of expertise.

Comer School Development Program Regional Professional Development and Training Center, Prince George's County Public Schools, Maryland

The Prince George's County SDP Professional Development Center supports in-depth dissemination of the Comer Process in the county school system and offers a large selection of training events for all levels of staff, which are open to participants from both inside and outside the district. These and other events are posted on their Web site (www.pgcps.org/~comer).

- A one-day team retreat held in mid-autumn for SPMT, SSST, and PT members. This annual event offers a broad array of workshop sessions led by local and visiting professionals, including SDP staff.

(Continued)

Box 4.1 (Continued)

- Comer Orientation, a two-and-a-half-day introductory training with an optional half-day site visit.

- Site visits to demonstration schools.

- Comer SDP Continuing Professional Development, a five-day workshop usually held in June.

The Prince George's County RTC also offers limited site-specific consultative services to schools and districts.

Comer School Development Program, Midwest Regional Training Center at Youth Guidance, Chicago, Illinois

Chicago's RTC is based at Youth Guidance, Inc., a nonprofit social service agency that serves at-risk students in Chicago's public schools by providing programs that guide them academically, socially, and emotionally. This RTC offers programs such as the Parent Leadership Conference and 101 SDP Leadership Training. More information on the center is available online at www.youth-guidance.org/csd.

(DEY) Regional Training Center: Detroit Public Schools, Eastern Michigan University, Yale Child Study Center

Starting in 1994, the Comer Process was implemented gradually in more than 30 Detroit schools under the Comer Schools and Families Initiative supported by the Skillman Foundation. Over a 10-year period, many Detroit teachers and administrators acquired experience in facilitating SDP and training others in SDP leadership.

Eastern Michigan University's (EMU) College of Education and the Detroit Comer schools joined together to build a pioneering preservice education program for EMU undergraduate students in elementary or secondary education who wanted to practice in SDP schools. As the EMU program evolved, it became evident that EMU resources together with Detroit experience could support an SDP Regional Training Center. The center has conducted basic 101 Leadership Training and offers consulting services for SDP implementation in Michigan. Professor Nora Martin, the university coordinator, says that prior to the organization of Comer schools in Detroit, EMU education students were not eager to be associated with Detroit schools. SDP opened many doors to what is continuing to be an ongoing, permanent relationship between Detroit Public Schools and EMU.

Carolina Comer Coalition, North Carolina and South Carolina

The newest regional support group is the Carolina Comer Coalition, a network of SDP school districts and schools in North Carolina and South Carolina. The coalition differs from other regional centers for SDP in that it is not tied to or supported by one district or organization. Bimonthly meetings are voluntarily sponsored by a different district each time. Team members meet to share ideas, solve problems, and discuss current state or regional issues. They also share local training opportunities. When one district offers training for its SDP schools, others are invited to attend at no charge. In 2001, the coalition organized a two-day training for member districts. Costs for participants were kept at a minimum by using an all-volunteer training staff. For the North Carolina and South Carolina region, which is experiencing major budget constraints, this kind of collaboration helps maintain the momentum of SDP.

Additional support came from an unusual community effort outside the district. The Education Coalition is an organization in the Asheville region of more than 40 businesses, nonprofits, institutions of higher education, community leaders, and school system educators and students. The coalition is committed to the success of students and their families; in their first year, they focused on improving the achievement of African American male students. The coalition has a Parent Involvement Team that works to empower parents, who have often been left out of the education process altogether. The chair of this team attended the Asheville parent training as well as celebrations of success at various SDP schools. The enthusiasm of the school communities was contagious. The chair subsequently adopted the process roles and guiding principles as the operating norm for her committee. She synthesized the fundamentals in an excellent one-page handout for parents.

SUSTAINING A TEAM APPROACH TO EDUCATIONAL CHANGE

In Asheville and other systemic districts, sustaining the team approach to educational change is ensured through visibility, organization, and integration. Asheville took an active stance in promoting visibility. Key reporters were involved in communicating the successes and problems of the Student Achievement Task Force as it worked to meet students' needs. They saw the potential of the emerging districtwide SDP and were willing to tell the story. Articles explained the program and reported on progress. When the administrative team invited Dr. Comer to visit the system, the media were supportive. Reporters interviewed Dr. Comer and, prior to his arrival, completed a comprehensive story about the delegation of students who attended a leadership academy at Yale.

Organization and integration were achieved through the district's strategic plan, which addresses the implementation of the program. All schools are required to include strategies in their own plans that will ensure full implementation. At stipulated intervals (at least annually), the system curriculum leadership team, associate superintendent, executive directors, and principals monitor implementation. This information is presented to the board as part of an annual review. Annual surveys delineate the progress of each school and the district. A local evaluator works with the district to assess stages of development.

AN ALTERNATIVE APPROACH TO INTRODUCING REFORM

Small districts may take a different approach to systemic educational change. In 1998, nearby Hertford County Schools, a rural school district, recognized the need for a districtwide approach to school reform and accountability. The superintendent became seriously interested in SDP and was encouraged by the assistant superintendent in nearby Guilford County, a system that had introduced SDP into about half of its schools. SDP's Edward Joyner also had strong associations in the community and was willing to help. The superintendent and school board as well as the School Improvement Team from each school, including parents and community members, participated in the decision to adopt the SDP reform model. An advisory council was formed, made up of principals and central office staff. A five-year time frame was set to replicate the Comer Process in all Hertford County Schools.

Hertford implemented the program in all the schools at the same time. This approach allows school leaders to learn from and support each other as they participate in the process. Districtwide implementation requires a strong district facilitator as well as opportunities for leadership teams from all the schools to meet and share issues and ideas.

SUMMING UP: TEAMWORK AND SUPPORT

The Carolina Comer Coalition's experience in working with rural and small school districts suggests the following key factors in quality outcomes for young people:

- involvement of all stakeholders in the decision-making process
- endorsement from key education leaders, including the school board
- long-term financial commitment from the school board
- establishment of a steering committee
- designation of one or more district facilitators, with the primary task of helping schools with implementation
- training of leadership teams and central office personnel
- training of Parent Team
- capacity building: the district takes responsibility for training new educators, the school board, and community members in SDP
- institutionalizing: the ongoing behavior of the adults in the school community embodies the Comer Process and mind-set

To this list, Alice Hart adds training the school board to use the Comer Process for their meetings; making SDP visible in schools with the use of banners, student work, and printed material; and celebrating successes!

Looking at the list of factors that contributed to the successful implementation of SDP in Asheville City Schools, it is apparent that having teams is not all that is needed. However, collaborative teams that have broad representation from the parents, community, and school make things happen. Through the efforts of these teams, the needs of the system are met.

5

Curriculum Structure and Teacher Planning

Balance, Alignment, and Student Assessment in the Standards-Based Curriculum

David A. Squires and Camille J. Cooper

The ideal curriculum eliminates needless repetition, creates an effective flow between grades, coordinates with the entire district, aligns with local, state, and national standards, and incorporates the six developmental pathways. Structuring such a curriculum is a complex but rewarding process. The authors discuss their philosophy and describe the structural characteristics of the process, which make it "specific enough to guide and coordinate instruction and . . . flexible enough to ensure teacher creativity." Offering five steps and 10 criteria, they demonstrate how to balance a curriculum within the school and within the district. The payoff—marked increases in standardized test scores—is greatest in schools that have most faithfully implemented the process.

WHY DISTRICTS NEED TO DEVELOP CURRICULUM

Curriculum is the district's or school's plan for assisting teachers in addressing state standards, benchmarks, and mandated tests. Without a curriculum, teachers must construct their own plans to address the state standards, often without the benefit of coordinated decision making between grade levels or courses. This chapter

- addresses the usefulness and usability of curriculum structure to assist teachers to plan instruction
- gives districts a process for deciding on their curriculum structure
- provides a way to rate the design of the curriculum structure when the plan is completed

Before considering curriculum, we examine tools districts use in place of curriculum: textbooks, state standards, and state assessments, and we provide reasons why these are inadequate.

WHAT DISTRICTS USE TO CONTROL INSTRUCTION AND WHY THESE OPTIONS DON'T WORK

Textbooks

School districts and teachers often rely on textbooks as a way to coordinate instruction. Most textbooks contain more material than a teacher can teach, so each teacher picks and chooses textbook material and activities that he or she likes. In this situation, the teacher's choice of activities is rarely coordinated among teachers of the same course, let alone teachers of different courses. Textbooks claim to be aligned to state standards, but 49 states have standards, and no one textbook can meet the needs of all of them. (Each district in Iowa constructs its own standards.) In the past, the textbook may have been an adequate tool. Now, however, textbooks need to be used as resources for instruction rather than the de facto curriculum because not enough emphasis will be placed on the various domains important for individual state standards and high-stakes tests (Squires, 2004).

State Standards

Why not just rely on state standards and state tests as a resource to guide instruction? Standards addressing a range of grade levels are not specific enough to guide instruction. For example, many states have standards saying, in one form or another, "Students should read critically for a variety of purposes." Such statements are not specific enough to help teachers plan instruction: The wording "read critically for a variety of purposes" does not define what each grade level should cover. The standards provide the outcome but don't tell us how to get there.

State Tests

State tests, on the other hand, are too specific, zeroing in on small content domains. For example, a persuasive writing prompt appears on a state test for the eighth grade. Does this mean that eighth-grade teachers should concentrate only on persuasive writing, as this is the only way writing is tested at this grade level? Making instructional decisions on the basis only of what is tested will artificially narrow instruction and cause problems at subsequent grade levels, because the full range of writing has not been taught. If other types of writing atrophy for a year, the curriculum is unbalanced.

Curriculum is the only tool districts have to coordinate the instructional program; textbooks, standards, and state assessments do not accomplish this. Coordination is needed among various teacher plans for the same course, and it must consider not only instructional activities and the scope of instructional units but also course sequence. *Curriculum* is a vague word that has many meanings to many people. In the next part of the chapter, we define curriculum and provide some options for designing its structure, with the assumption that some curriculum structures are better than others.

CURRICULUM DEFINED

Curriculum is defined as a district's written plan to help guide the instruction and assessment functions of teaching. Such a plan is aligned with state standards and with high-stakes and/or standardized assessments. Curriculum focuses on what students will be able to know and do, not what teachers are supposed to cover, thereby ensuring that students meet and/or exceed the standards. Curriculum functions to ensure that all students have equal access to quality instruction.

Curriculum is the only tool available to help a district's teachers coordinate decisions about courses, units, and instructional activities in a planned way. Teachers teaching the same course should address similar content in similar ways so that students have equal access to the most important content. Without coordination, teachers will emphasize what they personally feel is important, but when viewed from a systemwide perspective, these individual decisions don't benefit the development of all the children. Children going to the next grade level may not have the prerequisite skills necessary for success at that level, as teachers have not coordinated their decisions about what is most important for students to know and be able to do.

Further instructional coordination is needed to make sure the activities build upon one another sequentially, rather than randomly, and address significant outcomes of state standards. Instructional units should build upon skills and concepts learned in previous units. Planned units ensure students can and will master increasingly difficult material. Without planning on the unit level, instructional activities will not address all the areas specified in the standards. Curriculum can facilitate good decision making about the sequence of courses. Does the first-grade math curriculum provide the prerequisite skills necessary for the second-grade curriculum? Is there an appropriate sequence in middle school and high school so that all children can take algebra, the gateway to higher education?

DOES CURRICULUM MAKE A DIFFERENCE?

The School Development Program (SDP) Balanced Curriculum Process has made a difference in districts and schools. Scores on standardized and state tests have improved in all cases where the curriculum has been both written and implemented (Squires, 2004). Not everyone attempting the SDP Balanced Curriculum Process carries it out. Some get "stuck" in the curriculum-writing process, never finishing, so implementation cannot occur. Some distribute the curriculum to teachers but don't institute a management system that will tell them how the curriculum is being used. Others have produced the curriculum but have not had the organizational fortitude to ask their teachers to follow it.

The Third International Mathematics and Science Study finds that the structure of a curriculum makes a difference in how well students know math and science. In Japan, for example, students study one topic in depth until mastery is assured. In the United States, on the other hand, many more topics are covered during a year, resulting in a curriculum that is "a mile wide and an inch deep" (Howson, 1995, pp. 28–29).

Who has better results? Japan. Why? In part because the structure of the curriculum is different: The text helps focus the content of instruction. Content mastery is valued more than content coverage. Research is beginning to show that curriculum and its structure make a difference in student performance on tests (see Schmidt et al., 2001).

What we know from the emerging research and our experience in implementing the SDP Balanced Curriculum Process for eight years is that curriculum is the tool best suited to helping teachers plan instruction to meet standards and state tests and that the structure of curriculum used in the SDP Balanced Curriculum Process produces results.

In the next section, we examine the options for designing a curriculum structure; then, we provide a rationale for the choice of structure used in the Balanced Curriculum Process. Districts will need to choose from the options presented. A worksheet is provided that may be accessed from our Web site for that purpose (there is a link on SDP's Web site: www.balancedcurriculum.com).

QUESTIONS ABOUT CURRICULUM STRUCTURE

There is no standard way to structure a curriculum. The curriculum may be formulated in a general way, for example, as a list of grade-level expectations, or in detail, as in a series of lesson plans. All teachers may be required to complete the curriculum, or they may just be given a list of suggested activities. Assessments and provisions for monitoring and revising the curriculum may not be a part of the curriculum structure. In this section, we examine questions that districts will need to answer in designing their curriculum structures, including the following:

- What are the schedules in the schools (i.e., what time is available, and what time is allocated for instruction)?
- What will be the smallest component of the curriculum?

- Will the curriculum be disciplinary or interdisciplinary?
- What will be described in the curriculum, and how will the language be structured?
- Will the district suggest or require that the curriculum be followed?
- Will the curriculum be aligned?
- Will the curriculum be assessed?
- Will there be staff development related to the curriculum?
- Will the curriculum be implemented?
- Will the curriculum be monitored?
- If the curriculum will be monitored,
    Who will monitor it?
    What will be the monitoring procedure?
    How will monitoring records be kept?
    What will be the consequences of noncompliance?
- By what specific procedures will the curriculum be revised?
- What policies will support curriculum development, implementation, and revision?

We believe these decisions need to be made before large sums of money are spent on developing the curriculum documents, as documents are effective only if the content is implemented. The curriculum's effectiveness rests on how each of these areas is addressed. The questions need to be addressed in sequence, as the answers to the earlier questions determine the options for the subsequent answers.

Consider School Schedules

Schedules may seem like a strange place to start in designing curricular components. Nonetheless, curriculum places content within a time frame. Thus time and content are the two structures that curriculum directs and controls. Time in schools is defined by schedules. In elementary schools, there may be a reading and mathematics block. In self-contained classrooms, the blocks are flexible, while in middle and high schools, the blocks are more defined. Knowing the amount of time per day, week, or month that is allocated for subject area instruction is critical to developing curriculum, as the amount of time available will determine the scope and sequence of content.

We have worked in districts where one school may have two periods for reading/ language arts, while other schools only have one. Different schedules demand different curricula. In another district, the time for mathematics was increased from 30 minutes a day to one hour a day, because teachers felt more time was needed for students to get enough practice to master the curriculum. When specifying a districtwide curriculum, districts need to assist schools in deciding upon a schedule that is appropriate to accomplishing the curricular goals. Because all curricula rest on scheduling considerations, we do not recommend the practice of districts that accept different schedules for schools following the same curriculum. These districts make the assumption that different amounts of scheduled time are needed for all students to be successful. If schools' time schedules vary from each other, then a different curriculum should be developed for each schedule.

Consider the Smallest Component

Decisions need to be made about the specificity of the curriculum: What will be its smallest "chunk"? For example, state standards are examples of a curriculum whose smallest chunk is usually a grade-level range by subject area. In social studies (a subject area), standards are defined for a grade-level range: K–4, 5–8, or 9–12. In the grade-level range, there is no further delineation about time; usually a chunk like this is phrased, "By the end of Grade 4, students will:..." The smallest chunk then would be a grade-level range, such as K–4, because no further time division is mentioned. Some states, such as North Carolina, have narrowed the grade-level range to single courses, such as Algebra I or Grade 3 Reading/Language Arts. In this case, the chunk would be Algebra I and would read, "By the end of the Algebra I course, students will:..." District-level curriculum divide individual courses into units. Units are usually chunks of time shorter than a year, perhaps a few weeks or a month. If units are the chunk used, then the outcome statements for the units would be phrased, "By the end of this unit, students will..." Units may be subdivided further into lessons. If the lesson is the smallest chunk, then the curriculum would be written, "By the end of this lesson, students will..."

The larger the chunk, the more latitude teachers have to make decisions about when and where to include this in their plans. The downside is the more latitude, the more difficult it is to coordinate decisions among teachers. The less coordination, the less certain the district is that standards are being met. The more coordination, such as a district's developing daily lesson plans, the less latitude teachers have and the more likely districts will be to field complaints about too much structure and not enough latitude.

As mentioned earlier, one typical district approach is to have the textbook serve as the de facto curriculum. Of course, the difficulty is that most textbooks contain much more information and activities than can be taught, so teachers have maximum latitude, but districts have minimum coordination. In another typical structure, districts may have a curriculum, but it specifies "suggested" activities. Again, the teachers have maximum latitude, but districts have minimum coordination and no way of knowing whether the suggested activities were actually taught. Many districts have traded coordination for maximum teacher flexibility and then lament when that flexibility does not produce improved achievement. Achievement can improve, but only when the curriculum structure fosters both teacher latitude and coordination.

Consider the Disciplinary Nature of the Curriculum

Another decision about curriculum structure is whether there will be discipline-based curriculum, such as science and social studies, or some form of interdisciplinary curriculum. Crossing subject area lines in an interdisciplinary curriculum most frequently occurs in the elementary grades. Science and social studies content is integrated into units or lessons in language arts or mathematics, and vice versa. For example, a unit on plants may involve listening to stories about plants (reading), counting and predicting for a plant experiment (science, math), and listing how we use plants for living (social studies). The decision about a discipline-based versus interdisciplinary curriculum will affect the schedule and the choice of alignment categories. For example, if social studies and reading/language arts are combined in the curriculum, then the curriculum will need to be aligned to reading/language arts and social studies standards and the schedule might indicate "Reading/Language Arts—Social Studies: 9:00 a.m. to 11:00 a.m."

Curriculum theorists debate the merits of focusing on each discipline with its unique ways of viewing the world, or focusing on topics from various disciplinary perspectives. It is clear from the structure of most states' standards, assessments, requirements for teacher certification, and from the way higher education is organized, that these educational institutions are organized around subject areas. While schools serving pre-K and kindergarten may opt for an integrated curriculum, as grade level increases school structure becomes more discipline based; that is, classes are organized by subject area. An interdisciplinary curriculum then becomes more difficult to organize, not only because of the school's subject area bias but also because of teachers' discipline-based training.

Consider What Is Described in the Curriculum

Curriculum designers make choices about the extent to which they will stipulate both *what* will be taught and *how* it will be taught. Standards and accompanying benchmarks are useful in describing *what* the outcomes of courses or ranges of courses will be. Objectives, such as behavioral objectives, are useful in describing the outcomes of units or lessons. Both objectives and standards focus on describing what the outcomes are but, in general, say little about how to achieve those outcomes.

For example, the curriculum says teachers should teach "Reading for the main idea." One teacher thinks, "The state test is coming up, and I will just drill my students on multiple-choice items about the main idea. In this way, they'll be prepared for the test." Another teacher chooses to teach the main idea through creating headlines after understanding the structure of news articles. A third decides to use the social studies book to teach children how to read for the main ideas there. A fourth decides her students already know about the main idea; she'll proceed to something more important. While three of the four teachers address the main idea, their classes do so in strikingly different ways and with the probability of producing very different outcomes. When the students arrive at the next grade and are mixed into new classes, it's no surprise that the new teachers wonder whether the main idea was addressed. Generally, curriculum has been designed specifying the outcomes, and the teacher decides how to get to the outcomes. We address this choice in our later discussion of curriculum usefulness.

Consider Whether the Curriculum Should Be Required

Decisions about suggesting or requiring fidelity to the curriculum need to be made at the course level, at the unit level, and at the lesson plan level, depending on the decisions made in previous steps. Should individual curricula for reading, math, science, and social studies be suggested or required at fourth grade? This is an example of a decision made at the course level. With districts adopting longer time periods (block scheduling) for teaching reading and math, science and social studies in elementary and middle schools may be squeezed out of the required curriculum, although focus is achieved for reading and math.

Many curriculum documents are constructed as suggestions about objectives that teachers need to address at a particular grade level or course. Implied in the word *suggested* is that they are not required. Teachers can choose to focus their instruction on the objectives or choose other objectives. Embedded in this approach is the assumption that teachers can wisely choose which objectives to incorporate and which to leave out, based on the needs of their classes. Another assumption is that the decisions of individual teachers will not make a difference in student learning when test scores are tallied across grades or courses. Returning to the previous example of teaching the main idea: If for two years, a student had learned about main ideas through reading passages and filling in multiple-choice questions, that student would be less able to understand and identify main ideas than would a student who had learned about them through newspapers or a student who had learned about them through reading social studies texts. We argue that a required curriculum is more likely to ensure the coordinated impact on student learning that is necessary to improve on high-stakes tests and maintain a balance in the curriculum.

Consider Curriculum Alignment

Alignment means there is similar content in both the standards and the goals/objectives. Research indicates that alignment is a powerful indicator of academic achievement (Cohen, 1987; English & Steffy, 2001; Moss-Mitchell, 1998; Neidermeyer & Yelon, 1981; Porter, Kirst, Osthoff, Smithson, & Schneider, 1994; Porter & Smithson, 2001; Price-Braugh, 1997; Wishnick, 1989). Although there are many different processes and procedures for aligning curriculum to standards and assessments, the preponderance of the research indicates that an aligned curriculum can overcome usual predictors of student achievement, such as socioeconomic status, gender, race, and teacher variables (see Squires, 2004).

Curriculum designers must decide how they will accomplish alignment to specified standards. Many strategies exist. In some districts, teachers are required to indicate alignment when planning lessons. Although such alignment is usually not the time to determine what is emphasized and what is left out, the practice does ensure at a minimum that instruction addresses some of the standards and state assessment categories. Other districts also align materials, either required or recommended, to state standards and assessments. Again, these alignments are not often reviewed in summary within a course.

To deal with the many possibilities of alignment, we created (Squires, 2004) an alignment chart (see Figure 5.1). The chart indicates which curricular component can be aligned or compared with which other curricular component. The arrows on the chart indicate that national standards can be aligned with all of the other components on the right-hand side. District curriculum designers will need to decide which of these areas are most important to work on, as alignment takes time and effort.

The alignment octagon (Squires, 2004) is another way for district curriculum designers to decide what to align. Figure 5.2 shows an example of perfect alignment in which all components of the curriculum, instruction, and assessment are aligned with each other. Districts will, of necessity, choose something less than perfection.

Figure 5.1   Curriculum alignment chart

Alignment Chart

National Standards from Professional Organizations	National Standards from Professional Organizations
NAEP, SAT, ACT	NAEP, SAT, ACT
Commercial Standardized Tests	Commercial Standardized Tests
State Standards	State Standards
State Assessments	State Assessments
Textbooks	Textbooks
District Curriculum	District Curriculum
District Standards	District Standards
District Assessments	District Assessments
Teacher Lesson Plans	Teacher Lesson Plans
Teacher Assessment	Teacher Assessment
Teacher Instruction	Teacher Instruction
Teacher Assignments	Teacher Assignments

SOURCE: Copyright © 2004 by David A. Squires. Used with permission from *Aligning and Balancing the Standards-Based Curriculum,* by David A. Squires. Reproduction authorized for the local school site that has purchased this book. www.corwinpress.com.

For example, suppose the district decides to align their textbooks with state standards and assessments. In this case, the district is assuming that their textbooks are powerful enough to guide the instructional choices of teachers and that the textbooks need to be aligned with the state standards and assessments. In this case, lines would be drawn only between textbooks and state standards, and textbooks and state assessments. Districts can use the alignment chart and the alignment octagon to chart out their alignment strategies and question their assumptions about how alignment will produce greater achievement.

Consider Curriculum Assessment

Does the curriculum include assessment? Which components will assessment cover? Will the assessment be developed by the district or the teachers? Will the assessment be required or optional? Will it be aligned with both the curriculum and the state standards or with other components? Assessments strengthen

Figure 5.2   Curriculum alignment octagon

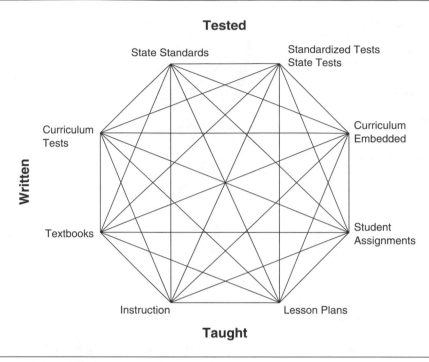

SOURCE: Copyright © 2004 by David A. Squires. Used with permission from *Aligning and Balancing the Standards-Based Curriculum,* by David A. Squires. Reproduction authorized for the local school site that has purchased this book. www.corwinpress.com.

curriculum by providing feedback that students learned what was taught. This information can inform further curriculum development, assessment revision, rules about course sequences for students, and remedial and enrichment programs for students.

Curriculum designers decide when assessment should occur, whether it takes place after the lesson, the unit, the course, or a certain number of courses. Again, time is a factor in determining structure for assessment and may be based on previous decisions. Some districts have begun testing on a quarterly basis, using state standards or frameworks as the template for showing that it is possible to conduct assessment in midstream, for example, between units and/or between courses. To be most effective, these assessments need to be aligned with both the curriculum and the state standards and assessments. This can be mapped on the curriculum octagon if the district intends to make sure the alignment happens. In some districts, quarterly assessments are aligned with state tests but with the instruction taking place in the district. In this case, the district is attempting to coordinate the curriculum through testing. Why not coordinate the curriculum directly?

All teachers of a particular course or all teachers in a particular school can use the same assessment. Sometimes it is left up to the discretion of individual teachers to develop assessments on their own. When this happens, individual teachers generate unit assessments or lesson assessments and the district and/or school generates final or quarterly assessments.

Consider Staff Development

Writing the curriculum is a staff development task. The decisions about who will write it and who will lead it, the time needed for writing, and the money to support the writing all come under the purview of staff development. We suggest that the curriculum be written by representatives of a grade level or course, consisting of the wisest, most caring, most influential teachers in the district. In this way, the district captures their knowledge, experience, and expertise and institutionalizes it in the curriculum document. The experience can build a culture of teamwork and improve adult relationships.

Once the curriculum is written, staff development is needed to support its implementation. Curriculum writers should help to develop the implementation plans and be involved in carrying them out. Who but the writers know best about the curriculum content? Involving the writers in actual implementation is another way to build relationships and teamwork. If representatives from across the district developed the curriculum, then they can also be involved at their own schools, working with staff they already know.

For example, one district had grade-level groups of teachers meet at their individual schools and divide the curriculum parts into three equal piles: (1) easily implemented tasks, (2) tasks or topics that would be moderately difficult to teach, and (3) tasks or topics that would be difficult to teach. Then, the groups set aside staff development time to discuss ways to teach the topics effectively. This strategy got groups of teachers involved in solving common instructional problems. Staff development can be very effective in strengthening curriculum implementation.

> In "It's All About Effective Relationships" (Chapter 12 in *Six Pathways to Healthy Child Development and Academic Success* in this series), J. Patrick Howley explains: "Human relationships are the cornerstone of school change and improvement. The relationships in our schools can either support or hinder efforts at improvement and growth." The task in this case is writing the curriculum. Paying attention to the process—how the adults on the team relate to one another—will ensure that the task is accomplished with excellence.

Consider Implementation

For a curriculum to have an effect, it must be implemented. Curriculum designers will need to consider staff development to (1) familiarize teachers with the curriculum, (2) help them to plan for and implement aspects that are new or changed, and (3) assist them with unfamiliar curriculum areas.

Curriculum designers will need to determine what measures will demonstrate that teachers have implemented the curriculum. What evidence will they accept as proof? It may be a teacher's lesson plans that indicate the recommended content has been covered. For a curriculum with uniform assessments, good scores on the assessments may serve as evidence of adequate implementation. Between actual implementation and the evidence, however, there is always an assumption. In this case, the assumption is that if a teacher implements the curriculum, the scores on the assessments (however they are structured in time) will be good.

Curriculum designers need to question assumptions in order to build curricular systems with integrity. In the example above, just because a teacher implements the curriculum does not necessarily mean that students will score well. What about students who were absent, not paying attention, not doing their homework, not studying for tests, or goofing off in class? Curriculum designers may decide that those who complete required work should score well on the assessments. Are we then assuming that implementation is best measured at the individual rather than at the classroom level? Is evidence of implementation drawn from teachers or from students?

Consider Monitoring Procedures

Determining whether a curriculum is implemented requires monitoring. Who will monitor? Is it the responsibility of the principal, the assistant principal in charge of instruction, the central office, the teacher, or some combination? What procedure will the person(s) follow to collect the information agreed upon? Monitoring is also determined by time and can take place on a daily, weekly, monthly, or yearly basis, or by semester. For a teacher who does not comply with the monitoring requirements, consequences need to be defined. Staff development for new and existing teachers will need to be conducted so everyone understands the information flow and the rationale for collecting the information. The collected information may need to be aggregated in some way and sent to the central office. Procedures need to be developed to determine who has access to the information and what they should do with it.

Consider the Procedures for Revision

Curriculum is typically revised once every five years or in-synch with the adoption of textbooks. Using this approach, even if a district has testing data on a yearly basis, that data can be used to impact curricular changes only once every five years. The frequency of curriculum revision determines in part how the curriculum is used in a school system. If a curriculum with only suggestions and no assessment and no monitoring requirements is revised every seven years, it may have great utility the first year, but will then fade into disuse and be shelved as the sixth and seventh years come along. On the other hand, a *required* curriculum that is revised on a yearly basis, with accompanying staff development efforts, and is aligned to needs revealed by the state test will have a better chance of surviving as a guide to instruction.

Curricular revision has budgetary implications, as teachers are generally paid for the extra work during the summer to revise the curriculum. Gathering input from staff members is important if the curriculum is to reflect gain through implementation. Is a unit too long or too short? Do units need to be combined? Do new state directives or district directives impact the curriculum? The specific procedures by which the curriculum will be revised are integral to the design process and should be specified from the design stage onward, not tacked on as an afterthought.

Consider Policy Support

The rules and regulations around curriculum development, implementation, and revision need to be backed by sound policies. These policies must spell out the roles of the school board administration, teachers, parents, and community members in developing curriculum. Once established, all of the procedures surrounding curriculum development should be inserted into the policy handbook to show how the policies will be implemented. Sound policy can clarify issues such as academic freedom and the school board's right to establish curriculum. The following is a quotation from the Curriculum Management Audit, a process created by Fenwick English:

> Quality control is the fundamental element of a well-managed educational program. It is one of the major premises of local educational control within any state's educational system.
>
> The critical premise involved is that, via the will of the electorate, a local board of trustees establishes local priorities within state laws and regulations. A school district's accountability rests with the school board and the public.
>
> Through the development of an effective policy framework, a local school board provides the focus for management and accountability to be established for administrative and instructional staff members, as well as for its own responsibility. It also enables the district to assess meaningful use of student learning data as a critical factor in determining its success.
>
> Although educational program control and accountability are often shared among different components of a school district, fundamental control of, and responsibility for, a district and its operations rest with the school board and top-level management staff. (*Northwest Independent School District Curriculum Management Audit*, 1996)

USEFULNESS AND USABILITY AS INDICATORS OF CURRICULUM QUALITY

Designing curriculum is a matter of consciously making decisions about how the curricular elements fit together to make a coherent whole. Each part of curriculum design—the schedule, decisions about whether it will be disciplinary or interdisciplinary, the curriculum components, the way the curriculum is described, whether the curriculum is required or only recommended, the degree to which it is aligned, staff development, curriculum monitoring, curriculum revision, and curriculum policy—all affect each other. The staggering number of permutations and combinations may leave us throwing up our hands and adopting the curriculum format from the district down the road, with all its unexamined assumptions. How do we make a choice? In this section, we discuss curriculum design using the criteria of usefulness and usability. Curriculum won't help if it isn't used and isn't useful to those making decisions about instruction.

10 Criteria for Structuring a Usable and Useful Curriculum

1. Useful and usable if it helps teachers use time to address content and appropriately pace instruction.

2. Usable if the content is structured so that teachers know what is most important to teach and if it outlines how to teach the content.

3. Usable if teachers have the flexibility to use their own creativity in planning instruction.

4. Useful if it focuses teacher instruction on the standards.

5. Useful if it helps teachers balance their instruction so that items aren't over- or underemphasized.

6. Useful if it helps teachers know that students have performed at high levels on instruction aligned with standards and assessment.

7. Usable and useful if the results of assessments embedded in the curriculum can be compared with results of state and standardized tests.

8. Useful if it brings teachers together to collaborate on designing the curriculum and planning instruction.

9. Useful if it has a structure for monitoring student and teacher completion of the curriculum.

10. Usable if it is revised yearly to take into account the most recent performance on state and/or standardized tests and teachers' experience with the curriculum.

THE SDP BALANCED CURRICULUM PROCESS MEETS THE CRITERIA OF USEFULNESS AND USABILITY

In this section, we examine the SDP Balanced Curriculum structure as one way that a curriculum can be designed to improve student outcomes. Then, we show how that structure meets the criteria of being usable and useful.

What are the structural characteristics of the SDP Balanced Curriculum Process? It is specific enough to guide and coordinate instruction, and it is flexible enough to ensure teacher creativity. The structure consists of units, significant tasks, alignments, assessments, and a management system. The process of building the curriculum involves five steps. Here they are in summary form:

1. Generate units.

2. Decide on 2 to 5 significant tasks for each unit, for a total of 35 to 50 significant tasks for the year.

3. Align and balance the significant tasks with standards and standardized tests, and with the developmental pathways (see discussion below).

4. Develop format and content assessments aligned to significant tasks, standards, and standardized assessments.

5. Ensure that the balanced curriculum is taught, assessed, managed, and improved.

After reading the rest of the chapter, you will be ready to design a curriculum that can make a difference for your district or school.

Step 1: Generate Units

The Balanced Curriculum Process asks schools to come to a consensus about what is most important to teach and assess. The model requires schools and/or grade levels to divide their reading/language arts or math curriculum into units with beginning and end dates. A Grade One English curriculum, for example, might have 10 units, with the first unit beginning in September and the 10th finishing in June. Everyone agrees to teach these units.

Step 2: Decide on 2–5 Significant Tasks for Each Unit, for a Total of 35–50 Significant Tasks for the Year

Author teams develop 2 to 5 significant tasks per unit to be taught by all teachers of the course. The significant tasks are larger than lesson plans, but smaller than units. A series of unit projects is a good way to think about significant tasks. The significant tasks are designed so they take up 60 percent of the unit's instructional time. Again, the team needs to reach consensus on these powerful tasks. Authors also review state standards and district assessments to make sure these elements are addressed in the significant tasks.

Step 3: Align and Balance the Significant Task With Standards and Standardized Tests and the Developmental Pathways

The author team learns how to align the significant tasks. Research suggests that if a curriculum is aligned with standards and standardized tests, student achievement is likely to improve. (Indeed, in every school and district that implemented the SDP Balanced Curriculum Process, student achievement improved.) Teams learn how to balance their curriculum so it meets both academic standards and students' developmental needs along the six pathways. A tenet of the SDP program is that the curriculum should promote the development of children along all six developmental pathways. If alignment to one or more of the pathways is not achieved during the first several passes, teachers might then need to reexamine the significant tasks and modify them to include the missing pathway(s). In this way, all are confident that all standards have been addressed and that the curriculum is balanced.

Step 4: Develop Format and Content Assessments Aligned to Significant Tasks, Standards, and Standardized Assessments

Author teams learn how to construct a format assessment and a content assessment. The format assessment, given once for each unit, provides students with practice on the format of standardized tests, a critical variable in enhancing student outcomes. The content assessment is given by all teachers to determine how well students perform on significant tasks and the standards aligned with the significant tasks. All who teach the course give all students the same format and content assessments. Districts can enter the schools' scores for each assessment on a consolidated form or district Web site, making it easier for the district to review and assess student data.

Step 5: Ensure That the Balanced Curriculum Is Taught, Assessed, Managed, and Improved

Central office and school administrators develop a plan to ensure that the curriculum is implemented. Each principal provides time for the faculty to plan their instruction and assessments using the balanced curriculum documents. A system for monitoring the completion of significant tasks by different teachers can be set up electronically; readers may wish to consult the Web site (www.balancedcurriculum. com). The SPMT and/or the principal may provide oversight of the faculty's efforts to complete the curriculum and develop strategies to assist those who experience difficulty. Grade-level or course-level meetings help the faculty to collaborate on instructional planning and implementation; teams at these levels should keep records of their suggestions about how the significant tasks and/or assessments can be improved the following year. Thus the Balanced Curriculum Process builds a district's capacity to continue improving the curriculum, instruction, assessment, and outcomes for students.

WEB-BASED CURRICULUM DEVELOPMENT AND IMPLEMENTATION

Curriculum development can be a tedious task, especially when there are many authors. Web-based curriculum development can help district leaders coordinate document production, make revision easier, and offer tools for administrators to check teachers' completion rates of the units and significant tasks throughout the year. Curriculum updates should be based on (1) student and teacher experience, (2) whether the curriculum specifically addresses state standards and assessments, and (3) whether the curriculum provides equal access to significant tasks based on best practices.

DO THE FIVE STEPS DESCRIBED ABOVE MEET THE 10 CRITERIA FOR A USEFUL AND USABLE CURRICULUM?

Let's examine each of the 10 criteria carefully.

Curriculum is useful and usable if it helps teachers use time to address content, and appropriately pace instruction. The SDP Balanced Curriculum Process addresses time through defining time-bound units that everyone teaches. The significant tasks take up about 60 percent of a unit's time. The first criterion is met.

Curriculum is usable if the content is structured so that teachers know what is most important to teach and if it outlines how to teach this content. The significant tasks define what is most important to teach (the objectives) as well as how to teach the task (instruction). The SDP Balanced Curriculum Process meets these standards.

Curriculum is usable if teachers have the flexibility to use their own creativity in planning instruction. As the significant tasks take up 60 percent of instructional time, the teacher can design his or her own instruction for the other 40 percent. In addition, most significant tasks are written in general terms so teachers can use their creativity in deciding the appropriate instructional sequence to meet the significant tasks.

Curriculum is useful if it focuses teacher instruction on the standards. The SDP Balanced Curriculum Process aligns the significant tasks with the standards. The significant tasks tell how the standards are enacted in the classroom.

Curriculum is useful if it helps teachers balance their instruction so that items aren't over- or underemphasized. The SDP Balanced Curriculum Process incorporates alignment of significant tasks with standards and then provides a review of the alignment for balance in the curriculum, ensuring that nothing is over- or underemphasized.

Curriculum is useful if it helps teachers know that students have performed at high levels on instruction aligned with standards and assessment. Two types of assessments are included: a format assessment, in which students practice in the format of the state test once per unit, and a content assessment that tells teachers and students how well they met the standard embedded in the significant tasks.

Curriculum is usable and useful if the results of assessments embedded in the curriculum can be compared with results of state and standardized tests. For individual students, good results on curriculum-embedded assessments should predict good results on state assessment items or clusters aligned with the local curriculum. The curriculum should be structured so the data are collected and aggregated in ways that show the prediction is true or untrue. If results of curriculum-based assessments don't predict scores on the standardized assessments, then the district needs to consider either revising the curricular assessment to increase predictability or abandoning it altogether.

Curriculum is useful if it brings teachers together to collaborate on designing the curriculum and planning instruction. Curriculum is written by a district's best teachers, discussing the best and the strongest ways to approach curriculum content through the design of significant tasks. Everyone teaches the same significant tasks, so cooperative planning is encouraged because it makes lesson planning easier for everyone.

Curriculum is useful if it has a structure for monitoring student and teacher completion of the curriculum. The SDP Balanced Curriculum Process has a structure for monitoring progress. Teachers are asked to keep a log of their completed significant tasks either manually or electronically, noting the date they completed the significant task. This information can be aggregated by subject area or teacher so administrators will know whether the students and teachers are progressing through the curriculum.

Curriculum is usable if it is revised yearly to take into account the most recent performance on state and/or standardized tests and teachers' experience with the curriculum. The SDP Balanced Curriculum Process asks teachers to record comments about their recently completed significant tasks. These can be valuable in the revision process. A yearly revision is strongly recommended, in which the most current results of the state or standardized test are examined to determine other changes needed in the curriculum.

The worksheet that appears on the Web site helps you to make systematic and thoughtful decisions about the structure of the curriculum for your district. You can download this worksheet at no cost from the Balanced Curriculum Web site (www.balancedcurriculum.com). We recommend tackling this task with a districtwide planning or steering committee before writing the curriculum. Coming to a consensus on the most appropriate design will build your capacity to actually implement the curriculum. The worksheet provides a framework for discussing the structure of the curriculum in your district. After completing the framework, rate your design using the 10 criteria for structuring a usable and useful curriculum. We hope you find this a useful way to approach developing curriculum for your school district.

REFERENCES

Ceperley, P. E., & Squires, D. A. (2000). *Standards implementation indicators: Charting your course to high achievement.* Lanham, MD: AEL/Scarecrow Education.

Cohen, S. A. (1987). Instructional alignment: Searching for a magic bullet. *Educational Researcher, 16*(8), 16–19.

English, F. W., & Steffy, B. E. (2001). *Deep curriculum alignment: Creating a level playing field for all children on high-stakes tests of educational accountability.* Lanham, MD: Scarecrow Press.

Howson, G. (1995). *Mathematics textbooks: A comparative study of Grade 8 texts.* Vancouver, Canada: Pacific Education Press.

Moss-Mitchell, F. (1998). *The effects of curriculum alignment on the mathematics achievement of third-grade students as measured by the Iowa Test of Basic Skills: Implication for educational administrators.* Unpublished doctoral dissertation, Clark University, Atlanta, GA.

Neidermeyer, F., & Yelon, S. (1981). Los Angeles aligns instruction with essential skills. *Educational Leadership, 38*(8), 618–620.

Northwest Independent School District Curriculum Management Audit. (1996). (Available from Texas Audit Center, Texas Association of School Administrators, 406 East 11th Street, Austin, TX 78701)

Porter, A. C., Kirst, M. W., Osthoff, E., Smithson, J. L., & Schneider, S. (1994). *Reform of high school mathematics and science and opportunity to learn.* Consortium for Policy Research in Education Policy Briefs. New Brunswick, NJ: Rutgers University, Consortium for Policy Research in Education.

Porter, A. C., & Smithson J. L. (2001). *Defining, developing, and using curriculum indicators* (CPRE Research Report Series RR-048, Consortium for Policy Research in Education). Philadelphia: University of Pennsylvania.

Price-Baugh, R. (1997). *Correlation of textbook alignment with student achievement scores.* Unpublished doctoral dissertation, Baylor University, Waco, TX.

Schmidt, W. H., McKnight, C. C., Houang, R. T., Wang, H. C., Wiley, D. E., Cogan, L. S., & Wolfe, R. G. (2001). *Why schools matter: A cross-national comparison of curriculum and learning.* San Francisco: Jossey-Bass.

Squires, D. A. (2003). *A structure for the analysis of district curriculum.* (Available from ABC Education Consultants, 3 Indian Woods Road, Branford, CT 06405)

Squires, D. A. (2004). *Aligning and balancing the standards-based curriculum.* Thousand Oaks, CA: Corwin Press.

Wishnick, K. T. (1989). *Relative effects on achievements scores of SES, gender, teacher effect and instructional alignment: A study of alignment's power in mastery learning.* Unpublished doctoral dissertation, University of San Francisco, CA.

AUTHORS' NOTE: This chapter is the outcome of a writing project undertaken by SDP's Teaching, Learning, and Development Unit. The chapter is based on the book *Aligning and Balancing the Standards-Based Curriculum* (Squires, 2004) and on a paper written for Appalachia Educational Laboratory, "A Structure for the Analysis of District Curriculum" (Squires, 2003), which proposes a design for describing all district curriculum in Louisiana. This paper informed the section "What's Included in Curriculum Designs?" The 10 criteria for structuring a usable and useful curriculum for assessing the curriculum structure are modified versions of Standards Implementation Indicators, by Ceperley and Squires (2000).

6

Comer-in-the-Classroom

Linking the Essential Elements of the Comer Process to Classroom Practices

Fay E. Brown and Valerie Maholmes

Historically, the Comer Process has been a whole-school reform model with a marked emphasis on governance and policy at the school and school district levels. In this chapter, SDP's director of Child and Adolescent Development and SDP's director of Research and Policy explain that Comer-in-the-Classroom represents a deepening of the implementation of the Comer Process within the school. Through Comer-in-the-Classroom, teachers and their students modify their own behavior according to the principles of consensus, collaboration, and no-fault. They come to understand and report on their own growth and development in terms of the six developmental pathways. They are able to have a clearer focus on the goals of the comprehensive school plan. When the Comer Process is in the classroom, parents become more involved and there is a rich and rewarding communication between the classroom and all other parts of the school community.

WHAT IS COMER-IN-THE-CLASSROOM?

Teachers often ask these questions: "How do the collaborative decision-making strategies of the Comer Process relate to what I do in my classroom?" "If I am not on a Comer team, what role do I play in implementing the Comer Process in my school?" "If the Comer process doesn't have a curriculum, how can it affect teaching and learning?"

Comer-in-the-Classroom refers to the specific ways in which teachers apply the principles of the Comer Process and link the qualities and characteristics of the nine elements to classroom practice. Thus teachers must have a working knowledge of these principles so that they may become highly observable in all aspects of curriculum, instruction, and assessment. As a result, these classrooms can be distinguished from the classrooms in which the principles have not been fully implemented. Figure 6.1 elaborates the qualities and characteristics of the Comer Process and shows how teachers can link these elements to classroom practice.

Figure 6.1 Classroom strategies linked to the Comer Process

Comer Process	Qualities and Characteristics	Strategies
SPMT	*Representativeness:* All students have opportunities to learn and to participate in leadership roles and activities. *Shared Decision Making:* Students have opportunities to participate in making rules and norms for the classroom. Students have opportunities to have a voice in important matters that pertain to them.	Cooperative learning. Peer-to-peer tutoring. Students serve as delegates to the SPMT. Students participate in rule setting. Students codevelop consequences for breaking rules and rewards for keeping rules.
SSST	*Problem Solving:* Individual level problem solving. Global classroom-wide problem solving. Instructional activities need to be informed by knowledge of the students and their particular needs.	Peer mediation. Conflict resolution. Class meeting. Application of the six developmental pathways.
Parent Team	Parents need to be engaged in a way that supports the learning and development of children both inside and outside the classroom.	Parents as substitutes. Parents assist in guided reading activities. Parents conduct workshops for parents on classroom strategies. Parents serve as chaperones. Parents observe and provide feedback.
Consensus	Teachers encourage consensus decision making in the classroom. Students take ownership through the consensus process. Students have choice in instructional materials/activities.	Perspective taking. Considering others' perspectives. Acceptance of differences in people and points of view. Listening skills. Respect for self and others. Negotiating skills.

Collaboration	Teachers, students, and parents work together, get along with one another, respect themselves and each other.	Teamwork in dyads and triads. Cooperative learning. Negotiating skills.
No-fault	No-fault is modeled in the classroom. A positive tone is set from the first day of school. Positive climate is experienced in the classroom. High expectations are evidenced through "words and deeds." Assessments are used to diagnose rather than to punish.	Teachers explicitly teach students descriptive, nonjudgmental language. Teachers and parents model no-fault language for the students. Developmental pathways are used as a framework for lesson planning and assessment.
Assessment and Modification	Teachers are reflective and thoughtful about the ways they carry out their instructional practices and how they relate to students.	Action research. Reflective teaching. Fair and appropriate use of data for instructional decision making.
Staff Development	Students develop skills to perform leadership functions in the classroom and to collaborate on projects. Parents develop skills to support classroom practices.	Teachers explicitly teach students leadership and social skills. Parent liaison/team conducts training to enable parents to support classroom practices.
Comprehensive School Plan	Lesson planning is a central component of a teacher's comprehensive plan for delivering developmentally appropriate instruction.	Lesson plans indicate which developmental pathways are being addressed. Plans take into account student learning styles and developmental needs.
Relationships	There is evidence of positive teacher-student, teacher-parent, and student-student relationships.	Community and team-building activities. Student dialogues. Class meetings. Conflict resolution skills.
Developmental Pathways	The classroom reflects the six developmental pathways.	Display of students' work. Activities that incorporate movement. Appropriate and flexible arrangement of the classroom. Language-rich environment, "healthy noise." Developmentally appropriate materials, strategies, and assessment. The classrooms are multimodal and multisensory.

While Figure 6.1 operationalizes the nine elements of the model in the classroom, there are also some specific, nonnegotiable standards that define the everyday practices of teachers, students, and parents in the Comer classroom. The adherence to these standards fosters a positive climate that is conducive to effective learning, teaching, and development. Presented below are seven standards that are foundational to implementing Comer-in-the-Classroom.

THE SEVEN FOUNDATIONAL STANDARDS FOR IMPLEMENTING COMER-IN-THE-CLASSROOM

1. Have High Expectations for All Students

Teachers have both implicit and explicit expectations for their students. The implicit expectations reflect the belief that all students can learn and have the potential to achieve. The explicit expectations encompass those that are verbally and behaviorally expressed to students, incorporated into the lesson plans, and prominently displayed in the classroom. Teachers have specific expectations for each child so that they can guide each one toward a specific outcome that he or she will accomplish by the end of the year. These expectations are then translated into goals for individual students and for the class as a whole.

- What are the goals that you have for your students?
- How are they reflected in behavioral terms to your students?

List some specific strategies for meeting this standard:

_____

_____

_____

_____

_____

_____

2. Teach From a Challenging and Rigorous Curriculum

If we have high expectations for our children, we will provide a challenging and rigorous curriculum to meet those expectations. Teaching from a challenging curriculum enables children to perform to their highest potential, whereas teaching from a watered-down curriculum limits their potential. Brain research suggests that when we stimulate children's thinking, neural connections are made, and when we don't stimulate or challenge the children, these connections are underdeveloped and the capacity to make these connections is diminished (Jensen, 1998).

List some specific strategies for meeting this standard:

_____

_____

_____

_____

_____

_____

3. Develop Positive, Healthy Relationships

Learning to high levels demands a partnership between teacher and student. They both have a responsibility in creating that mutuality. A healthy relationship is the foundation that allows that partnership to develop and to thrive.

> Where there is a good climate of relationships, there is academic achievement, and you can accomplish the business of socializing kids and making gains at the same time. One need not interfere with the other. (Comer, cited in the National Center for Effective Schools Research and Development, 1989, p. 43)

> Rogers maintained that "the teacher's skills, knowledge of the field, curricular planning, lectures, and selection of books and other learning aids are all peripheral; the crux of the learning situation is the relationship between the facilitator and the learner which should be characterized by realness, valuing, and empathy. (Ryan & Cooper, 1995, p. 46)

List some specific strategies for meeting this standard:

_____

_____

_____

_____

_____

_____

4. Cultivate Mutual Respect and Trust

If you have high expectations and demonstrate those expectations in attitudes and behaviors toward students, it fosters mutual respect and trust. Attitudes and words that students and teachers use toward one another reflect the level of respect that exists among them. Respect and trust are consequences of the initial tone and climate established in the classroom during the first few days/weeks of school.

List some specific strategies for meeting this standard:

_____

_____

_____

_____

_____

_____

5. Honor the Three Guiding Principles of Collaboration, Consensus, and No-fault

The guiding principles give teachers the tools for learning how to conduct their classrooms in ways that promote healthy relationships, respect, and high expectations. They enable teachers to challenge students to their highest potential, because they have built this respectful, achievement-oriented climate. The guiding principles remove the excuses that students have for not performing to high standards and the excuses that teachers have for not teaching to high standards.

Collaboration allows the teacher to engage students in meaningful ways as they work together. It sets an expectation that says, "We will all work cooperatively, not competitively." It also teaches students certain social skills that they need in order to work in that kind of environment. Students learn that in order to work in this climate, there are certain roles they have to play, certain responsibilities they have to take on, and certain behaviors they have to demonstrate.

Consensus allows the teacher and the students to come to agreement about the things that will foster an effective learning community. It allows both teacher and students to listen to each other and to make decisions about classroom norms, rules, and consequences. Thus it is a process that gives teachers, students, and parents a forum for expression in a safe and respectful climate.

No-fault in the classroom calls teachers' attention to the messages they send to students through words, deeds, and attitudes. They are always cognizant of the fact that children can be easily turned on or off by the messages that are sent to them on a daily basis. This no-fault attitude of teachers allows children to feel valued and to feel that they can be successful. When teachers are thinking no-fault, they are more prone to provide opportunities to promote, rather than to stifle or impede, students' learning and development. In a classroom where no-fault is evident or in operation, teachers tend to see children's potential, not their limitations, and they tend to reward efforts in increments, rather than wait for explosions of academic excellence. They understand that rewarding students incrementally can lead to high performance. Teachers don't blame students for not knowing, but celebrate with them and scaffold the little that they know into the vast expanse of what they will know—the zone of proximal development—moving students from budding to blossoming to flourishing.

No-fault builds students' confidence and sense of efficacy and academic self-concept. From the students' perspective, no-fault allows them to accept each other with the understanding that each one is a learner and that each one needs help along the way. Students respect each other and use appropriate language that reflects this respect. They understand that mocking, jeering, or criticizing other students' weaknesses is not acceptable. Teachers use appropriate, nonjudgmental language to provide feedback to students. Thus no-fault is a problem-solving strategy that is used to address the little things that can happen in a classroom in the course of any given day.

List some specific strategies for meeting this standard:

_____

_____

_____

_____

_____

_____

6. Operate From a Developmental Perspective

The six developmental pathways (physical, cognitive, psychological, language, social, and ethical) enable teachers to view children from a developmental rather than a deficit perspective. These pathways serve as a framework within which teachers can develop lessons as well as diagnose and respond to student behaviors. In addition, they extend the concept of no-fault into the classroom. The core of what we do is to develop children, because we believe that when children develop well, they learn well.

List some specific strategies for meeting this standard:

_____

_____

_____

_____

_____

_____

7. Know Your Students

When teachers know their students, they have a heightened awareness of their individual and collective needs and learning styles. This knowledge should extend beyond the classroom and outside the realm of academic tasks. Teachers are also aware of the different ways in which they can work with students to promote their learning and overall growth and development. Thus teachers use the pathways as a tool for diagnosing, assessing, problem solving, and strategizing. Essentially, when teachers know their students, they understand that in "every interaction they have with every child, they are either helping to promote development or to impede development" (Dr. James P. Comer, March 1999, personal communication).

List some specific strategies for meeting this standard:

_____

_____

_____

_____

_____

COMER-IN-THE-CLASSROOM LIFE CYCLE

Knowledge of how the nine elements link to classroom practices and an understanding of the importance of the standards prepare a teacher for the effective implementation of Comer-in-the-Classroom process. Just as the SDP Implementation Life Cycle guides the implementation of the Comer Process in the school, the Comer-in-the-Classroom Life Cycle and the accompanying checklists (see Figures 6.2 through 6.8 at the end of this chapter) may be used to implement and assess the Comer-in-the-Classroom process. The Life Cycle consists of five phases:

1. Planning and Preparation

2. Foundation Building

3. Transformation

4. Institutionalization

5. Renewal

The phases of the overall SDP Life Cycle are expected to be implemented in the school over a five-year period, while the Comer-in-the-Classroom Life Cycle is intended to be accomplished during the course of the school year. Although the phases are listed sequentially, in practice, they will not unfold as such. While implementing one phase, for example, Institutionalization, situations such as high mobility, behavior problems, and low achievement may necessitate revisiting the earlier phase of Transformation. In addition, the day-to-day realities of classroom practice may result in multiple phases of the process being implemented simultaneously. Thus the Comer-in-the-Classroom Life Cycle is intended for use only as a guide for continuous improvement of classroom practices and interactions. The following is a delineation of the phases of the Comer-in-the Classroom Life Cycle and specific expectations for implementation.

Planning and Preparation

During the first part of the year, teachers are encouraged to start with a plan that articulates objectives and strategies for meeting the standards of Comer-in-the-Classroom. This plan should also specify academic and other outcomes along each of the six developmental pathways. The following are indicators and benchmarks that characterize this phase of implementation:

- Reflection and Analysis
  - Use the developmental pathways framework to reflect on teachers' own needs, strengths, and overall readiness to teach and interact with students and parents.
  - Conduct a needs assessment using the pathways framework to identify the needs, strengths, and possible challenges of the students they will teach for the year.
  - Ascertain the functionality of the physical space for promoting students' development along each of the six pathways.
  - Determine availability of resources to promote high achievement and overall student development.
- Comprehensive Classroom Planning
  - Articulate in writing teachers' expectations for students individually and collectively.
  - Have a plan for what they hope to accomplish during the year to meet the holistic needs of students.
  - Have a plan for how they hope to meaningfully engage parents.

Foundation Building

During the first couple of weeks of the school year, activities and strategies that characterize this phase may unfold simultaneously or overlap with some aspects of the Planning and Preparation stage. The essence of this phase is the building and maintaining of positive relationships between and among teachers, students, and parents.

- Creating a Shared Vision
  - Each teacher should have a vision for teaching and reaching every child.
  - Teachers should help students to develop their own visions for learning, interacting, and achieving.
  - Parents need to be encouraged to have visions that promote successful outcomes for their children and that support the attainment of goals for all students in the class.
  - Through respectful, open communication, and consensus decision making, the different visions of teachers, parents, and students become a shared vision.
  - Teachers, parents, and students know and practice the guiding principles of consensus, collaboration, and no-fault problem solving.
  - Teachers establish the use of class meetings as a foundation for building relationships and engaging students on all levels.
  - Teachers should make deliberate efforts to know aspects of their students beyond the classroom.
  - Teachers collect baseline data based on academic, behavioral, and performance indicators to know students and to plan effectively for them.

Transformation

At this stage, Comer classrooms can be distinguished from classrooms that are not implementing Comer-in-the-Classroom. The components of Comer-in-the-Classroom should be observable and practiced regularly. Outcomes should include, but not be limited to, achievement gains, a safe environment in which students can take risks, and reduction in behavior problems. More specifically, the following characteristics should be observable:

- There is a shift from an adult-centered orientation to a child-centered orientation.
- Students have more opportunities to take on leadership roles in the classrooms and participate in decision making.
- There is strong evidence of the practice of the guiding principles by teachers, students, and parents.
- There is strong evidence of a developmental focus in instructional practice, in management and organization, in order and discipline, and in assessment of student performance.
- The physical organization and resources of the classroom reflect an intentional effort to promote student development through a variety of strategies.

- There is strong evidence that teachers are making deliberate connections between curriculum, instruction, relationships, and development.
- The plan outlined at the Planning and Preparation stage is in full operation.
- The goals and the vision articulated at the Foundation Building stage are actualized.
- Teachers, students, and parents celebrate their accomplishments thus far.

Institutionalization

At this phase, practices and interactions that define the standards of Comer-in-the-Classroom should be highly observable and practiced at optimal levels. There should also be evidence that these practices are filtering outside the classroom to permeate the entire school and, by extension, the home. The following are characteristic of implementation at this stage:

- The guiding principles and developmental pathways frame a common language that is communicated and responded to in the classrooms and throughout the school.
- There is meaningful and consistent parent involvement.
- Teachers are behaving as critical friends, sharing effective strategies and providing feedback.
- Rules and logical consequences are practiced consistently across classrooms and permeate the school building.
- Same-page behaviors are practiced in the classroom, across grade levels, and throughout the school.
- The content and tenor of conversations in the teachers' lounge reflect no-fault language, valuing, and positive regard of all students.
- Students are aware of themselves along the developmental pathways and can measure their own progress on academic, social, and behavioral criteria.
- Teachers are more cognizant of themselves along the developmental pathways, which fosters greater understanding between the teacher and the students.

Renewal

This stage is characterized by the teacher's assessment of the level of implementation of the Comer-in-the-Classroom components and the extent to which the standards are being met. The following problem-solving questions may be used to guide the assessment process: What is working well? What is not working well? What should be done differently?

Along with this assessment, teachers are encouraged to do a thoughtful self-assessment using the developmental pathways framework. The self-assessment may uncover areas in which there appears to be a need for a recommitment to the philosophy and principles of the Comer Process as it is applied to the classroom.

ASSESSING THE OBSERVABLE ELEMENTS OF THE COMER PROCESS IN YOUR CLASSROOM

The Comer-in-the-Classroom checklist (see Figures 6.2–6.8) operationalizes the philosophy, principles, and strategies of the Comer Process so that teachers may have a clearer picture of their role in a Comer school. This checklist provides a sampling of practices for selected components of the Comer Process. These practices serve as a framework for answering the following questions: "What are the characteristics of a classroom in which the Comer Process is fully integrated?" "What practices need to be strengthened?"

The checklist is designed to give teachers a way to self-assess their progress in linking the Comer elements into the classroom. Thus teachers may be encouraged to use the checklist at the beginning of the year to establish a baseline, at the middle of the year as a benchmark, and at the end of the year to examine progress over time. By doing so, teachers will be able to assess and modify their practices as they move along the Comer-in-the-Classroom Life Cycle. Since collaboration is a central part of the Comer Process, teachers may choose to use the checklist with peer coaches or colleagues with whom they work closely, as a means of documenting and recording collaborative work.

While the checklist is not designed to be an evaluative tool, it can be used by administrators as they work with teachers to support their growth and development in the Comer Process. The administrator may check a response option that best fits the characteristics observed in a single classroom and then give a rating for each component of the Comer Process. He or she may use the *averaged* ratings as a way to help a teacher make progress in a specific area. The administrator may also use the checklist as a general barometer of overall implementation, and not target a specific classroom. Insights gleaned from observing particular classrooms using this checklist may be addressed directly with the individual teacher, a grade-level team, or a faculty meeting. However, to ensure schoolwide implementation of all the Comer components, patterns observed across classrooms should be identified and brought to the School Planning and Management Team (SPMT).

Healthy and nurturing learning environments are the hallmark of the Comer Process. The standards, strategies, and the Implementation Life Cycle offered in this chapter will help teachers, administrators, and other school staff to ensure that an enriched learning experience is provided in every classroom for every child.

Figure 6.2 The guiding principles

The guiding principles of collaboration, consensus, and no-fault are practiced in the classroom by teachers, students, and support staff.

	Highly Observable (5)	Observable (4)	Moderately Observable (3)	Minimally Observable (2)	Not Observable at This Point in Time (1)
I. Collaboration					
Parents, aides, and teachers work together to design academic and social development activities.					
Students engage in collaborative, problem-based learning activities.					
Students have opportunities to teach others and share what they have learned.					
Students have the opportunity to practice different leadership roles in group projects.					
The rules for teamwork are posted clearly on the walls or on class bulletin boards.					
Visitors are welcome and become a part of the learning process.					
Teachers work in teams to present thematic lessons and collaborate on class projects.					
Summary Score					

(Continued)

Figure 6.2 (Continued)

	Highly Observable (5)	Observable (4)	Moderately Observable (3)	Minimally Observable (2)	Not Observable at This Point in Time (1)
II. Consensus					
Teachers and parents model the consensus decision-making process for students.					
Students are knowledgeable about the consensus-building process.					
Teachers design lessons that allow students to practice consensus decision making.					
Students use data to make decisions by consensus.					
Students engage in inquiry processes, learn to question and seek information.					
Students have opportunities to make important decisions that affect the classroom environment.					
Summary Score					
III. No-fault					
The classroom environment is emotionally and psychologically safe for students, teachers, and parents.					
Teachers model no-fault problem-solving strategies for the students.					
Students have opportunities to learn through trial and error without being penalized.					

Students are treated fairly and have equal access to classroom resources.						
Neither the teacher nor students yell or use fault-finding language in the classroom.						
Students know what is expected of them in academic performance and social behavior.						
Teachers develop lessons and activities that reflect high expectations for student learning.						
Teachers use assessments as a way to diagnose student learning problems.						
Punishment is used as a last resort strategy for problem behavior.						
Teachers use a research-based system of rewards and consequences to foster positive student behavior.						
Summary Score						

Figure 6.3 Developmental focus

The six developmental pathways: cognitive, physical, social, psychological, language, social, and ethical, are evident in classroom practice.

	Highly Observable (5)	Observable (4)	Moderately Observable (3)	Minimally Observable (2)	Not Observable at This Point in Time (1)
Class assignments foster the development of effective communication skills, including listening and speaking.					
Teachers design lessons that help students develop prosocial skills and values.					
Students have opportunities through class discussions, writing assignments, and other venues to express feelings, needs, and concerns.					
Teachers incorporate movement and kinesthetic activities into lessons and class activities.					
Students have the opportunity to develop social skills and relationships through class assignments and projects.					
Teachers create opportunities for students to work according to their particular learning styles and strengths.					
Students use appropriate language and speak respectfully to the teacher and to classmates.					
The curriculum units and lessons promote critical and higher-order thinking.					
Class activities and lessons allow students a variety of opportunities to achieve success.					

Classroom rules are posted.				
Teachers do not yell or use disrespectful language with children.				
Teachers model rather than lecture about desired behavior.				
A class meeting is held daily in every classroom.				
Teachers do not "put down," "single out," or embarrass students.				
Summary Score				

Figure 6.4 Parent involvement

Parents play an important role in supporting student learning and development.

	Highly Observable (5)	Observable (4)	Moderately Observable (3)	Minimally Observable (2)	Not Observable at This Point in Time (1)
Teachers involve parents in activities that directly relate to improving student performance.					
Parents work with students in small-group or one-on-one activities when appropriate.					
Parents model the guiding principles in their interactions with teachers and students.					
Parents help teachers with outreach efforts to other parents.					
Opportunities exist for parents to work with students according to the students' particular learning styles and strengths.					
Class activities and lessons give parents a variety of opportunities to work in meaningful ways with students.					
Summary Score					

Figure 6.5 Assessment and modification

Critical reflection and analysis of teaching and learning.

	Highly Observable (5)	Observable (4)	Moderately Observable (3)	Minimally Observable (2)	Not Observable at This Point in Time (1)
Teachers use research findings to make instructional decisions.					
Teachers seek to improve their practice through classroom observations of other teachers.					
Teachers incorporate ideas and information from staff development activities to improve their planning and teaching.					
Teachers assess students' social development as well as academic achievement.					
Teachers use authentic performance assessments to determine students' academic strengths.					
Teachers use data to adapt lessons to match students' learning styles.					
Summary Score					

Figure 6.6 Relationships

Teachers create a positive atmosphere that fosters positive relationships among students and with adults working in the classroom.

	Highly Observable (5)	Observable (4)	Moderately Observable (3)	Minimally Observable (2)	Not Observable at This Point in Time (1)
Teachers know students' family backgrounds, extracurricular activities, and personal interests.					
Teachers work to establish a positive classroom climate.					
Classroom rules are consistent with schoolwide expectations and are regularly reinforced.					
Classroom management strategies are used to foster positive behavior and interaction among the students.					
Teachers model good listening skills.					
Students use peer mediation and conflict resolution strategies.					
Teachers, students, and parents use the Comer guiding principles.					
Parents feel welcome in the classroom.					

There is a process for welcoming new students into the classroom.				
All students are treated respectfully.				
Teachers clearly articulate expectations for student behavior and interaction.				
Teachers establish an emotional bond with all the children in their classrooms.				
Summary Score				

Figure 6.7 Comprehensive planning

Teachers set achievable goals and develop plans to promote students' learning and development.

	Highly Observable (5)	Observable (4)	Moderately Observable (3)	Minimally Observable (2)	Not Observable at This Point in Time (1)
Teachers collaborate with students and parents to set achievable goals for the academic year.					
Teachers' weekly lesson plans reflect the six developmental pathways.					
Teachers plan and carry out a variety of ways for students to represent their learning about particular subjects.					
Teachers plan activities that reflect the students' cultures and backgrounds.					
Teachers have identified students in the lowest quartile and have developed strategies to meet their individual needs.					
Teachers know students' learning styles and plan activities that take into account individual preferences and abilities.					
Summary Score					

Figure 6.8 Summary scores

Teacher Name: [   ]   Grade Level: [   ]

Number of students in class: [   ]   Date of Observation: [   ]

Summary Scores for Comer-in-the Classroom Components

Component	Summary Score	Comments
Collaboration		
Consensus		
No-fault		
Developmental Focus		
Parent Involvement		
Assessment and Modification		
Relationships		
Comprehensive Planning		

General Comments and Observations:

REFERENCES

Jensen, E. (1998). *Teaching with the brain in mind.* Alexandria, VA: Association for Supervision and Curriculum Development.

National Center for Effective Schools Research and Development. (1989). *A conversation between James Comer and Ronald Edmonds: Fundamentals of effective school improvements.* Dubuque, IA: Kendall/Hunt.

Ryan, K., & Cooper, J. (1995). *Those who can, teach.* Boston: Houghton Mifflin.

READ MORE ABOUT . . .

In Chapter 7, "A Demonstration of Comer-in-the-Classroom," by Carol Pickett Ray, an elementary school principal offers a real-life case study in which Comer-in-the-Classroom transformed an almost-failing school into the school with the greatest improvement in its district.

For a detailed description of the SDP Implementation Life Cycle, see "The School Development Program Implementation Life Cycle: A Guide for Planned Change," Chapter 18 in *Transforming School Leadership and Management to Support Student Learning and Development: The Field Guide to Comer Schools in Action* in this series.

7

A Demonstration of Comer-in-the-Classroom

Carol Pickett Ray

Comer-in-the-Classroom continues the SDP tradition of pioneering new ways to promote children's learning and development. The principal of a formerly low-performing elementary school in North Carolina reports on the power of Comer-in-the-Classroom to magnify positive changes throughout the school. The teachers have responded with increasingly creative programs, some high-tech and some no-tech, relying solely on interpersonal awareness. The improvement in the school's performance since implementing SDP has been staggering: from 42 percent of students demonstrating proficiency to almost all of the students, in just five years!

Had we known three years ago what we know now, we would have moved the Comer Process into the classroom the very first year we adopted the School Development Program (SDP). When we moved Comer into the classroom, it made everything come alive at Hall Fletcher Elementary School in Asheville, North Carolina. When we started to teach the developmental pathways to the children, it meant we as the adults in our school had to understand them. As the children learned about the pathways they were also teaching us. They were saying things to us about the pathways that we never thought of before. It energized our entire school.

THEY TOLD ME IT COULDN'T BE DONE . . .

Hall Fletcher was always a very special school to me. I leaped at the opportunity to move from the school district's central office to become the school's principal. My own daughter, who at that time was a fourth grader, had been a student in that school since kindergarten, and I had a lot of respect for the faculty and staff. During a transition meeting, I was told about the school's recent test scores: "It's not good. It looks like we're not going to meet our expected growth again this year, but at least we're over 50 percent proficient. So we're not in low-performing status. We're 50.2 percent proficient." Then a person said to me in all sincerity, "Get used to it. It will never get any better than this." That hit me just like someone had kicked me in the stomach because, remember: I wasn't just the new incoming principal—I was also a parent of a child in that school. When that comment was made to me, in essence, my child had been written off, just like every child in that school. And I said to myself, "By God, I'll show you."

> INCOMING PRINCIPAL: I was told, "At least the school is over 50 percent proficient. Get used to it. It will never get any better than this." That hit me just like someone had kicked me in the stomach.

By the end of my first year, we had improved to an overall proficiency rate of 66 percent. People have said to me that it had to be more than the Comer Process. I maintain it was *because* of the Comer Process: The process was the overarching framework through which we planned all of those direct strategies and nurtured all of those relationships—not just adult-to-adult, but adult-to-children and children-to-children—to really turn the school around. After the third year of SDP implementation, our proficiency had risen to 77 percent. In 2003, we were in the 82 to 83 percent proficiency range. Our kids haven't changed. Our student population is still the same. We are still 68 to 70 percent African American. The school still serves nine federal housing projects, and our low-income level is still 85 percent. When we achieved exemplary status in North Carolina (due to our achievement growth being better than 110 percent of the state's expected growth) and discovered our achievement growth percentage was larger than any other elementary school's growth percentage in our system, I had T-shirts printed up for all of my faculty and staff. At the meeting at which the school board handed out the certificates recognizing the schools that had met exemplary status, we all appeared wearing our Hall Fletcher T-shirts. The front of the shirts read "Hall Fletcher Dream Team." On the back, in big, bold letters, it proclaimed, "Exemplary Status, Who Said It Couldn't Be Done?"

. . . AND WE DID IT ANYWAY!

So how did we move Comer into the classrooms? Different teachers explored different ways to integrate the process with the academic curriculum.

Keeping Journals

The fourth- and fifth-grade classroom teachers decided they would implement the Comer journals. The children made contracts with themselves. For example, one student journal entry might read: "I, Carol Ray, am working on developing my social pathway. This pathway deals with the following. . . ." Then, the children wrote in their own words what that pathway means. As educators, we know that for children to really internalize something, they should put it in their words and write it down. Students committed to write in their journals at least once a week for six weeks, and focused on the success they were having in one particular developmental pathway. In addition, for many of our students, if they were encountering adversity within their pathway, or something happened that had really interfered, they included that in the journal entry as well. Remember: We were always encouraging them to use the concept of no-fault while trying to overcome problems they were facing.

Pathway Collages

Other classrooms integrated activities such as pathway collages. In a third-grade classroom, the students learned at the beginning of the year about the developmental pathways and what each pathway represented. There was an activity in which they formed Comer learning groups. Each group was assigned a developmental pathway, and its members hunted through magazines and such, to cut out pictures that represented that pathway. A lot of discussions occur during this kind of group activity. One child might say, "That picture really ought to be on the physical pathway because it's the doctor with a little boy there, and he's listening to his heart." And another child adds, "No, that picture fits our language pathway because the mother and that little boy are listening to the doctor and what the doctor is saying to them." That's what we want to happen with kids. We want them to see that these pathways overlap and interconnect. In addition, this is a good hands-on activity for children to do in the classroom.

Comic Strips

One of our second-grade teachers loves using comic strips in teaching. Her classes really enjoyed the following activity: When the teacher introduced the developmental pathways to her class, the class reached consensus on a comic strip that would represent each of the pathways. Maybe there was something going on in the comic strip that just really jumped out at them. This is the comic strip that they decided represented the speech language pathway: There are two kids, and the little girl is holding a homemade telephone—a tin can with a string connected—and the little boy is across the room holding the other end, and they're saying, "What did you say?" "What did you say?" The mother is saying, "I wonder if Graham Bell had it this hard." For the students, this comic strip represented the language pathway. This is another example used to help kids bring the developmental pathways to their own level.

Current Events

Current events are wonderful opportunities to link with the developmental pathways. In one of our special education classes, the children posted the insignia of the Olympics under their physical pathway display. They made an obvious connection to the physical pathway. Here, the teacher was helping students to understand that the concept of the developmental pathways is not just something at Hall Fletcher; it's something that applies to all of us as humans.

Self-Portraits as a Cognitive Display

The first-grade teachers wanted to find ways to display student work and connect it to the Comer Process. Student work is displayed in a huge corner at one end of the first-grade hallway. The teachers mounted a display along this hallway: "First Grade Displays Their Cognitive Intellect." Each of these displays represents a child. There is a child's self-portrait, and then right underneath it, there is a matted picture of the child taken by the teacher with a digital camera. So, if no one recognizes Jaime from his self-portrait, they will know this is Jaime because they can see his photograph.

All children in every first-grade classroom have their work displayed in the hall. The children's proud work for the week is posted for the world to see. It might be a product from their writer's circle. It might be a display of their handwriting. It might be a sheet that recapped a science project or experience that they participated in. It might be something that they produced within a Comer group. Their proud work is displayed, it stays up, and it grows all week long. And then, on Friday, the pieces that need to be sent home are sent home, and the pieces that need to be photocopied for their portfolios are photocopied and retained by the teachers.

Video Recitals

I was excited when one of my first-grade teachers came to me with the idea of weekly "Friday Recitals." Some of the goals in North Carolina's Standard Course of Study in language arts use the verb "demonstrate": "The student will demonstrate mastery of . . ." So in an effort to reach those goals of demonstrating mastery, the teachers have a video camera that they set up, and each child comes out to the hall and does a Friday Recital. It might be reciting a poem that he's memorized that week. It might be spelling some spelling words he's worked on. It might be reading from one of the take-home reading books that he's worked on all week long. The child has his recital in front of the video camera, and the teacher, or the teacher assistant, records it. Each child has his or her own videotape, and each Friday Recital is added to those that were recorded earlier in the school year. When the parent comes in for a parent-teacher conference, the teacher can cue up the videotape of that child and share with the parent the types of things he's been working on, and show the progress that's being made. The best aspect of this occurs at the end of the year: Parents receive videotapes of their children's Friday Recitals for the whole year, and they have a family treasure documenting that tremendous progress from August through May.

The most productive investment of school money has been in video cameras and tapes so that these teachers can do this. The parents love it. They absolutely rave about it. Here, again, teachers have taken the Comer Process and just flown with it. And, boy, if you don't think that pulls in parents to be involved! Suddenly, parents want to come in: "If you need any help in recording the recitals, I'll come in and help you," because they want to be sure the project keeps going.

USING THE COMER PROCESS TO INTRODUCE TEACHERS TO SOMETHING NEW

The hardest part for teachers in thinking about anything new is their immediate reaction of, "Oh no, here we go again! I've got to change everything I've done and find a different way to do it!" Not so with the SDP. Once you've put the basics in place, you can "Comerize" a lot of the activities you're already doing just by attaching some new words and phrases to them. Let's consider some of those that we did at Hall Fletcher.

Book Reports on *"SMTV News"*

We are a science, math, and technology magnet school, and we have a closed-circuit television system. Our media specialist trains the fourth and fifth graders to write and produce—including anchoring, and operating the camera and other equipment—a news show we call *SMTV News.* Every morning on *SMTV News,* we broadcast our morning announcements. And every day on *SMTV News,* we broadcast "The Comer Minute." I am one of the guest anchors (I would never say I'm one of the main contributors, because I'm not one of the fourth or fifth graders). Guest anchors are allowed to appear every morning, and I anchor "The Comer Minute." That Comer Minute could be a book-talk by a child I introduce on the show. The student holds up his or her book of choice, talks about the book, and relates it back to the developmental pathways.

There's some history behind this. At the beginning of this school year, when we wanted to really pull out all the stops on Comer-in-the-Classroom, we wanted to target our school improvement goal of getting our kids to read more. We decided to have every faculty and staff member come on *SMTV News* during the first several weeks of school. One at a time, each gave a guest book-talk on a book of his or her choice, a favorite book. We wanted all the kids in the school to see that we were modeling being readers and that we were reading for pleasure, not just reading for assignments. I'll never forget the time our physical education teacher gave a book-talk on the autobiography of Michael Jordan. She talked about how Michael Jordan had developed his physical pathway from the time he was very young with his basketball skills, and developed his cognitive pathway when he was at the University of North Carolina. She talked about how it was important to him that he not only excelled on the court but also in the classroom. She described how he developed his study habits. That was a beautiful example of infusing knowledge of the pathways with literacy in our school.

It wasn't long before kids were picking up on the idea. The teachers gave the kids a format for their book reports, and there was always a little snippet at the end: "How does this relate to any of the developmental pathways?" This makes the connection very obvious for the children—and when we do that, we also make it very obvious for us as adults.

Shining Stars Program

We have created many opportunities to recognize students through special activities in our building. It's important for any elementary school to celebrate the students, and with our student demographics, it is particularly important that our kids are celebrated at every opportunity, because many of them don't have opportunities to be celebrated at home and in the community.

The Shining Stars program existed at Hall Fletcher long before I became the principal. This student recognition program was actually the brainchild of several teacher assistants who wanted to find some way that they, as a group, could recognize students in a number of ways. Every month, the teacher and the teacher assistant (if there is an assistant in the room) collaborate on naming the classroom's "Shining Star" for the month. This student is not voted on by students, because it's not a popularity contest.

Since we have integrated the Comer Process, we choose a Shining Star from each classroom based on the student's modeling of the guiding principles and development in the developmental pathways. So, a child is recognized not for having the best grades, but for exemplifying tremendous growth in one of the developmental pathways. For example, a child could be recognized for "exemplifying the guiding principle of maintaining a no-fault attitude with others."

Every month, when a teacher and a teacher assistant name the Shining Star for their classroom, they submit a Comer statement about that child. I then recognize each Shining Star on our school's *SMTV News* during the Comer Minute. Sometimes we do that with a couple of kids at a time. I introduce them to the rest of the school as the Shining Stars from last month from Mr. Anderson's room and from Miss Drake's room, and then read the Comer statement that their teachers have written about them. As one of my kids said, "You read that in front of the whole world!" Yes, I do. I read that right here on *SMTV News*. And that child is sitting right beside me, and they just sit so tall, and they're so proud, because not only are they hearing the statement written about them for the first time, but everybody in the school is hearing this good statement too!

In the beginning of the year, the Comer statements were very simple. The teachers just wrote Comer statements about the things that the children were doing or how the children were developing in their cognitive pathways. Then, as the year went on, the teachers started getting a little competitive with this, as teachers often do. One teacher would write a Comer poem about a student, and then another teacher would try to top it the next month with something else. This is one example of a Comer statement that came from a second-grade teacher later in the school year:

> Shining Star Report: If Dr. Comer walked into our second-grade classroom to examine Eric, what would he find?
>
> A healthy child who enjoys running, playing, and getting exercise? "Yes," says Dr. Comer. A child who can talk about his feelings in a way his friends can understand? "Yes," says Dr. Comer. A child who respects his classmates? "Very good," says Dr. Comer. A young person who can think in different ways and come up with creative answers? "Very interesting," says Dr. Comer. In short, Dr. Comer would give Eric a clean bill of physical, verbal, emotional, ethical, social, and intellectual health. "This is a fine, well-developed young man!" says Dr. Comer.

The teachers have fun with this kind of thing, and the kids just love it. And this has become a program that is as much fun for the teachers as it is for the kids.

The "Modeling Matters" Program

By seeing what teachers do and hearing how they talk, children and parents learn by example. Depending on what the teacher is doing, something good or something bad could be reinforced. When teachers talk about developmental pathways and when they make good choices, children and parents learn how to do that, too. Our kindergarten faculty and staff thought that modeling our guiding principle of no-fault was a wonderful way to teach their students about the Comer Process: We don't want to place blame; we want to solve problems!

So with kindergarten, there was an all-out focus on adopting a slogan of "Modeling Matters." Within two weeks of its inception, every time I would go into a kindergarten classroom the kids would come up to me and say, "Oh, Mrs. Ray, Mrs. Ray, modeling matters!" And I would say, "Yes, it does! Thank you very much for remembering that!" Or I would be in the hallways, and the kindergartners would pass by, and inevitably someone from the line would say, "Good morning, Mrs. Ray! Modeling matters at Hall Fletcher." And I'd say, "Yes, it does! Thank you so much for showing us that you know what that means!"

Well, it wasn't long before first graders heard kindergartners getting this response from the principal. So, the first graders would come up in the cafeteria, and they'd say, "Modeling matters, Mrs. Ray!" And I'd say, "Yes, it does. Thank you so much for remembering that!" The kids were doing it, of course, to get this positive affirmation. I think that's okay. It certainly helped us spread the word quickly around the school of the importance of remembering Modeling Matters in everything we do.

Pretty soon, the Modeling Matters theme in kindergarten became a schoolwide motto. In the 2001/2002 school year, the front of our T-shirts read, "Hall Fletcher Elementary School," and the back read, "Where Modeling Matters Every Day." That became the motto for the school. Now we have some buttons printed with the words "Modeling Matters."

We used to have a program our guidance counselor initiated called "Caught Being Kind." Whenever a kid was "caught" doing an act of kindness, he or she was presented with a little button to wear during the day that read "Caught Being Kind." At the end of the day, the recipients of these buttons could go to the guidance counselor's office and exchange the button for a trip to the treat box. Our School Planning and Management Team (SPMT) acted on a suggestion from our Comer Kids Student Leaders that we change the slogan "Caught Being Kind" to "Modeling Matters to Me." And when a child is observed modeling a good deed or a guiding principle, the presenter of the "Modeling Matters to Me" button tells the child what it is that we're so pleased to see. Each faculty and staff member in our school has two of these buttons with his or her name on the back to present to children during the day. Then, at the end of the day, the counselor collects them as the kids bring them in and exchange them for the treat box. She places them back in our mailboxes the next morning, so that we can give them out again. This is another example of a preexisting program that changed just slightly in its terminology in order to fit under our Comer umbrella.

THE KIDS REALLY GET IT

A research team from the University of North Carolina at Chapel Hill has been gathering information on SDP's systemic reform process. They're trying to design an evaluation system that schools can use for themselves. They came to Asheville to observe the implementation of the Comer Process, and our school was one of the schools they "lived in" for three days. They didn't want us to do anything differently; they just wanted to observe and take notes. We provided focus groups of parents, focus groups of teachers, and focus groups of children of every age available for the researchers to speak with—all without administrators. And I said to our researchers, "You'll probably hear a lot about Comer-in-the-Classroom from our fourth and fifth graders because they're older and they can articulate those concepts. You're probably going to hear about Modeling Matters from kindergartners and not so much the talk about the developmental pathways. Just understand that." I guess you could say I was putting forth our disclaimer!

Well, when the researchers finished, they debriefed us about everything they'd experienced for three days. They said, "You know, you were right: We did hear a lot from not only fourth and fifth graders but also from third graders about developmental pathways. We heard a lot about what they're doing with their activities and how they're incorporating them and making their decisions for personal goal setting. But what you were wrong about is this: We heard even more of it from kindergartners, first, and second graders." They recalled this story about the kindergartner focus group: The researchers were talking with the children, and they asked them about the colorful wheel displayed in our lobby. The children told them it was the developmental pathways wheel. The researchers asked, "Well, what is that?" A little girl explained that each piece of that pie on the wheel represented a pathway that helps us to be a better person and helps us to grow and be healthy and to be smart. One of the researchers asked, "Well, is there a part of that wheel that you have learned a lot about this year?" The little girl said, "Well, yes, I'm doing very well in my ethical pathway, and that means I'm making good choices." That's what it's all about! They *do* know what that means!

A second grader talked with them during their focus group session about how he had grown in his language pathway. He reported to the researchers that not only can he stand up and recite a poem and not cry when he starts talking (as he did at the beginning of the year) because he's not afraid, but he also knows how to listen very closely when the teacher is talking so that he knows what to do later.

I share these stories with you to tell you that if it can happen at Hall Fletcher, it can happen at your school, too. We are no different. We may talk with a little more Southern drawl, but we're no different from any other school in any other place. We are an inner-city school, not a school of the elite. We are not a school of the gifted. We are a school of children, and we are a school of happy children, of happy folks. And that's because we've learned to work together and become a family as we go through anything new.

BRINGING THE MESSAGE TO A NEW SCHOOL

In July 2002, I was transferred to another school, Claxton Elementary School. It was a very emotional month of May as we ended the school year and I said goodbye to my dear friends and students at Hall Fletcher. They were concerned when it was announced that I would be going to another school. I would love to tell you they were concerned because they just didn't think they could live without me. But the fact is, they were most concerned about "What's going to happen to Comer? We've worked so hard, and we've come so far with Comer, and now they're moving you, Mrs. Ray. What's going to happen with Comer?" And I said to them, "Comer is not about charisma. Comer is a model of school reform. It's not one person, it's not three people, and it's not one tiny group. Comer is a philosophy, and just as you don't want to lose Comer, you must remember this. The only people who can take that away from you are yourselves. And that's only if you decide you will no longer follow the guiding principles and you are no longer going to use child development theory in making decisions for kids. You are the only ones who can take that away."

To me, the greatest legacy that any principal can leave in a school that uses the Comer Process is to be able to step aside and to go somewhere else and have the Comer program continue. If the only reason the program is in place is because a particular principal was there, something's missing. It's got to be bigger than any one person. I'm confident it would not be possible to "blow the Comer School Development Program out of Hall Fletcher Elementary School with bazookas!" There's just no way it's going to happen. The faculty and staff of Hall Fletcher Elementary School are committed to doing wonderful and great things for children. They know the importance of building relationships and helping children to develop in all areas fully. They know this, and they have proven the effectiveness of the Comer School Development Program.

POSTSCRIPT: THE TEST SCORES WENT UP

In the first year of implementation of SDP, the percentage of students at or above grade level was 42 percent, as measured by their performance on all three exams (math, reading, and writing) that are administered as part of North Carolina's ABCs of Public Education program. In Year 2, 66 percent passed all three exams. In Year 4, 78.6 percent passed all three. In Year 5, almost the whole school passed. On August 26, 2003, the following appeared in *The Asheville Citizen-Times,* in an article by Barbara Blake on how Asheville elementary schools were closing the achievement gap:

> The most significant improvement was seen at Hall Fletcher Elementary, where the gap between African-American and white students was 33.3 percent in math in 2001–02, and only .07 percent last year. A gap of 28.8 percent in reading in 2001–02 dropped to 6.7 percent in 2002–03. (p. 1)

The school accomplished this without changing children or staff. The school still serves the same percentage of minority students (70 percent). It's still the school with the highest percentage (88 percent) of students eligible for free or reduced-price lunches, a poverty indicator.

CLASSROOM ACTIVITY 7.1: DEBRIEFING A FIELD TRIP (OR SIMILAR ACTIVITY)

Pretend that you are my fifth-grade class, and yesterday was Adventure Day. On Adventure Day, we had college and university students come into our fifth-grade classrooms and conduct day-long activities on team building. It started at 8:15 a.m., and it ended at 2:30 p.m., and you worked in groups as a class all day long. You did various activities. While Adventure Day was going on, I, as your classroom teacher, took digital pictures as we were doing these activities together.

"Today, I have set up in our classroom a bulletin board that has pictures with captions of some of the activities you were doing yesterday. I've also set up, in the center, some word choices. Who can tell me what these words are?"

"Developmental pathways."

"You are right. Absolutely. It's our list of developmental pathways. Now, in your Comer groups, what I will want you to do is to move to the bulletin board. I want your group to please take some time in front of the bulletin board. On your table, you have some blue yarn, and you have a roll of Scotch tape. I want you to collaborate with your group and decide which pathway you are going to connect to the various activities that you did yesterday. And you're going to need to talk about what's happening. For example, preparation and cooperation. You remember when we got started, the first thing we did was to meet with our counselors as a whole group and talk about the rules for the day? We talked about the kinds of things that we would be able to do and what would not be tolerated. Remember that discussion? And we all listened to one another? Now, which pathway could we connect to this one right away?"

"Language pathway, because we were listening to the directions and using our words to contribute to the discussion of the rules and procedures."

"Good. I want you to take one of those pieces of yarn and place one end of it in this picture and take the other one right across to language. Is there another pathway that this could connect to?"

"Respect the integrity of others."

"Absolutely. The ethical pathway. Guess what? It can connect to more than one. So, connect it to that one as well. You get the picture? I want you to move now and take about 10 minutes to complete the activity with your group at the table. We'll take care of our physical pathway while we're doing this. Now remember, as good Comer groups, we're going to make certain that everyone in our group is involved in the discussion. Remember our rules for collaboration. We want everyone's input. Timekeepers, monitor our time. Please be sure to tell us when we are at the halfway point with our time."

8

Mobilizing Schools for Instructional Excellence

Instructional Leadership Is a System Responsibility

Edward T. Joyner

Instructional leaders are the chief agents and the chief role models for school improvement. Whether dealing with global issues or minute details, instructional leaders must excel at being part executive, part relationship coach, part organizer, part psychologist, and part pure motivator. SDP's executive director reflects on these topics and describes the work of an exemplary school superintendent, who has used SDP's framework and strategies to great advantage in a challenging district in Brooklyn, New York.

Instructional leadership is the critical element in improving student achievement. It requires the support of the superintendent, central office staff, and even school board members. All of these people help to create the conditions that allow the principal to orchestrate a process of profound change. Through this process, parents, students, teachers, support staff, and other administrators are mobilized to elicit higher levels of student performance. This team effort ensures that the skills and content on local, state, and national assessments are taught sequentially across all grades and subject areas. Effective instructional leadership ensures that teachers are provided with the support to teach and that students are provided with the support to learn. In an instructionally effective school, parents are also asked explicitly to support the academic development of students by frequently checking their children's progress and by providing a quiet place at home for study and homework.

The job of an instructional leader is to lead a team effort to initiate, motivate, and support school improvement. According to Shoemaker and Fraser (1981), there are four themes that are critical to this process:

1. Assertive, achievement-oriented leadership

2. An orderly, purposeful, and peaceful school climate

3. High expectations for staff, students, and parents

4. Well-designed instructional objectives and evaluation systems

Any school and/or district that effectively addresses the challenges inherent in these themes will be well on its way to becoming instructionally effective. Effective instruction requires a strong central office presence in schools. In fact, Jerome Harris, the former superintendent of the Atlanta Public Schools, has suggested that superintendents spend 50 percent of their time in schools and that principals should spend at least that much time monitoring and supporting instruction in classrooms.

ASSERTIVE, ACHIEVEMENT-ORIENTED LEADERSHIP

Leaders must be willing to let followers know what they will and will not stand for. Assertive, achievement-oriented leaders model appropriate behavior, vigorously oppose education malpractice, and involve their followers in collaborative planning and decision making. They are well informed in their respective areas of responsibility and seek continuous growth both personally and professionally. They consciously and aggressively facilitate the development of values and acceptable behavior within their areas of influence. Such values and behaviors support the achievement of system goals and outcomes. Assertive, achievement-oriented leaders learn from successes and failures and encourage followers to do the same.

The instructional leader works with staff to clarify and publicize the critical skills and content that each grade and subject area must impart for student progression to the next level. The leader also provides teachers with enough time to plan together and to evaluate what they are doing instructionally, encourages students to work diligently for self-improvement, keeps parents engaged in the academic life of the school, and procures the resources that are necessary for teachers to teach effectively and for students to learn.

ORDERLY SCHOOL CLIMATE

Education and psychosocial growth are best facilitated in an orderly environment characterized by fairness, justice, and clear standards of behavior that are supported and enforced by all stakeholder groups. Order may take many forms: in a well-designed and well-maintained building, in meetings that start and end on time, and in students' and parents' clear sense of what will be learned and how it will be assessed. Harmony and synergy are inherent in order, as is the sense that things are well organized and working together for the common good. On the other hand, disorder threatens the potential for achievement in virtually every area. Consequently, the first order of business is to build structures, processes, and helpful mechanisms that move schools and school organizations from chaos to order.

HIGH EXPECTATIONS

The ability to communicate and support high standards of behavior for school teams in every aspect of the school's operation is key to instructional leadership. Holding high expectations suggests to followers that you have faith in them and that they are capable of outstanding work. On the other hand, it is not fair to hold people to high expectations without supporting them in meeting those expectations. High expectations bear fruit only when leaders hold themselves to high standards and when they provide the support necessary for staff and students to achieve. Setting high expectations with measurable outcomes energizes staff, parents, and students. Frequent feedback allows for adjustments, and praise and encouragement provide staff, parents, and students with the will to continue in the struggle for excellence.

WELL-DESIGNED INSTRUCTIONAL OBJECTIVES AND EVALUATION SYSTEMS

In his classic primer on curriculum, titled *Basic Principles of Curriculum and Instruction*, Ralph Tyler (1949) identified four fundamental questions that must be answered in developing any curriculum and plan of instruction:

1. What educational purposes should the school seek to attain?

2. What educational experiences can be provided that are likely to attain these purposes?

3. How can these educational experiences be effectively organized?

4. How can we determine whether these purposes are being attained?

States attempt to answer these questions through assessments. State-mandated assessments clearly suggest that schools are to be held accountable for certain student outcomes. However, states are not alone in imposing assessments. When you combine local, state, and national assessments, the picture is complete. In the present reform environment, assessment drives instruction. The public will not have confidence in schools or school systems in which significant numbers of students fare poorly on local, state, and national assessments.

Assessment is a way of life in American society. Examinations are given to individuals at every level of the civil service system and for entry into the military, colleges, and graduate schools in law, medicine, and other fields. Exam preparation has become a multimillion-dollar industry. Companies like Kaplan, Princeton Review, Arco, and Barron are helping students to pass the Scholastic Aptitude Test (SAT), the Medical College Admissions Test, the Law School Admissions Test, the National Teachers Examination, and the Graduate Record Examination, to name a few. The great majority of these students come from families that recognize the power of high test performance and the label that is assigned to children on the basis of what is believed to be "quantified intelligence."

Tyler's four questions in the current education environment lead us to the following conclusions:

1. The school's education purposes are driven by national, state, and local performance objectives in the form of tests, such as the SAT, state proficiency tests, and to a much lesser extent, standardized tests that are locally determined.

2. Schools and school systems must organize curriculum content and skills to be in direct alignment with the student performances that are measured on such tests.

3. Schools and school systems must set their standards higher than the tests.

4. Schools and school systems must organize their students, staff, resources, and time as efficiently as possible to prepare students to become high achievers.

5. Schools and school systems must develop strategies to evaluate the instructional delivery system in a timely manner and to provide staff and students with resources to self-correct.

6. Schools and school systems must engage parents and others in an effort to make student achievement and character development a priority.

When schools and school systems rigorously pursue strategies related to these six areas and learn from the work that ensues, student achievement will begin to rise.

FUNCTIONS OF INSTRUCTIONAL LEADERSHIP

Similar to teaching, instructional leadership can be divided into broad functions. Arends (1994) identifies the executive, the interactive, and the organizational functions; to this, the School Development Program (SDP) adds the psychological and motivational function.

Executive Function

As the chief executive, the superintendent is expected to provide leadership, acquire and deploy resources, direct staff, work with the school board to develop policy, and coordinate the activities of system employees to accomplish instructional goals. Planning, use of time and space, developing supportive learning environments, and assessing and evaluating personnel and programs are the ultimate responsibility of the superintendent at the central office level. This function, however, cascades down the system through department heads at the central office, to the principal, assistant principal, and, finally, to the teacher. Parents are legally required to send their children to school. Moreover, they are expected to support learning in the home. If the latter doesn't occur, schools must not use parental neglect as an excuse for not delivering quality instruction.

Interactive Function

The interactive function of instructional leadership refers to the face-to-face contact that leaders at every level of the system engage in to improve individual and team performance. Leaders must know the instructional goals of the districts and the assessments that will measure the level of student performance. They must provide staff members with the fair and consistent performance appraisal that is necessary for continuous improvement. Critical skills in this area include (1) setting relevant performance objectives through a collaborative process, (2) defining performance standards, (3) creating an ongoing professional development plan, (4) providing clinical, nonjudgmental feedback in the formative stages of the instructional improvement process, and (5) providing a final summative evaluation based on performance indicators and standards at the end of the school year.

Organizational Function

The organizational function of instructional leadership refers to the essential activities in which a leader engages to improve instruction. A school is a complex social organization in which people's attitudes, values, and mores come together to create a unique culture and belief system. Arends (1994) highlights the interdependency necessary for schools to provide purposeful learning experiences for students and provides the following actions to describe what is needed to provide even one day of instruction:

- Paper, pencils, and chalk have been ordered.
- Rooms have been cleaned.
- Curriculum guides have been prepared, and textbooks ordered.
- Parents have chosen to send their children to school.
- Teachers have chosen to be professionally trained.
- Buses have been driven, and breakfasts and lunches have been prepared.
- Schedules have been determined, and children assigned to classes.
- Health services for students have been planned and managed.

The point is clear. Successful instruction is complex and does not begin and end in the classroom. It requires synergy throughout the system.

Psychological and Motivational Function

In addition, the psychological and motivational needs of teachers and support staff must be satisfied for them to perform best. People are motivated to invest energy into three domains: achievement, affiliation, and influence. Achievement manifests itself as staff members work individually and collectively to be competent professionals. Affiliation is important as educators turn to their peers for support and affirmation. Influence addresses the need of adults to have a voice in decisions that are made in their workplaces.

PROVIDING STRUCTURE AND PROCESS

Mobilizing All the Stakeholders in the Learning Community

SDP provides schools and school systems with a structure and a process for mobilizing stakeholders within the broader school community to improve instruction and overall child and adolescent development. Learning communities cannot be created without such a structure and process because relationships must be built between the critical stakeholders through collaborative assessment and planning, consensus decision making, and no-fault problem solving. There must be an upfront commitment to using the existing knowledge base about effective instruction and holistic development, as well as opportunities for staff and parents to contribute their experiences. Good schooling is a balance between the science of education (pedagogy, child and adolescent development, cognitive neuroscience) and the experience base of effective educators and parents. It also must draw on what we know about human relationships and organizational behavior. A community of learners must develop the personal and organizational discipline that will allow for rigorous examination of policies, programs, plans, and strategies aimed at improving student performance and personal development on an ongoing basis if the district and its schools are to continually improve.

In addition, as students mature, they must begin to take more responsibility for learning. Students and families must match the commitment of the educators who teach the children. There are troublesome signs in some communities that some students have not accepted their role in their own intellectual progress. And in some cases, educators have had to shoulder much of the blame when students do not perform well in school. Schools can do more, but parents and students must realize that they are also accountable for achievement.

I grew up in a community where it was expected that everyone would work hard in school and be kind to others. There was no patience for students who showed up without the tools of the trade—notebook, pencil, textbooks, an inquiring mind, and a good heart—unless poverty or extenuating circumstances made them too hard to come by. My parents walked several miles to school in the South when they were children. An ink pen was a luxury item, and they told me stories of breaking a single pencil in half so that they could stretch the supplies—with the eraser half going to the youngest child. Parents had little patience for what they regarded as foolishness in school. The prevailing axiom was that where there is limited opportunity, there must be great desire and commitment. Our culture faces a great danger if we cannot restore respect for learning as well as service to others within our young people. The achievement gap closes when everyone realizes that when it comes to excellence, everyone must contribute something to the effort.

SDP Strategy for Achieving Instructional Excellence

James P. Comer, M.D., is the leader of a school reform group that has been working in schools for more than three decades. The Comer Process provides the infrastructure for schools and school systems to pursue goals related to the physical, cognitive, psychological, language, social, and ethical development of students. Comer insists that schools develop all aspects of the child in order to create balanced young people. This balance maximizes students' academic potential. Moreover, he suggests that to promote children's learning and development requires "an active conspiracy" on the part of educators, parents, and members of the community.

The Comer Process provides the participation structures that are necessary for planning, identifying staff development needs, evaluating and modifying school programs, and addressing the critical issues that schools must confront to be instructionally effective. Comer stresses a developmental orientation that approaches students on the basis of strengths rather than deficits. As a physician, he emphasizes that we "first do no harm" when making decisions about the destiny of children and adolescents. Comer suggests that individuals and teams within organizations must accept the responsibility to work to acquire increasing proficiency in these critical areas in order to become learning communities.

SDP THROUGH THE LENS OF SENGE'S FIVE DISCIPLINES

Peter Senge (1990) has also contributed to our understanding of organizations and has collaborated with SDP to generate the collective wisdom that informs school reform. He lists five disciplines that members of organizations must cultivate to contribute to organizational effectiveness. These disciplines are force multipliers: When there is a conscious effort by everyone in the organization to cultivate personal mastery, rigorously examine the way they see the world and the people they serve, work together on creating a common vision, learn together, and think systemically, the whole becomes greater than the sum of its parts. Below are Senge's disciplines as they relate to schools and school systems.

Shared Visions

Visions are what we see in our mind's eye with respect to our work as educators. If we envision a school in which achievement is largely attributed to race and class, then this is the school that we will get. If we are pessimistic about the future of students from materially deprived families, then we will guarantee such a future for them. Educators must be engaged in continuous conversations related to how they envision themselves, their students, the school, and the district. A collective or shared vision of what the child, classroom, school, and district can become is the driving force behind any successful program. Students and parents must also participate in the process. To do this, they must stretch their visions of the possible.

Mental Models

As we engage in the rigorous self-examination that is a part of personal mastery, we may have to challenge our own mental models and the education malpractice that characterizes far too many American classrooms and schools. Mental models are what we carry in our minds about ourselves, other people, institutions, and every aspect of the world. They consist of images, assumptions, and stories that we use to make judgments about people and things. They are the substance of our deeply held beliefs. The bell curve and deficit theories are examples of mental models that educators carry, models that act as barriers to higher levels of student achievement.

The bell curve paradigm suggests that student performance should be distributed across a bell-shaped curve, with some students destined to be below average. According to this erroneous viewpoint, someone must be in each quartile, and the poor and/or minority children will usually be found in the bottom quartiles. There is, however, incontrovertible proof that schools can overcome the unearned disadvantages of poor and minority students when they use sound pedagogy, apply principles of child development in all aspects of schooling, constructively engage the parents and community in the education process, maximize use of resources, and use ethical principles in all of the above.

The bell curve mental model and pseudoscientific theories attributing intelligence to racial and genetic factors influence beliefs, and beliefs lead to actions. Actions based on such beliefs are a major factor in the low expectations held for poor children in general and, because of their unique history, held in particular for children who have a slave heritage. Bloom's (1984) counterposition that most students can perform well when there is an alignment between what is taught and what is tested has proven to be the belief underlying the success of schools that teach poor children. Consequently, if our mental models include the belief that students' achievement is a product of students' experiences, then we will look to manipulate children's school environments and not penalize them for unmerited disadvantages. We will invest our energies in providing students with opportunities to learn and develop, knowing that performance is linked to both nature and nurture. As we begin the struggle to change our mental models and see the fruit that such a change bears, we increase our faith and develop our capacity to create the substance of change through our collective will and energies.

Team Learning

Team learning is more likely to occur when educators have invested time and energy in clarifying their vision of the good school in which teachers teach well and students learn well. Team learning requires structures that allow members to engage in ongoing conversations about developing a high-achieving school. Through teams, we identify instructional priorities and pool our collective intelligence to create the tactics and strategies that, in our best estimate, will accomplish our goals. Leaders must establish time during the school day for teams to reflect and plan, and to learn from their work. Leaders must also provide the resources that staff teams need to do their best work. Team learning should be enhanced by quantitative and qualitative data related to the school system's goals, student performance, and any other measures of school effectiveness. If the purpose of school is to educate the hearts and minds of students, then common sense dictates that the substance of team meetings should be discussion that leads to better ways to deliver instruction and facilitate students' character development. SDP provides the structure that maximizes team learning and teamwork, and engages all the adult stakeholders in planning and executing strategies for school improvement. The assessment and modification process allows for the learning that leads to corrective action. Relevant data are critical to team learning: The capability of accepting reality and the responsibility to accept it rather than deny it are crucial to continuous improvement.

Personal Mastery

Personal mastery is a discipline that must be pursued by students, parents, and educators. The knowledge, skills, and attitudes needed to be effective teachers and learners start with personal mastery. Senge, Kleiner, Roberts, Ross, and Smith (1994) define mastery as follows:

> The capacity not only to produce results, but also to master the principles underlying the way you produce results. You produce results by your ability and willingness to understand and work with the forces around you. The central practice of personal mastery involves learning to keep both a personal vision and a clear picture of current reality before us. (p. 194)

It is reasonable to assume that educators in general want all students to achieve. The discipline of personal mastery requires that we deliberately set forth on a path to acquire the knowledge, skills, and mind-sets to make student achievement a reality for our children. Noble deeds and noble visions require the passion and lifelong commitment that personal mastery suggests.

Systems Thinking

Systems thinking helps us see the connections necessary to accomplish our goals and that everything we do has an influence on the system. There are direct connections between student achievement and clean, orderly schools, parental support, clear instructional objectives, excellence in teaching, adequate time and resources, productive leadership, staff development, policy, and central office engagement in the reform process. Schools also have to consider the cultural influences that children face that impact how they feel about school and academic excellence. Systems thinking insists that we do nothing in isolation, but work to create a collective response to challenges and opportunities based on our unique place in the school system.

CURRICULUM ALIGNMENT

Curriculum alignment provides SDP with procedures for engaging the school's faculty in a grade-by-grade process to identify the skills and content measured by national, state, and local assessments, and in developing a system to ensure that they are taught.

Cohen (1987) describes the curriculum alignment process, which includes the following steps:

1. The faculty determines the skill and content that a child should know in any subject measured by national, state, and local assessments. Skill and content

domains are translated into performance objectives and sequenced from easiest to most difficult.

2. Each grade determines its instructional responsibilities and promises the next grade that it will, in fact, teach the students this content and skill set.

3. Each grade organizes this information into units and produces a realistic timeline that ascertains how many weeks are needed for each unit.

4. After all grades have their unit titles, there is a "gallery walk," during which all faculty teams judge how their own timelines fit into the whole plan.

5. The administrative staff works with teacher leaders to produce a school document that contains the instructional targets for each grade.

6. After the gallery walk, each grade level writes activity-based objectives for each unit. Each activity must be
   complex (critical thinking skills across subjects)
   student focused (students actively engaged)
   reality based (involves students' experiences)
   stimulating (involves multiple senses and intelligences)
   inclusive of whole-group activities, small cooperative group tasks, and
      individual tasks

7. Some activities lend themselves to becoming performance assessments, and rubrics are developed for the assessments (e.g., writing).

The process of writing the activities requires the staff to collaborate in teams, make decisions by consensus, and be responsible to each other for the implementation of the curriculum. This alignment process creates the necessary consensus for what is important, how it will be taught, and how it will be assessed. The curriculum becomes the whole-school plan of instruction, and each faculty member becomes responsible for its implementation. This whole-school instructional plan is incorporated into the comprehensive school plan and is monitored by the School Planning and Management Team (SPMT). It becomes the task of the SPMT to support all faculty in the implementation of new instructional strategies incorporated into the new activity-based curriculum.

Appropriate central office staff members develop the support system that provides buildings with the services that are needed for maximum impact. Parents receive a syllabus that is a brief summary of the skills and content that students will be taught during the year, and each school conducts a quarterly self-assessment so that they can self-correct.

THE SUPERINTENDENT AS INSTRUCTIONAL LEADER: THE CASE OF BROOKLYN'S COMMUNITY SCHOOL DISTRICT 17

Dr. Evelyn Castro was the superintendent of the school district that was formerly known as Community School District (CSD) 17. The district no longer exists, due to

New York City's restructuring of its school system in 2003. CSD 17 was the largest school district in Brooklyn and the third largest in New York City. The district was composed of a highly diverse student population from the Crown Heights, Bedford Stuyvesant, and Flatbush sections of Brooklyn. In CSD 17, 18 elementary schools and six middle schools served 24,000 children. Eighty-nine percent of the students were African American, 9.1 percent Hispanic, 0.7 percent White, and 1.3 percent "Other." Eighty-nine percent of the students were eligible for free or reduced lunch, a poverty indicator. CSD 17 had the highest number of immigrant Caribbean students in the nation. About 65 percent of the students in CSD 17 were English speakers from the Caribbean, and of those students, about 25 percent were newcomers to the country. The district served students representing 78 nations. Conditions that threatened the improvement of student and school achievement included inadequate physical facilities, difficulty in recruiting and retaining a stable staff of professionals at all levels of the system, unfunded mandates, and an urban community ecology characterized by third-world poverty, drugs, gangs, and an insufficient number of family and child service providers to support the mission of the schools.

Superintendent Castro was the longest-sitting superintendent in recent memory in CSD 17. Prior to her assuming the position, there were 11 superintendents with an average tenure of two years. Castro worked with the staff of SDP over the course of her tenure as superintendent to develop a protocol for improving student achievement and social behavior. She mobilized the school board, parents, central office staff, teachers, and paraprofessionals to come together around a common vision for children, and to maximize the use of the system's resources to support the work of teachers in classrooms and the leadership of building principals. She held community meetings and seminars, planning retreats, staff and parent development activities. She also spoke directly to students about their role in working to overcome inherited disadvantages by being responsible, working hard in the classroom, and being good citizens in and out of school. She established the developmental pathways as the framework for staff and parents to evaluate the developmental progress of students and as the focus for academic and social programs during and after school. She used the SDP Implementation Life Cycle to guide the work of the district and as a benchmark to assess progress.

Superintendent Castro made it clear that large-scale systemic change required that everyone do something to achieve the mission of the district. She and the principals developed a win-win working relationship with the union leaders in the schools, and this allowed them to avoid major confrontations around contract issues. The great majority of the teachers were driven by their commitment to the children and enthusiastically supported district initiatives.

Each of the stakeholder groups in the CSD 17 community attended annual retreats, where they looked at the system from their perspectives. All groups agreed to focus on the needs of the children and to sacrifice personal agendas for the best interests of children. The retreats created a no-fault environment, where participants could assess the strengths and weaknesses of the schools, and also identify ways in which each could contribute to the goals of higher student achievement and personal development. No data were sacred, parents had access to school data, and all groups received training related to the developmental needs of children and adolescents at school and in the home. As a result of the parent retreats and the staff retreats, a plan to improve achievement and psychosocial development was crafted.

The principals and central office staff agreed to develop an ongoing staff development program that included the following content:

- Building-Based Staff Development
- Instructional Leadership: Curriculum, Instruction, and Assessment
- Action Research
- Supervision and Evaluation of Instruction
- Public Relations
- Developing Effective Relationships
- Literacy Across the Content Areas
- Child and Adolescent Development

Principals also made the following recommendations to be implemented district wide in order to raise student achievement:

1. Initiate a systemwide use of the superintendent's *Vocabulary List*.

2. Develop an independent reading program.

3. Develop a Writing Across the Curriculum program, and inspect the schools to make sure that they are in compliance with the new program.

4. Develop an intensive math program for students in the bottom two quartiles.

5. Convene a districtwide, "whole-village" discussion of holistic development to get broad community input, direction, and support.

6. Work with teachers to identify training needs; implement staff development.

7. Balance and align curriculum; have written documents that specify what will be taught, and when and how it will be measured.

8. Continue *Leadership Academy*; create *Parent Academy*.

Parents met at least twice per year in a retreat to develop a strategy to engage all the district's parents in school support activities and to plan for large community events designed to educate, inform, and act as a unified vehicle to solicit support for their children and the schools. The vice chairperson of the school board, the superintendent, central office staff, and the executive director of SDP attended all the two-day retreats that were held out of the district. The parents created an organization that met monthly with the superintendent and a board representative to monitor their plans and to address concerns. All of the groups adopted the guiding principles of SDP (no-fault problem solving, collaborative planning, and consensus decision making). The first annual Community School District Parent Retreat was held on September 29–30, 2001. About 500 families participated. The retreat itself was organized by the parents. Agenda items included "Education in Minority Communities: Historical Factors and Contemporary Challenges" and "The School Development Program: Vehicle for Constructive Change." The objectives of the parent retreat were as follows:

- to provide parents with an opportunity to identify their individual strengths and weaknesses as they relate to their status as advocates for the children of CSD 17

- to provide parents with an opportunity to understand the historical and contemporary forces that affect the education of African American, Afro-Caribbean, and Hispanic children
- to provide parents with strategies they could use to support the academic achievement of their children
- to provide parents with an understanding of how the structure and processes of SDP can be used as a vehicle for constructive change

The role of parents in school effectiveness was discussed in depth. Subsequent retreats were held, and an organized group of parent activists was created in the district, with plans to connect to other parents throughout the borough of Brooklyn. The past three years has seen significant academic growth in CSD 17.

Evelyn Castro mobilized all the resources within her community to support student achievement and personal development. In the 2002 school year, CSD 17 had the greatest reading gains in all of New York City. Castro focused on the outcome and the process thereby creating a system culture that enabled every stakeholder to make a meaningful contribution. She used conceptually sound structures and a process that placed children's needs at the center of the effort. She created opportunities for all the key participants in the education and development of students to learn together and to contribute based on their respective roles. CSD 17 became a disciplined organization that built its own capacity for continuous learning and improvement.

INSTRUCTIONAL LEADERSHIP IS A SYSTEM RESPONSIBILITY

Instructional leadership is a system responsibility. School districts must establish standards of delivery and accountability systemwide to ensure that all children are given maximum opportunity to learn. The work of Comer, Cohen, and Senge can inform the work of educators as they create the structures and processes to facilitate student achievement and overall growth.

Although much of the past and current literature regarding instructional leadership focuses on the principal, superintendents must lead the process at the district level, even as principals lead instruction in the schools. Academic achievement is a function of organizational and personal commitment, shared vision, examination of traditional mental models, and development of positive images of student potential. It is also a function of involvement of the entire system in the planning process through systems thinking and team learning.

The Comer Process provides an infrastructure, a focus on holistic child and adolescent development, a process for comprehensive planning and staff development, and a set of guiding principles that sets standards for adult behavior. Cohen's work informs the strategies for developing the instructional delivery systems; Senge has identified the disciplines that are critical to successful organization development.

School leaders must develop the personal commitment to master these ideas and their underlying principles in order to have an impact on the lives of students—particularly those who are labeled as "unworthy," "marginalized," and "disadvantaged."

REFERENCES

Arends, R. (1994). *Learning to teach.* New York: McGraw-Hill.

Bloom, B. S. (1984). The search for methods of group instruction as effective as one-to-one tutoring. *Educational Leadership, 41,* 4–17.

Cohen, S. A. (1987). Instructional alignment: Searching for a magic bullet. *Educational Researcher, 16,* 16–20.

Comer, J. P. (1993). *School power: Implications of an intervention project.* New York: Free Press.

Senge, P. M. (1990). *The fifth discipline: The art and practice of the learning organizations.* New York: Doubleday.

Senge, P. M., Kleiner, A., Roberts, C., Ross, R., & Smith, B. (1994). *The fifth discipline fieldbook: Strategies and tools for building a learning organization.* New York: Doubleday.

Shoemaker, V., & Fraser, H. W. (1981). What principals can do: Some implications from studies of effective schooling. *Phi Delta Kappan, 63.*

Tyler, R. (1949). *Basic principles of curriculum and instruction.* Chicago: University of Chicago Press.

READ MORE ABOUT . . .

To read more about SDP's approach to aligning the curriculum, see Chapter 5, "Curriculum Structure and Teacher Planning: Balance, Alignment, and Student Assessment in the Standards-Based Curriculum," by David Squires and Camille Cooper.

It takes approximately three to five years for districts and schools to create the appropriate structures, develop a comprehensive reform plan, see significant achievement and social behavior gains for students, and compile the research documentation of the program effects. The SDP Implementation Life Cycle guides the work of school districts and schools over a five-year period. See "The School Development Program Implementation Life Cycle: A Guide for Planned Change," Chapter 18 in *Transforming School Leadership and Management to Support Student Learning and Development: The Field Guide to Comer Schools in Action* in this series.

9

Maintaining Student Momentum Through Instructional Leadership

"And We Will Do It Again"

Marie B. Chauvet-Monchik

P.S. 138 in Brooklyn, New York, which serves 1,400 students from pre-K through eighth grade in a low-income neighborhood, led the city in self-improvement on standardized tests in 2002 and 2003. Its principal explains how she and her staff have done it: continuity, continuous professional development at the top, dedication to improving classroom practice, nurtured creativity in the staff, community outreach and partnerships, parent involvement, and Comer in every classroom—all supported by SDP principles, mechanisms, operations, and the concept of the six developmental pathways.

I received so many phone calls when the newspapers announced that P.S. 138 ranked first among all New York City public schools in its rate of improvement over its own spring 2001 results on the statewide eighth-grade English Language

Assessment and State Math Assessment. Everyone wanted to know our secret. I told them the secret was to believe that children can achieve, and to put the structures in place to address every child's needs.

THE CHALLENGES ARE MANY

I have taught in this school for 16 years, and I know and understand the community. The challenges are many. P.S. 138 serves 1,400 students from pre-K though Grade 8. We are in an enormous school building that spans an entire city block and spills over into a small annex in Brooklyn, New York. The two wings of the main building connect through the auditorium. School starts at 8:00 a.m., and many children arrive early because their parents drop them off on their way to work. The parents have nowhere else to leave them. The schoolyard is their safe haven. At 7:00 a.m., we have about 15 children in the yard, and by 7:30 a.m., there are about 150 children. The building is scheduled to open at 7:40 a.m., but I do not want the children to get into trouble, so we open it at 7:30 a.m. and the children play basketball in the gym with the coach. As a result of this initiative, we have a boy's basketball team that competes with other schools in the district. We also conduct an early-morning academic intervention program in literacy and math with children who are academically behind. The children are in the yard early, so I just use this time to give one-to-one instruction to those who are most in need.

I would like all the children to reach the highest standards. However, they need more time. Just 8:00 a.m. to 3:00 p.m. is not sufficient. It seems that in many instances when they go home, they are not reinforced in any skill that is taught in school. They are not being exposed to enough intellectual activities to enrich them academically. They sit in front of the television, and that is their babysitter. It is more beneficial for them to be in a school environment where they are safe and are being exposed to more intellectual and positive social activities. Therefore, we also have after-school programs.

I extended the school day by having classroom teachers remain with their students for an additional 90 minutes daily. This procedure enables teachers to reach students who are in need of additional instruction for the purpose of remediation or enrichment. There are two community-based organizations in the building that allocated funds to pay these teachers. Some teachers have opted not to be employed by these organizations; instead, they volunteer their services by providing small-group instruction before, during, and after school to targeted students. Their dedication to the children's achievement is quite beneficial to the participants.

Ten teachers work in Project Read and Extended Day. They serve about 200 students. These students are actively engaged in instructional activities Tuesdays through Thursdays, for six hours a week. Participants are selected based on their performance in last year's New York City and State assessments. The two community-based organizations extended their services to the community up to five days a week from 3:00 p.m. until 6:30 p.m. by sponsoring after-school programs that include a snack and dinner for 400 pupils who come.

Times have changed. Most of the students I taught back in 1982 are now in their 30s. Quite a few of them are very successful: They are doctors and lawyers; some of them are teachers of science and other subjects; and others are business people who have their own stores. They visit the school and elaborate on their accomplishments. It makes me feel good to hear what they are doing with their lives. Others are still struggling, but they are trying to better themselves. Quite a few of the students I taught in the second grade are now parents. They enroll their children at P.S. 138 because they trust the school.

Not all of the students are success stories; some of them became parents at an early age. They still try to make something out of their lives. They experience much difficulty in accomplishing their dreams because of added responsibilities at their young age. Some of them are bitter. When they do not see hope, they become angry at themselves and at their situations. But if there is life, there is hope, so we try to help them. Quite a few of them are trying to find their own paths. We offer the GED program. We refer some to Restoration Plaza (a community center that has computer training) and to other agencies in the community. The Beacon Program helps people in the community to develop their careers.

Stability of the staff is important. Sixty percent of the teachers have been here 15 years or more. So the community knows the staff. Because the community knows the staff, the staff knows some of the problems the community faces, as well as some of the problems the parents and children are having. I think that is why I have so many staff members volunteering before and after school: They know, "Yes, there is a problem, but there is also a solution to the problem." And that is where I think things are changing. Today, most of the children that we are teaching are more focused than those we taught years ago.

We also offer parents workshops on how to help children and themselves. If the parents do not have anyone exposing them to other ways, how are they going to make it? The school is an extension of the home, and that seems to be very important for the parents in our community.

DEEPENING MY UNDERSTANDING OF THE CHILDREN, AND BROADENING MY VISION OF SCHOOLING

When I started teaching here as a science teacher, the children were motivated to work with me because they wanted to perform experiments, and do their research. But I was dismayed to see that the children could not read or write. I said, "How am I going to teach them science when they are missing the basic skills?" I had a conversation with the principal at that time (this was three principals ago), and I asked her, "May I please move into a regular classroom? I would like to know what is preventing these children from learning." And she said to me, "But Ms. Chauvet, you are bringing me so many trophies!" I said, "You know, I understand that I could bring lots of trophies, but my job is more than just trophies. I would like to see our children actually learn how to read." So she told me, "Okay." She was trying to convince me not to take the job, so she gave me the low-achieving level of the second grade.

When I met the children, they couldn't read, but they recognized the alphabet. I said, "At seven years old, they are having so much difficulty learning! What is going on? Let me go back and look at my college notes and see how I should teach these children how to read." I noticed that reading was one difficulty that they were having and that the other difficulties were their self-esteem and their lack of motivation due to constant failure. I said, "This is a multiple problem. It is the social impact that is preventing these children from excelling."

Engaging the Parents

So, I took my record book and searched for the children's phone numbers and started calling the parents on a regular basis. Only 2 parents from a class of 32 attended the first conference, but I was not disappointed. I spoke to my 2 parents, and I felt I had an alliance with them. I told the 2 parents how their children were doing. At the next conference, more parents attended. The following year, I had about 28 parents. I was delighted to see them. I talked to them about how they could help their children. I did not put their children down. The parents of failing students are very reluctant to ask for help because they know what the school system is thinking about their children. I had to convince them that there was something positive about their children. Then, because they had developed that trust, I was able to teach the children further.

The following year, the principal left, and Dr. Pierre-Louis became principal. When he heard that I was a science teacher, he asked me, "Why did you abandon science when we are looking for science teachers?" I said, "Before they can be scientists, they have to be readers. Please leave me in the second grade." So, he gave me another low-level class because, he said, "I am sure that after three years, you are going to give this thing up. You are going to go back to your field."

I enjoy teaching science because it gives me opportunities to have children explore scientific facts and perform experiments, but I did not miss teaching science. I was really convinced that I could do this job because I felt rewarded to observe youngsters learn the art of reading. I felt that I was making a difference in their lives. I wanted to learn more about teaching reading. Although I had earned a master's degree in bilingual education in 1984, which had a strong focus in language acquisition, I went back to school to study more about teaching reading. I received a professional degree in curriculum development in 1986.

By then, I was really convinced that I could do this job. Even though I taught the lowest quartile, I was able to move about 50 to 52 percent of the children up above 50 percent (which was below grade level back then). So Dr. Pierre-Louis decided he wasn't going to bother me anymore; he was going to let me be who I am. One year I asked him, "May I please go up with my class?" He asked me, "You have the bottom, and now you want to go up with them?" I said, "They're not the bottom class. Look at this, I gave you 50 percent. If I go up with them, I'm certain that they will do better." So, he said, "Okay. You can go to third grade with this class." When the children got to third grade, not only were their academics improving, but their behavior and their demeanor were improving too, because they felt like leaders. Everything we did had to be something that would be true to life. For example, before going to a play, we would read the book from which the play was drawn, and investigate. Instead of being out of control, as they had been in first grade, the children became the leaders of the school.

Focusing on Reading

After I did that for about four years, Dr. Pierre-Louis told me, "You should be the reading teacher because you would be able to touch more than 32 lives." So I went into the field of reading. He assigned me to teach reading to students in the upper grades. He gave me all the nonreaders because I knew so much about phonics and balanced literacy (although we did not call it "balanced literacy" in those days). I was always reading to them. If children who do not hear English spoken at home listen to people reading the English language in school, they are able to mimic and to read the utterances and to become independent readers. The fifth- and sixth-grade children were motivated, and they couldn't wait to get to the reading lab.

Although I was a reading teacher, I used some of my English as a Second Language training to address the needs of the limited English speakers who attended the reading lab. It was a challenge for me because the children were functioning below level, yet they were being asked to score 50 percent or above within an eight-month period. It did not take long for the teachers to buy into the success of the program. They brought their entire classes to the reading lab. The children were instructed according to their functional abilities. The educational assistant had the high-ability students; the classroom teacher worked with students who were on grade level; and I taught the lowest-functioning group. Children were assigned homework and book reports on a regular basis. I met with classroom teachers regularly for consultation on students' progress. Dr. Pierre-Louis was satisfied with the strategies being used to improve student achievement.

One of the assistant principals encouraged me to return to school to study supervision, and she indicated that I had leadership skills because I was a motivator for other teachers around me. That's when I started taking administrative courses. But I still remained focused on instruction. I enjoyed being with my peers and performing collaborative projects that promoted teaching and learning.

Building the Third-Floor Team

When I became the grade leader, I said to myself, "You know what? I want the third floor to be the mecca of 138." (Our school has 10 floors, 5 in each wing of the building. The third floor then had second-grade classrooms on it.) The teachers thought I was weird. "What do you mean—we're not working hard enough?" I said, "That's not it. We have to be the example. When someone comes up to this third floor, I want them to say, 'This is where education is happening.'" So, they asked me, "How are we going to change the third floor?" I said, "Let's have each person develop the hallway bulletin boards. We are going to develop this third floor, and no one will want to go to any other floor but the third floor." So, I started with developing hallway bulletin boards, and the other teachers said, "You know, it is not a bad idea. I love the way your room and your bulletin board are matching. Let us all try it."

The third floor had the Thanksgiving dinner right in the hallway. We invited the parents to come and sit and listen to their children report about Thanksgiving. We had Christmas dinner the same way. We closed down the hall, brought all the desks outside, and had the children sit in a long row. The parents sat in the classrooms with their babies. This was a family time. So "the third floor" became a buzzword. When the superintendent heard about this, she said, "We have to come to the third floor." This is one building with 10 floors, but one floor attracted the superintendent to come and have dinner with us!

Thanksgiving and Christmas were celebrated in this fashion for years, even after many of the teachers left the third floor to assume other roles in the school and to spread the vision. (Eventually, everyone on that third floor became an educational leader, at P.S. 138, at other schools, or at the district level.)

On the third floor, all the test scores were rising because everybody was always motivated to do something instructionally, then create a culminating activity afterward. The parents couldn't wait to come to see their children perform. The parents realized that the students' performance was excellent not only onstage but also in their everyday work. All 10 classrooms along the whole hall were performing well. It was so beautiful to see the result of pedagogues collaborating for a common goal.

Dr. Pierre-Louis was amazed to see what was happening with the third floor. He said, "We have to do more than just the third floor. You have to find a way to coordinate this whole thing to make the second floor, the fourth floor, and the other side of the building do it."

Expanding the School to Save the Children

Once the parents were talking more openly, we started thinking about ways to save the children from some of the peer influence that they would experience in junior high schools. Everyone was so happy with what was going on here. But when the children would go to the junior high school, many would join gangs, they would drop out, and they would come back pregnant. I was so upset. These children were my babies. It was not fair to see our hard work go to waste due to negative influence in the junior high schools. Starting in 1991, the parents said to us, "How can we keep these children at P.S. 138?" One parent's child was to graduate in two years. She asked us, "Do you see what is happening? You have given these children an oasis from the very beginning in kindergarten until the sixth grade. Then, they go away for two years in the junior high school, and they go backward academically, they join the wrong social groups, and they do not even make it to high school. We are lucky if one child makes it out of the junior high school without being stained. The only solution to this social dilemma is to allow students to stay in the same environment until they reach high school age—to extend the school from prekindergarten through the eighth grade."

In 1995, Dr. Pierre-Louis decided we were ready to try it. He said that the only way he could do it would be if the team agreed. There was also the question of finding teachers with expertise in junior high school math and science. We started looking at who we had in-house who qualified to teach content area subjects needed for junior high school students, and we learned what teachers have to do to obtain appropriate state certification. We really did not want to hire junior high school teachers because if they were failing to teach in junior high school, why bring them to our school?

We identified teachers already at P.S. 138: Ms. Duncan for the science component, and Ms. Lawes and Ms. Straker for the math component. Next, we advertised for a social studies teacher and hired Mr. Ambrose to fill the position. He was a high school social studies teacher who wanted to teach in Brooklyn, near his home. I said, "Here we go: We have our team. We will be able to keep the children now."

We had to start small because we had never experimented with it before and did not know how it was going to work out. That first year, we kept two classes for the sixth grade. The following year, we had three classes, and the following year, we had four classes. Now we keep all six classes. And I have to say that it has worked for us. After the children graduate from here and go to the high schools, they are above level. They leave here having taken the biology Regents Examination.

Until recently, students took the math Regents Examination in addition to the science Regents Examination. We discontinued administering the math Regents two years ago because high school math departments no longer accept the Regents scores from junior high schools. This regulation prevents students from participating in the math Regents program, but it does not impede us from teaching students an accelerated math curriculum. Many of our graduates return to school expressing their gratitude for the quality of education they obtained at P.S. 138. Most of the students who study French take the French Regents on completion of their first year of high school because they are introduced to basic French in the fifth grade. The course gets more challenging as they are promoted from grade to grade. They also write in French to their pen pals in Québec, Canada.

Up to that point, I had been a staff developer. When school became a pre-K through eighth-grade school, I became the assistant principal for six-and-a-half years. In 2001–2002, I became principal.

Changing the School Culture Through Partnerships

After I became the reading teacher, it was important for me to see what was going on outside the building, because all I had known all my life was P.S. 138. I really got involved outside the school. I kept working at P.S. 138, doing professional development for the teachers and parents, giving one-to-one instruction to children who needed additional help, and I also started working at the New York City Board of Education doing professional development for new teachers. That is when I obtained a real perspective on what they were going to need to become successful teachers later on in their careers.

We started training new teachers on Saturdays. Every Saturday morning, I would wake up at 6:00 a.m., drive to Manhattan, and train new teachers at J.H.S. 144, where the board of education conducted all their professional development workshops. And everything I used on Saturday I would bring back to P.S. 138 to further develop the staff.

The new teacher-training workshop was unique compared with my experience at P.S. 138. Every Saturday, I would face a new group of professionals who came to acquire knowledge. It made me quite organized, because I had to be well prepared to present in front of my peers. I wanted to extend my expertise to new teachers. The more workshops I presented, the better I became at presenting. It was also a very important experience for me to learn what the board felt was needed in the general educational setting, compared with what was needed at P.S. 138.

Then, we started working with the colleges. We invited Brooklyn College Center for Educational Change into the school; they worked closely with us, training the teachers. We also invited Isoke Nia, a writing professor at Columbia University.

Once Isoke Nia started to work with a cadre of teachers on the Writing Process and the Whole Language approach, the teachers' instructional styles improved dramatically. They began to discuss teaching practices. They looked at students' work in depth and they applied Isoke Nia's practices with their pupils. Once Isoke Nia started working with the teachers, they developed books by the children. At the children's book reviews, which we hold in a huge room, we have the authors stand in the front and present their books to an entire grade.

In addressing the needs of language development, we invite real authors to read aloud with students. Students are also encouraged to become authors. Quite a few of our students have their poetry and short stories published in children's autobiographies. In 2002, a sixth grader won a free trip to Disneyland as a reward for winning the national Hawaiian Punch contest.

Although P.S. 138 was directly involved with Isoke back in 1991, some teachers are still involved with her study group. They attend her Saturday workshops sponsored by Community School District 17. The teachers really began to believe that they had to sit together and be trained. Our study groups developed from that type of training. Teachers now coteach each other and observe each other. They now have a critical friend.

When we first began this practice, each person had a turn as observer and had to explain what he or she saw in the lesson and how the lesson would improve children's development. Then, the observers had to explain one or two points they thought could be added to that lesson to make the lesson more efficient. The first teacher they observed was Ms. Mingo, who really is a master teacher. She had been teaching for about 20 years, and all the other teachers had years' less experience than she did. We agreed that we wanted the other teachers to be a little critical of her; we wanted them to understand that it's okay for someone to receive a negative comment, because that can help you learn how to improve yourself and become effective in that area. Ms. Mingo was willing to take anybody's criticism. The next time, they observed a teacher who had been teaching for only five years, but they all felt okay about the critique because they understood that if the master teacher could have some flaws, so can the person with only five years' experience. It was very interesting to see that they were accepting other people's criticism.

After a while, we began to videotape the teachers in order to share their practices with their colleagues in the school. This was the best professional development model that I participated in. Ms. Mingo volunteered to be videotaped first. She taught an interactive read-aloud with the class. It was such a fabulous lesson! Despite some nervousness due to the number of adults present (we had invited the district staff developer), she delivered one of the best lessons of her career. Other teachers followed Ms. Mingo's lead. We have different study groups. For example, the third-grade teachers do a "Lunch and Learn." We give them a common planning time with their immediate supervisors and staff developers. That gives them 100 minutes every week to discuss what they have read in the books and how they can apply it in the classroom. Sometimes, we use three periods. They all go to each other's classrooms, observe their colleagues teach, and offer constructive criticism about their observations. They explain what is working and what things the teacher needs more help in, and they do a focused observation of each other. It is really good for them.

They explain the content of their observations and comment on good practices and what needs to be done to improve the lesson. I encourage a no-fault approach to providing feedback. We do not want to discourage the presenter from inviting others to his or her classroom. I want them to focus on instructional strategies instead of other concerns. This is now a common practice throughout the school. That's how we changed the school culture. The teachers who have bought into the program have really been willing to stay together.

IF I AM NOT IN THE CLASSROOMS, I AM NOT DOING MY JOB

I do a walk-through every day, which is very hard because it is a huge school: In the main building, we have 65 regular classes, 11 special education classes, 15 cluster rooms, and two science labs. The annex contains three classrooms, an early childhood gym, a room filled with blocks, a parent room, and an office. When I observe a teacher in a walk-through, sometimes I do not document the observation, but if I see something that I think needs to be addressed, I will tell them, "See me during your lunch time." At that point, I will sit and discuss instructional strategies and good or bad practices, and the teacher and I will have a dialogue. My main purpose is to improve the quality of instruction that takes place in the class.

If I am not in the classroom, then I am not doing my daily job. In the classroom, you get to see what the teacher is doing. You get to see the children interacting. The children tell you things. One little girl told me, "I am so happy. Today is my mother's birthday." I did not have to know that, but it was important to her, and she shared it with me. And I said, "Oh, wonderful! I am so glad to see that your mother was born in February." It made her happy. But if you are not in the classroom seeing and inspecting what the teachers are doing and seeing how the children are interacting with the teachers, then you have a program only on paper.

In addition to the two guidance counselors, there is a dean of discipline for the junior high school component of the school. All three handle some of the disciplinary issues of students in need. They also provide small-group counseling, conflict resolution, and parental outreach. On quite a few afternoons each week, I have cabinet meetings at which everyone tells me what is happening in the building, because I really want to be aware of daily occurrences and plan for their resolution.

USING THE SIX DEVELOPMENTAL PATHWAYS

In 1999, when I was still assistant principal, Chancellor Ramon Cortines instructed schools to have leadership teams. Dr. Evelyn Castro, the district superintendent, provided professional development for principals and parents to help them work collaboratively as a team. She brought the Yale Child Study Center's School Development Program to train us. That is when I met Ed Joyner. When he started talking about the six developmental pathways, it was like the light at the end of the tunnel that I needed to see. When he spoke about the physical pathways, I said, "You know, he is correct. If the child is ill, he cannot learn. If the child is hungry, he cannot learn. If the child cannot see, he cannot learn." Looking at all the things that stop children from learning, I said, "This makes sense." Dr. Joyner described language development, psychological development, ethical development, cognitive development, and social development. All of them are important to the total development of children. I said, "I really want to read more about Ed Joyner, and I want to hear more of what he has to say. He is quite knowledgeable in his field. He connects children's development with the factors that affect children's lives. Dr Joyner is the conveyer of information from Dr. Comer's initiative."

From that point on, every time there was a meeting at P.S. 138, we would bring in some parents and teachers to make sure that they understood the developmental pathways and how we could apply them in the school. We decided to extend the developmental pathways to our after-school programs in order to reach more children.

I said to Dr. Pierre-Louis, "You know, we have to find how to integrate what Ed Joyner is saying about the developmental pathways and make it visible in the school, make it become a living document." So, we started exploring different ways to do it. For example, we made our school-based support team (our child study team) more involved in the school: going to observe the children, counseling with the classes, creating focus groups based on students' interests, being able to give parents references to outside help when it is necessary.

We assisted families in obtaining medical benefits. You see one child in the school, but they have younger siblings who have not been to the doctor. We started having a doctor make monthly visits to the school nurse's office to inoculate the children of parents who fit the criteria. When the doctor comes, she sees 15 to 20 people. Sometimes, she has to make another visit to finish what she started. For example, she has been helping a mother with seven children, and we have been able to contact other social agencies to give this family a much better living environment for the children. Now that the mother's life is more stable, the children are doing better in school.

In terms of their cognitive development, we want to get the children more involved in their own education. We extended the school day for the purpose of remediation, enrichment, and language development. We now have a music program that starts in the second grade, in which the children are playing the violin, saxophone, drums, all kinds of instruments. And our chorus sings at a nursing home two blocks away. The children are now looking at senior citizens in a different way. For some of these senior citizens, our children's visit is the one positive visit that they have had for the whole year. We have a dentist whose office is two blocks away. He takes five of the eighth graders into a dental program he has created so that the students will develop an interest in science. We are using the community in such a way that our local merchants and other professionals interact with the school positively, offering apprenticeships to some of the youngsters in the school.

EVERY TEACHER IS A LITERACY AND MATH TEACHER DURING "DROP EVERYTHING AND TEACH"

To promote children's learning and development, I looked at the data and realized there was a common trend: Some children were doing better in some areas than other areas on the reading and math standardized tests. I wanted to know the number of children performing at Level 1, 2, 3, or 4 in all the literacy and math skills. I would have to put each group together and work on different strategies with them to make them understand the concept of sequencing. The next time they took the test, not only would they achieve Level 2 in other things, but they would also achieve Level 2 or above in sequencing.

I had to come up with a strategy to address their difficulties. Then, I could set up a structure to address the missing skill so that I could help them become successful overall. Schools need structures to help students succeed. P.S. 138's structure is the differentiated targeted-instructional hour. It is called either "Drop Everything and Read" (which we do in three hour-long periods per week) or "Drop Everything and Do Math" (which we do in two hour-long periods of math per week). During that time, all the cluster teachers (content area specialists who usually provide coverage while classroom teachers are on their preparation periods) are sent back into the classrooms, and the cluster teacher is assigned a very small group of students. The teachers must use assessment documents to see what is needed for these children to learn. One group works with the classroom teacher, and another group works with a music teacher or gym teacher. I do not want to have only gym teachers: A gym teacher must also be a literacy and math teacher. A music teacher must also be a literacy and math teacher. Everybody must teach literacy and math during the differentiated targeted-instruction periods.

When I introduced this program in September of 2002, the cluster teachers were furious. One asked me, "Why am I teaching reading and math? I am a French teacher." Another said, "I am a science teacher, why am I teaching reading and math?" I said to that teacher, "In the long run, not only will you be able to teach science, but you will learn how to integrate science content into literacy and math."

In the beginning, when they walked into the classrooms, the cluster teachers were not comfortable with their new assignments because they were afraid to teach the children subjects they were not accustomed to teaching. So, I had meetings between the classroom teachers and the cluster teachers. I explained the purpose of the differentiated targeted-instruction periods: All of the children who did not meet the standards must be separated from those who performed at Level 3 or 4 so we can give the children on a Level 2 or Level 1 the scaffolding that they need in order to turn into 3s and 4s.

I conducted faculty conferences to discuss this matter. The cluster teachers gradually became more comfortable with their new roles. They became familiar with students in their groups. They referred to the students as "their" students. For the cluster teachers who did not have a common planning time, I had a luncheon for only 17 of them. I explained to them the importance of them going into the classrooms and helping children make the gains that they need to get to the next level. The union representative was very supportive of this initiative. The cluster teachers became convinced that this initiative would highly benefit the children in the long run.

After three weeks, I conducted individual conferences with each of the 17 cluster teachers regarding the progress of students in their groups. At some point in this process, each person who was scheduled into the classroom realized, "I am not here just because Ms. Chauvet wants me out of my room; I am here because I am going to make a difference in the children's lives." The French teacher said, "You know what? It works, even though I teach French. I understand: Now I can see the importance of my work with the children. If a child is not doing well in French, it may be that he is having problems with his own language and with his reading and the math skills." I said, "You see? You made relationships that you would never have made if you taught only French." I was able to get the teachers to believe that they are here to make a difference in the children's lives, and it does not matter what content area they teach. When they are here with the classroom teachers, they are here as a partnership to change the educational outcome. So, whether the teacher is an art teacher, a science teacher, or whatever, during Period 3, they go in there and do differentiated targeted instruction. They are actively involved in increasing students' aptitude in the area of reading and mathematics.

A FINAL THOUGHT

There is no magical secret to helping children learn and develop. We believe in children, and we put structures into place. Some of the structures that have worked well for us are the teams, the teacher study groups, the extended school day, bringing cluster teachers into the classroom, using data to drive instruction, relationships with the community, and an educational plan addressing the needs of individual students. I am also unpredictable sometimes, which keeps everyone on their toes. I make myself visible all over the school. I always remember that to be an instructional leader, I have to be in classrooms because that is where students are learning the cognitive skills that they will need in order to be successful academically.

AFTERWORD: WE RANKED FIRST IN RATE OF IMPROVEMENT

In spring 2002, P.S. 138 ranked first among all New York City public schools in its rate of improvement over its own spring 2001 results on the statewide eighth-grade English Language Assessment and State Math Assessment. In spring 2003, P.S. 138 did it again: It ranked first among all New York City public schools in its rate of improvement over its own spring 2002 results on the statewide fourth-grade English Language Assessment and State Math Assessment.

10

"And This Is How We Will Do It"

Comer Youth Voice Their Opinions About the Comer Process

The Comer Club Ambassadors of P.S. 138, Brooklyn, New York

The proof is in the students. In this chapter, fifth through eighth graders at P.S. 138 in Brooklyn, New York, speak about the Comer Process directly to the students in your school. The chapter ends with a useful glossary.

A FEW WORDS ABOUT DR. COMER

James P. Comer, M.D., is a medical doctor who continued his studies and became a child psychiatrist. He is a professor at the Yale University Child Study Center and an associate dean at the Yale University School of Medicine. Dr. Comer has written many books, book chapters, and journal articles for doctors and educators. He has spent his whole adult life helping children, and a lot of this effort has gone into the School Development Program (SDP).

A FEW WORDS ABOUT THE SCHOOL DEVELOPMENT PROGRAM

In 1968, Dr. Comer began trying to help two schools in New Haven, Connecticut, in which the students were very disruptive and the teachers were very disheartened. He was convinced that those schools could improve if everyone worked together toward the same goals. He met with the principals and assistant principals, the teachers, the parents, and the students and taught them the three guiding principles of no-fault, consensus, and collaboration. These are useful ways for people to work with each other while keeping a positive outlook. The people in the schools worked together in this new way, and they made a real difference both in schools and in the schools' neighborhoods.

Over the years since then, Dr. Comer and his colleagues have organized their thoughts into a model they can teach to many schools at the same time. The model they created is called the School Development Program. SDP is now used in hundreds of schools throughout the United States. The goals of SDP are (1) to enhance students' social and emotional development, (2) to improve students' academic learning, and (3) to enlarge and strengthen school communities.

INTRODUCING THE COMER CLUB

KALEEL BETHEL:
The Comer Club is a great place to be,
that's why it's for smart kids like you and me.
It deals with things like food and mood,
and even some things about your attitude.

Many of us go there to learn,
hoping that an education is what we'll earn.
Kids from grades five to eight debate,
on topics to which they can relate.

We try to do what is right,
which is why we never fight.
I enjoy the time we share together,
sometimes I wish it would go on forever.

THE THREE GUIDING PRINCIPLES

No-fault

FATOUMATA BAH:
I think no-fault should be adopted in a lot of classrooms, because in a lot of classrooms, there are a lot of accidents and blaming going on. Students need to learn how to work together so they can find a solution to the classrooms' problems.

KESHIA M. G. PITT: When things happen, don't waste your time trying to find out who did it. You should be focusing on how to solve the problem. What's done is done. Instead of pulling your hair out or throwing a temper tantrum, try solving the problem.

Consensus

KESHIA M. G. PITT: Consensus means no voting. Consensus is very important when you are in a group with a lot of different people. If one person has an idea, and another person has a different idea, you could try blending both ideas, and later on maybe you could add another idea to it. This way, no one would feel backed into a corner or left out, and the club would have a pretty good idea that would help the club get a little bit closer to their overall goal and purpose.

Collaboration Also Helps Us Achieve Consensus

SHONTESE ASH: One person could have an idea, but someone else would disagree with this because they have an idea they think would be better. Some people will be on either side of any of these debated ideas. But the best thing to do is *collaborate*. Collaboration will prevent chaos. The debating groups should just calm down, work together, and create an idea that they both agree on. The crowd that was on one side or the other will think about this new idea, and agree on this.

Collaboration

ANGELINA MEZIER: Many people in our world don't believe that working together is one of the most important things. We fight, we argue, we go to war, we kill, and—most of all—we suffer. I don't believe that we have to go through trouble to get peace. What is so hard about a group of people just getting together and collaborating? If I had the opportunity to be friends with everyone and to help everyone, and if everyone had the same ideas as I have, believe it or not, the world would be a better place.

ANTHONY GEATHERS: Collaboration is a major word. It means "working together." Whether you work with 2 or 10 people, you want to make sure that you do these things:

1. Listen to someone in the group when that person is speaking, and don't interrupt.

2. When speaking, speak in a mannerly way.

3. When debating over an issue, try to talk to solve the problem and come up with a solution.

4. If you disagree with someone's statement, don't yell, scream, or be disorderly.

These points should help you to work better in a group. Group work helps because it gives fellow students the opportunity to learn about each other. They learn about each other's strengths and weaknesses. It also helps when students are placed in groups to work and study together. They can see what they have accomplished and learned as a group.

Group work motivates the students into learning and working together. If they have a project dealing with everyday issues (for example, diseases or homelessness or teen pregnancy), the students will want to know why these things happen. Group work also brings friendship. When one student doesn't know something, another might know it and could share it. Then the four or five will work together and get to know more about their partner(s).

THE SIX DEVELOPMENTAL PATHWAYS

TIKI MORRIS: The six developmental pathways have a good impact on me, my school, and community because they teach us a lot about respect and may even give us a personality check.

These are the six pathways:

Physical: the way you nourish yourself and keep physically fit

Cognitive: the way you think (mental processes, brain function)

Psychological: the way you feel and think about certain things

Language: the way you talk to others

Social: the way you communicate with others around you

Ethical: the way you respect others

I like the six developmental pathways developed by Dr. James P. Comer because they set a positive example for the younger generation and help the role models (upper grades) to think about more positive things and ways of solving problems.

The Physical Pathway

ROMA BEGUM: Did you ever know that some things could affect our learning? Well, maybe you have heard, or maybe you haven't. One of the important things that can affect our learning is the physical pathway.

The physical pathway is all about health. Lack of sleep, which is part of the physical pathway, can affect your learning. When you have a vision problem and you can't see, that can also affect your learning. When you're sick and you're not feeling too well, that can stop you from learning. Laziness is another thing that can also affect your learning.

Lack of nutrients is another thing that I believe can stop you from learning. If you don't eat anything when you come to school, you will be hungry, and you will not be able to concentrate. You have to watch what you eat. If you eat junk food, you will not get any nutrients. It will make your health worse. You have to eat healthy food such as fruits. You have to balance what you eat. If you eat a junk food, in order to balance your food, you have to eat a healthy food.

GARRICK JEFFERS: The physical pathway is the pathway along which people grow and develop physically. Some physical behaviors people do are smelling, eating, seeing, hearing, and feeling. These things can affect your physical pathway.

For example, if you don't eat nutritional food, you would not want to do your schoolwork. Another example is not getting any sleep: Sleeping is important to your body because it affects you in many ways. One way is this: Not sleeping could make you want to sleep in class. Also, not sleeping would make you want to not do your homework because you would want to sleep.

One more example of growing on the physical pathway is not being clean (for instance, not taking a bath). If you don't take baths, you might feel bad because some students will say bad things about you. Now, this is what I think of the physical pathway.

APRIL LYNCH: The physical pathway is based on what kids and adults really want in life in order to keep going on in life. This pathway is one of my favorite pathways because it helps me to realize what I really need for my body to have the right shape and health.

CLINT THIERENS: The physical pathway is about your physical needs. We all have physical needs such as eating and sleeping. The use of the bathroom is considered a physical need. If you do not eat breakfast, you would not have the right nutrients to think, and without the right amount of sleep, you would not be able to perform well in school because you would feel drowsy. If you have problems seeing and you are far from the blackboard and you don't have glasses, that too would affect your learning.

The Cognitive Pathway

KYOSHA PIERRE
FRANCOIS: *Cognitive Pathway*

This is a pathway that connects with your brain,
And when you don't think, it's in pain.
This pathway is always yearning
For some thinking and learning.

This pathway is working whether you're
Thinking positive or negative.
Do you know which pathway this is?
This pathway is the cognitive!

AOMI CASTRO: The cognitive pathway is about manipulating something (meaning when you learn something) very fast, for example, your math multiplication.

The Psychological Pathway

FATOUMATA BAH: *My Feelings Towards You*

You say I have no respect for you.
You say the only feelings I have
towards you are hate and anger.
You say one day I hope you'll find someone who you will respect.
You say that I don't do nothing for you,
and will regret all of this one day.

But truly the only thing
I have towards you is love, and respect.
My love for you is as strong as Mother Nature,
And my respect for you is as wide as this earth.
There are no words that can express
how I appreciate, love, and respect you.
If it wasn't for you I wouldn't be here.
To me you are larger than life.

KESHIA M. G. PITT: Being wholehearted or halfhearted deals with how you feel about a certain project or task. This is in tune with the psychological pathway. It also has something to do with the ethical pathway, too.

When you're wholehearted, you put your all into whatever you have to do. You spend all the time that's possible, whether it's needed or not, on that task, and you try to contribute to the task as much as necessary. You come up with new ideas to further the progress of the project, and you're willing to help any member of the group with anything concerning the project.

When you're halfhearted, you don't really care about your task. You wouldn't do it at all if you had the chance. You don't bother to come up with ideas and suggestions, and if you are given a job to do that would benefit the group, you do any old thing or you don't do it at all. You don't care for the task, you don't care for the other people working on the task, and you want it to stay that way.

We should all try to be wholehearted in whatever it is we have to do. It's not right to say that you're going to do something when you know that you're not going to be able to do it. Sometimes, that's the polite thing to do, but it's not always such a hot idea. You have to learn when to say "No" to something, and you can't allow your thoughts and feelings to get in the way of the progress of the group. It's not fair to the others who actually care about doing the project and doing it right. Just because you don't want to do something doesn't mean you should ever try to discourage others from reaching their goal.

The Language Pathway

KENITA WILLIAMS: SPEECH [LANGUAGE

S – *Speaking* what's on my mind
P – The *parts* of my speech
E – The *excellence* within words
E – The *eloquent* sounds of words in my head
C – The *characteristics* of speech
H – The *humbleness* of words

[– The sign of bond between Speech and Language

L – The *learning* of words
A – The *act* of making words

N – The *neatness* of speaking
G – The *guaranteed* love of words
U – The *usual* speech
A – The *assistance* you get from words
G – The *generousness* of words
E – The *exotic* words

The Social Pathway

AOMI CASTRO:

The social pathway is about getting along with a person in a positive way and not a negative way. It also means you can socialize with a person or a group of people and become a pair, a team.

AOMI CASTRO:

Dr. Comer, do you have a favorite pathway?

DR. JAMES P. COMER:

Yes: the social pathway. It's the key to a rewarding life.

The Ethical Pathway

KYOSHA PIERRE FRANCOIS:

I like the ethical pathway because it has to do with your respect. The ethical pathway is to respect the rights and integrity of others. I think this pathway is necessary because if you want respect, you have to give respect. Also, with respect, you can go far in this world.

COLIN WOOD:

Some people use the ethical pathway, but some of us do not. I like using this pathway because it deals with respect, and I always say "lend a hand and you will be respected." Dr. Comer lends a hand and is now respected, just as I said.

Don't be a fool and drop out of school. Do not rush your childhood, go to the park and enjoy yourself. Why rush your childhood when you could be in school playing basketball? Respect yourself and give your body time to grow, and eventually you will be old.

Respect your teachers and mostly your elders. Don't curse at your teachers or your elders. Why cut class when you can be in class developing a new skill? Why would you like to talk in class when you can wait until lunch? Talk when you are asked a question, not when you like to talk with your friends.

Respect is not something you get, but it is something you earn. Respect goes a long way.

CHRISTINA SIMPKINS: The ethical pathway is about respecting others. The reason why I like this pathway is that without respect, you will not get anywhere in life. Another reason why I like this pathway is that you would want people to treat you with the respect with which you have treated them. This pathway is also important to everyday life because we should respect other people even if they are younger or older than we are.

KENITA WILLIAMS: To me, being halfhearted is the experience of having one part of you that wants to do something—for example, helping—but another part says, "No." Being half-hearted is like having a piece of you torn off—even though really it's not.

To me, being wholehearted is the experience of having every part of you say, "Yes." You want to help with what's going on. Being wholehearted can be like two pieces of a charm being put together. Both sides say, "Yes."

For example, let's say I told my mother that I'd help her with her chores, but only one side of me said, "Yes." The other side would have been saying, "No. Don't help your mother. Hang out with your friends and have fun!" But if I am wholehearted, I do the task asked of me by my mother and get rewarded (which is actually what I do).

This is what I think about being halfhearted and being wholehearted.

RELATIONSHIPS

ROMA BEGUM: Teachers' and students' relationships can affect the future. The way you or the teachers work is one main thing. If you or the teachers work poorly, then you have no chance to have a bright future. You have to understand what the teachers are trying to say, and the teachers have to make sure that you understand what they are trying to say. That way, everything will be easy for you, and you will have the feeling of believing that everything will be easy later on. If you or the teachers work closely and with understanding, then you will have the most "intense" future ever.

What you or the teachers are looking forward to is another important thing that can affect the future. If you or the teachers are looking forward to an appalling future, then you have no chance to accomplish something. If you or the teachers are looking toward an excellent future, then you have the chance to achieve something. You have to have the willingness to go to college or to other high-quality places to have a nice future. You cannot be lazy about your education, especially not when you are looking forward to accomplishing something.

BEING A POSITIVE ROLE MODEL

KYOSHA PIERRE FRANCOIS:

Being a positive role model is an important thing in life. By being a positive role model, you can set an example for kids younger than you are. When they see you behaving well, very often, they'll behave well, too. When you see other kids behaving well because of you, you'll think, "I might've set a good example for that child." You might also feel good about yourself.

Another reason you should be a positive role model is that when teachers and other people see you acting in a positive way, they'll think well of you.

AUTHORS' NOTE: The authors gratefully acknowledge Rhonda Haynes and Olivia Delaine, the coordinators of the Comer Club.

EDITORS' NOTE: These writings were responses to workshops conducted during the 2002–2003 school year by Michael Ben-Avie and Trudy Raschkind Steinfeld. They were edited with each author's collaboration for inclusion in this field guide.

GLOSSARY OF SDP TERMS

Compiled by the Comer office of the Prince George's County Public Schools.

Child Psychiatrist: a psychiatrist who has been specially trained to work with children *[see also Psychiatrist, below]*

Collaboration: a guiding principle of SDP that focuses our attention on speaking respectfully, listening attentively, and working together cooperatively and effectively on projects and problems *[see also Consensus, Cooperation, and No-Fault, below]*

College: an independent institution of higher learning in a professional, vocational, or technical field offering courses leading to an associate's or a bachelor's degree; a part of a university offering a specialized group of courses *[see also University, below]*

Comer Facilitator: a highly trained person who works with teachers, parents, students, the principal, and other members of the school community to help them implement SDP at their schools; a role model for members of the SDP school community *[see also Implementing, Model, and School Community, below]*

Comer School Development Program (SDP):   a program begun in 1968 by Dr. James P. Comer and developed since then by Dr. Comer and his colleagues to (1) improve the academic learning and the social and emotional development of school children in grades pre-K through 12 and (2) enlarge and strengthen school communities *[see also Community and School Community, below]*

Community: people with common characteristics and/or interests living together within a larger society; a group linked by a common policy; a neighborhood *[see also School Community, below]*

Consensus: a guiding principle of SDP that focuses our attention on general agreement; in SDP schools, a type of decision making in which each person must (1) share his or her thoughts and feelings, (2) if necessary, gather additional creative ideas and information from the wider community, and (3) be willing to support the group's action plan after it has been thoroughly discussed, even if the decision seems less than ideal to that group member; a way of arriving at decisions that increases the likelihood that all group members can help shape the decision and can therefore support it *[see also Collaboration, above, and No-fault, below]*

Cooperation: acting and working with another or others; acting together; associating with another or others for mutual benefit

Dean: one of the highest-ranking administrators at a college or university

Facilitating: making easier; helping to bring about *[see also Comer Facilitator, above]*

Implementing: carrying out; accomplishing; providing instruments or means of expression for ideas

Model: a description, diagram, structural design, or other small version of a thing, system, or process; a pattern of something to be made; an example for imitation or emulation; a person or thing that serves as a pattern

No-fault: a guiding principle of SDP that focuses our attention on (1) finding solutions rather than assigning blame and (2) keeping a positive attitude and sharing responsibility for making things better *[see also Collaboration and Consensus, above]*

Problem: an intricate or unsettled question or situation that is hard to solve or with which it is difficult to deal; a question raised for inquiry, consideration, or solution

Professor: one of the highest-ranking faculty members at a college or university

Psychiatrist: a medical doctor who has had many years of special training in helping people solve personal mental, emotional, and behavioral problems [see also Child Psychiatrist, above]

School Community: this includes but is not limited to the students, parents, teachers, staff members, administrators, community organization members and leaders, businesspeople, government and law enforcement officials, and public and private policymakers—all those who are involved in making a school an even better place in which students can learn and develop well

SDP: [see Comer School Development Program, above]

Team: two or more people whose task it is to work together on achieving a goal

Teamwork: work done by several people, with each one doing a part and each one considering his or her personal needs to be less important than the efficiency of the whole team

Three Guiding Principles: [see Collaboration, Consensus, and No-fault, above]

University: an institution of higher learning whose faculty members teach and conduct research; an institution that grants undergraduate and graduate academic degrees [see also College, above]

11

Performance Management

The Principal's First Priority

M. Ann Levett-Lowe

Hundreds of seemingly important demands are made on principals every day. With so many distractions, it is easy for them to lose sight of their first priority, which is to make sure that every teacher is doing his or her best to instruct every student. The remedy for this is for principals to concentrate on performance management: developing their staff's instruction skills through monitoring and mentoring. SDP's deputy director, a former school principal and interim superintendent, deputy superintendent, and chief academic officer, offers the benefit of her experience so that principals can monitor and mentor their staff members—and themselves.

I served as a principal. It's one of the toughest jobs around, but for me, it has been among the most rewarding. I always speak of principals as a group of wise people who are extremely underappreciated. Most people from the world outside education do not know what it takes to make a school thrive—or even just to make a school run! A principal's day is an unending series of challenges to one's ability to organize and prioritize in general, and to cope with the physical plant, district policies, lack of human and material resources, and myriad other concerns. One of the most significant challenges for a principal is performance management. This includes managing the performance of administrative, teaching, and support staff and of students, as well as managing the involvement of families and community partners, all the while responding to the conditions created by the community at large.

An excellent school is made up of excellent classrooms, and excellent classrooms are headed by excellent teachers. You increase the likelihood that your teachers will perform excellently when you (1) are clear in your expectations, (2) provide appropriate and sufficient resources, and (3) provide support when and where necessary. If you want to have a thriving, academically sound, nurturing environment for all those who live in the school, as the principal, you must fulfill your ethical and legal responsibilities for creating those conditions.

This chapter is about setting appropriate expectations and defining appropriate actions needed for everyone in the school community to perform at their best—including you. As principal, you must focus on what is important and put performance management, which includes instructional monitoring and mentoring, at the top of your "to do" list. More important, you must help other people understand why you have made performance management your primary focus.

MONITORING: DISCOVERING WHAT'S REALLY GOING ON IN YOUR BUILDING

The way to know what's really going on in the building is to get information regularly and directly about what's going on in the classrooms. To do this, first, you need to develop and implement strategies to increase your opportunities to get out of the office and into those classrooms. Second, you need to determine how you will respond to what you discover once you're there.

Get Out of Your Office and Into the Classrooms

When I started out as an administrator, I was in the classroom maybe 5 to 10 percent of the time. Based on the population I served and the context in which I was working, if I got into a classroom, it was typically to respond to a disruption or to do something else related to creating order. Only rarely was it to observe instruction. But I learned that if I was going to have a direct impact on instruction, I needed to be in the classrooms a larger percentage of my time. When I did my own library research on effective principals and successful schools, I learned that effective principals spend about 85 percent of their time in classrooms, monitoring, giving feedback, coaching, and mentoring. When I started spending more time in classrooms observing instruction and coaching teachers, the students' outcomes improved consistently. I came to understand and believe that spending purposeful time in the classroom and working with the faculty on improving their instructional practices were critical to improving student achievement.

Years later, when I served as an assistant superintendent, I would not call principals during the school day unless it was really an emergency. If I called a school and the principal was always able to answer the telephone, I wondered why. My message to him or her would be, "Your first responsibility is to be in the classroom and to focus on order and instruction. That's the way to turn a school around, make it a success, and keep it that way."

Just being in the classroom, however, is not sufficient. You can go into some classes and fall asleep, given how little is going on. You can sit in the back of the room, ignore the lesson, and just process your mail or complete paperwork. But when (1) you're in the classroom regularly, (2) you know what to look for, (3) you have made sure that everyone else knows what you're looking for, and (4) you have a way of documenting and keeping track of what you've seen and what you haven't seen, then you've got well-organized monitoring. This is the first part of the formula for ensuring successful student outcomes. It is essential, however, that well-organized monitoring be accompanied by well-organized mentoring. You need to act on what you've seen. So, the second part of the formula is a good feedback process for teachers and a structure for mentoring them.

Employ Personal and Administrative Strategies to Increase Your Opportunities to Monitor Instruction

Because you are trying to make virtually everything else secondary to your being in the classrooms, you need to use effective strategies for ensuring that you can meet your goal of increasing the opportunities to monitor classroom instruction. This monitoring includes classroom observations and examining artifacts that reflect what is happening in classrooms.

Check to Make Sure Each Person *Really* Understands Your Goals

Even if you think your goals and strategies are clear, ask each staff member to describe them to you in detail. For example, take the learning goal of raising the math test scores by at least 15 percent. You must make sure that the specific components and strategies implied in this message are clear to everyone who is designated to carry it out. What gets measured gets done. If staff members know you're not paying attention to something, some of them may not follow the established plan and the learning goal will not be met. If you want to improve student achievement, the teachers, families, and students must know what you expect and that you will inspect for it. Put the learning goals in language that staff, students, and family members can give back to you. Share the data and all the essential information in a way that allows each person to understand why the goals have been established and the exact role each plays in meeting those goals.

We would be wise to use a strategic approach, as do generals of the armed forces. The generals at headquarters can create the plan, but they must communicate it clearly to their commanders. If the commanders on the front line don't understand what the plan is, they will be less than effective in meeting the established goals. Because we are fighting for our students' futures, we must all know the plan, check for each person's understanding of it, and monitor our progress regularly.

Become Clearer When You Communicate Your Focus on Being in the Classrooms

A principal's behavior and language must say it all: "I am going to be out of my office and in the classrooms because that is the only way to make sure that our students and staff are meeting our learning goals." Ask people whose opinion you value to help you assess and improve the way you communicate this message. It is important to remember that to increase the likelihood that you have been understood, you need to be (1) in rapport, (2) specific, and (3) congruent, that is, all channels of your communication—the tone and tempo of your speech, your posture and gestures, and your words—agree with one another. Of course, it should be evident that you are focused on positive student outcomes. Respond to the feedback given to you so that you can improve and model responding appropriately to input and feedback.

Let People Know That Everything Else Will Have to Wait

The scope and nature of the responsibilities assigned to you as a principal dictate that the majority of your time should be spent among the students and staff throughout the campus. You must tell people consistently, in memorable language and with memorable behavior, that being in classrooms is your priority. I often said, "Unless you have 99 bullet holes (a *real* emergency), it can wait!" Your actions, body language, and tone of voice must match your words. If you don't make this message clear, people will expect to have access to you at all times.

The most difficult part of making everything else wait is the conflict a principal may feel about this approach. No one wants to wait. Each person has a dilemma he or she feels that only the principal can address, and that dilemma is a crisis that must be addressed right now! And since the principal is "in charge" of the building, he or she must be responsible for solving all of the problems! Some principals even promote this thinking through their behavior.

Nonetheless, if the students and staff are not performing well and the principal does not address that, there's an even bigger crisis in the building. To avoid this situation, the principal must make sure everyone understands that the first priority is to monitor instruction and that everything else will have to wait.

Protect Academic Time by Learning How to Say "No, But . . ."

One of a principal's major responsibilities is to protect academic time so that the students receive consistent and adequate exposure to all facets of the curriculum. You also must make sure that the academic time you are preserving is organized so that each learning opportunity is maximized. If the students are not in the classroom or if someone else is leading them, you may not have a chance to observe the planned instruction, the students' response to the learning experience, or how the teacher is performing.

Special activities, assemblies, parties, field trips, and guest speakers may all be enriching to students but may cost you time on task. Instruction time may already be reduced by some administrative functions, such as fire and other safety drills, public announcements, building maintenance, and other events. Disorder and disruptive events can also reduce instructional time on task. In combination, all these activities can greatly reduce the number of hours with focused instruction. Thus the impact of each learning experience proposed and undertaken must be considered carefully in relation to attainment of established learning goals, cognitive and otherwise.

Each learning experience, formal and informal, should contribute to the attainment of the stated learning goals. To ensure that a learning experience will indeed advance student learning, criteria about which types of experiences should yield the desired results must be established by the staff and administration, and communicated to all. Through discussions with key stakeholders, these criteria should be established and applied uniformly across all activities to ensure that instructional time is used wisely and that all learning experiences provided for students will yield maximum benefits.

Many well-meaning persons, staff as well as community partners, propose and plan valuable learning experiences for students. Each experience, undoubtedly, can enhance the development of students in some way. Yet each learning experience (inside or outside the classroom) must be evaluated for its value in the overall plan to attain the established learning goals. Since instructional time is so limited, the timeliness, student readiness for, cost/benefit ratio of, and direct link to the learning goals must be examined (especially for those experiences planned to take place during the school day).

While schools frown upon rejecting the creative ideas of staff and the offers of assistance from parents and community partners, it is sometimes necessary to respond with a diplomatic "No, but . . ." response. Counter each offer that does not meet the criteria the staff has established for all learning experiences with a request for what the school *really* needs: experiences directly related to your school goals. Make suggestions that allow the person making the offer to understand your needs and how that person can help you reach those specific goals. Perhaps you can adjust that person's plan or offer of assistance to better suit your identified needs.

For example, a community partner has offered to host an all-day track-and-field event in early fall. The following might be a suitable response to such an offer: "We appreciate your offer to host the field day event in October. Devoting a full day to such an activity would delight all of our students. At the same time, however, the staff and I have decided to get our students focused on specific skills during the fall. The activity would work better for us if we could do it in the spring. As well, we could benefit from your volunteers' help with our tutorial and reading program throughout the school year. Volunteers could participate as often as they are available. Could this plan work for you?"

This kind of response expresses appreciation for the offer and maintains the community partner's interest in the school, yet amends the offer to better suit the school's academic pacing plan. The partner is also advised of other ways to be involved with the students in an ongoing, substantial way. This should produce a win-win situation for all parties, with the students gaining the most benefit from this partnership.

Have Gatekeepers to Protect Your Time

There are persons designated to assist a principal and the school. Those persons, generally, are other administrators and your secretary or administrative assistants. They can create access to you for themselves or others, becoming "gatekeepers." Gatekeepers must understand your needs and the goal of increasing your time in classrooms. Thus one of their most important roles is to limit the access others would have to you in order to help protect your classroom observation time.

Remember that a task unscheduled is a task undone. If you really wish to increase your time observing classroom instruction, you must schedule yourself into classrooms. Not only should you set aside time daily for classroom observations, you should also schedule such observations over weeks and months. Set a weekly goal of a reasonable number of classrooms to visit. Begin the school year with a calendar of dates set aside throughout the year for observations. Be sure to build in makeup dates. Frequently evaluate your progress in keeping the schedule. Make adjustments as necessary to keep yourself on track.

When you are scheduled to visit classrooms or conduct observations, have your gatekeepers behave as if you are off campus. Be very clear about the circumstances or conditions that demand *your* immediate attention and warrant *your* forsaking an observation task. When you must miss an observation, it is also important to reschedule it. I suggest that you direct your gatekeepers to call you only if the building is on fire!

Create Several Backup Plans for Handling Crises

You are not the only person in the building who can handle a crisis. In a school, the definition of a "crisis" can range from a highly disruptive classroom situation to an emergency that puts people's lives at risk. In any situation, a team response is recommended. Develop a plan that encourages each staff person to take an active role in handling crises. Work with the staff to develop such plans, and make sure the plans are communicated and reviewed often. Communicate clearly that everyone has a responsibility to assist in establishing and maintaining a safe and orderly environment.

Establish procedures and roles for handling the typical "critical incidents" that may happen in your building. Communicate them widely and employ them as needed to reduce the chaos and mistakes bound to occur if these procedures and roles are not well established. Have those responding evaluate their responses, to promote their reflection about handling such incidents.

Furthermore, conduct research and have conversations with peers in your district and others, and conduct emergency preparedness exercises, the same way that communities do. Based on feedback sessions evaluating those exercises, refine your emergency preparedness plans to the point at which they are second nature. Not only will this help you free up the time you need, it will also serve as professional development for your staff.

If you don't delegate some of the responsibilities and also empower others to fulfill those responsibilities, you end up having no energy, no time for yourself, no time for your family, feeling frustrated, and being far less effective. Tell people that you're delegating in this way because instructional monitoring is your priority and because each staff member can and should play a critical role in responding to events in the building. Unless you've become omnipotent, you will need everyone's assistance to get most things done.

Share Your Leadership Tasks and Responsibilities

Effective leaders manage best and most effectively when they distribute some of their tasks and responsibilities to team members according to the situation and skills of the team members. This act of sharing leadership can be scary. However, once a leader recognizes that he or she cannot complete the job alone, it will become easier to distribute some tasks to capable leaders. Delegation, a key part of this sharing process, can serve to motivate and develop other leaders in an organization. When tasks are delegated, the person or group assigned to a task can be trusted to make the decisions about how best to accomplish it. This must be done, of course, with clear guidance given up front to those now charged with this responsibility. Not all major tasks should be delegated, however, since the principal is the person most accountable to all stakeholders!

Those who help maintain the committee structures—the assistant principals, the formal leaders, and the informal leaders—must feel your trust in them to assist in the process of leading. The principal must demonstrate respect for their work, recommendations, and input. It is best to avoid mishaps, bad feelings, and loss of credibility by ensuring that all expectations and parameters for decision making by other leaders are communicated clearly before any work is done. Checking periodically with the person or group often can help you determine whether any clarifications or modifications should be made.

Chart the School's Instructional Course

Teams can help you chart your school's instructional course. These teams can examine data and make suggestions or decisions based on what they learn about all aspects of the school program. They can create valuable tools and procedures that allow all stakeholders to monitor the school's performance at established points in time.

Review and Assess the Data

What data can you share so that all those involved in the educational process know what it is you're trying to measure and how well you all are doing? Make sure that the data are in a form that can be easily understood. Sharing data is one way to challenge the ineffective practices you may observe in the classroom. Remembering that your first obligation is to students will help you to challenge adults' ineffective practices and identify the actions necessary to advance student achievement.

Share your data regularly with the School Planning and Management Team (SPMT) for their analysis. This sharing is both a skill builder and a way of bringing more people's insights to the problems. Let the SPMT draw their own conclusions and ask their own questions. Present this data and ask, "What is it that you see here?" Give them time to examine the information fully. Give them the data in advance and say, "I want you study this and tell me what you see." Then they can come to a meeting prepared to share their observations. Sharing observations can "jump-start" the problem-solving process.

Sometimes, it really does matter who brings the message. You can come in and say to the faculty as a whole, "Our students are performing very, very poorly in this particular area." In response, you may get blank stares, or blaming may begin. However, if a team of teachers who have studied the data come in and share the same message, the message may be received differently. Having the SPMT help you review and report the data creates a culture in which you are not the only one taking the news forward. The SPMT members are going to talk informally and formally about the data with their colleagues. The conclusions reached and the questions asked will promote real problem solving on a wider basis, involving more staff members. In fact, there would probably be a stronger commitment in the future to looking at the data and questioning current practices.

Dedicate Specific Times of the Day for Certain Tasks

Dedicating specific times of the day for certain tasks is a sure way to manage your time more efficiently and ensure that you can focus on the areas and tasks that deserve your attention. Establish procedures and guidelines for you and your staff to ensure that paperwork, nonemergency tasks, and meetings are scheduled at times of the day that do not interfere with your classroom observation time. This will take practice and skill, but it can be done.

Reflect on your weekly activities. Identify how you are using your time and the kind of changes you will need to make to reach your goals. Establish your priorities and solid time estimates for the tasks you must complete daily. Note things that must be done at certain times, at any time, or by someone else. Unanticipated meetings, emergencies, or last-minute schedule changes may be a routine part of your life. You cannot control for them all of the time. So, when others can handle things or when things are fairly quiet for you, find your way into the classroom.

For example, if your school day typically ends at 3:30, you may decide to take phone calls, return calls, sign paperwork, and hold conferences between 3:45 and 5:30. You might direct your office staff to schedule conferences between 4:00 and 4:45. Have your staff get as much information to you as possible in advance so that your time may be used efficiently. Set time limits as necessary. Advise your office staff of your desired schedule and your priorities. Review the schedule with the staff at least twice a day to determine whether adjustments must be made.

Take more control of your time, because then you can do what you really need to do. When parents call, have your gatekeeper say, "She is in classrooms; she's doing something very important. If it's an emergency, I will ask her to call you back. If it's not an emergency, she will call you back between 4:45 and 5:30. If you need her to call you back at some other time, please let me know, and we'll see what we can arrange."

If there are extracurricular or night activities that you must support, be sure to alter your schedule to allow a break between the end of the day and the next activity.

Set a reasonable time to end your day. Doing so will help you maintain a good life outside of work.

Turn Other Situations Into Opportunities to Get Into the Classrooms

A principal must be intentional about getting into classrooms. The only way that you will create the time you need is to create a plan that places you in the classrooms, given all the other forces at work to keep you out of them. Therefore, you must create a plan that forces you into the classrooms and around the building.

If a teacher wants to see you, go to his or her room instead of having him or her come to your office. If a teacher calls and asks for help with a discipline problem, go to the room. Do this especially with the teachers who continually ask for help with minor infractions. Go to the room, and sit and observe. Even if you remove the child from the room, sit and observe. You may learn a lot about the conditions that created that situation.

Circulate throughout the building, stopping in classrooms to get a mental snapshot of what is happening at any given moment. You may find something that warrants your attention. Some things you see may be especially exciting and indicate what is going well in the school. Other things may confirm your previous ideas or inform you of needs that should be addressed privately or collectively to promote student or staff performance improvement.

Let's say that one day you may not be able to spend ample time in classrooms. You may decide that you're going to visit five classrooms for five minutes for an informal visit to see what's going on. Create a private "five-by-five" chart listing which classes you'll be visiting. If you're in classrooms every day, after a while, your presence is not a novelty, and people will not be surprised by your presence. You can learn a lot about what else is really going on in five minutes.

Walk visitors to the classrooms or places in the building they would like to visit. Have your students take you (with or without visitors) on a tour periodically of the building to see things from their perspective.

Be creative in finding ways to see more of what is happening in most or all classrooms every day.

EMPLOY CURRICULUM-RELATED STRATEGIES TO INCREASE YOUR OPPORTUNITIES TO MONITOR INSTRUCTION

It is also important to use a variety of curriculum-related strategies to learn about what is happening daily in the classroom. Typical strategies include examining artifacts like lesson plans and student work samples, and talking with students and families about what students are learning.

Use Lesson Plans as a Monitoring Tool

Lesson plans are an essential element of effective teaching. The plans are a road map, outlining the critical information necessary to ensure that the teachers and learners meet the learning goals. Some teachers are quite experienced and effective and can explain exactly what they are teaching, why they have chosen to use particular strategies, and how they will know if they have been successful. Even with these teachers, it is best to have a written plan available for your review. These plans are particularly useful should an emergency arise. They can also serve as expert models for less experienced teachers.

It is the leader's responsibility to outline for all teaching staff what you expect to see in the lesson plans and in the lessons taught. Be clear about what you expect to learn when you review the lesson plan. Many districts provide a suggested format for lesson plans.

Lesson plans can indicate the degree to which the teacher is keeping pace with the required content and skills. They can show where a teacher is focusing his or her attention, where things are going well, or where progress is not being made. Lesson plans may indicate where a teacher needs assistance or guidance. This helps an administrator facilitate improvement of performance of students and staff.

On your computer, keep a list of learning objectives for each grade and each subject. You only have to organize these lists once. The district or state department makes some of these lists available. You can update them periodically and print them out whenever you need them. When you look at a particular grade area or department, you'll know which specific learning objective you are looking for. Make sure that the teachers know those learning objectives and include them on your observation checklist. Check them against any instructional pacing guides that you may have.

I don't believe in administering or teaching by number. But I also don't believe in teaching by happenstance. For those of us who may not be familiar with pacing or perhaps have not given it as much attention as is needed, it's important to establish some pacing benchmarks, because you want to make sure that teachers cover the right amount of information in a timely manner. This is not the same as covering the textbook. It means that the teaching staff is moving students through the curricular objectives at an appropriate pace. Check the learning objectives for relevance. Make sure that the materials or resources teachers use are an appropriate match for the population, context, and established learning objectives.

A caveat: Review all lesson plans and give teachers feedback. Don't collect them if you do not plan to review them. It is also wise to check the lesson plans against what you actually see happening in the classroom when you observe. Note the adjustments the teacher makes (if any are needed) based on the students' responses to the learning experiences.

Examine Student Work

Some of the best indicators of how and what students are doing and not doing are samples of student work. You may collect such samples directly from students and teachers or from other places students often leave work: on the floor, in their desks, in the schoolyard. All such samples of work, complete and incomplete, can inform you of what students may or may not be learning.

Staff members generally post their students' best work on the classroom or corridor bulletin boards. When you peruse this work, think about the learning objectives reflected in the work. Comment to the teachers about what you see and how it relates to the established learning objectives.

Request copies of a recent test, seatwork, or independent assignment that the teacher has given and review the students' submitted work. These are important artifacts. Do this especially if you find that there is a day when you cannot get into the classrooms. Compare the samples to the teachers' lesson plans and the established objectives for learning. You will learn a lot by engaging in this review of student work. When the staff and students are aware that you are examining student work to confirm that students are performing as needed and that teachers are teaching as expected, each will learn that monitoring instruction is your priority.

Some samples you will find are of work that isn't so good—work that shows misunderstanding or no understanding. They may be left in a desk, thrown in the trash, or left in a place that may reflect the students' feeling about the work. These pieces are also important to review because they may indicate areas of difficulty for students and/or teachers.

A way to empower your teachers is to encourage them to examine samples of student work as a group. The results of such a process can influence the choice of teaching strategies, student grouping practices, and the assignments given to students.

Interview Students

Another effective strategy for determining what students are learning is to talk with them directly about what they are learning and how they feel about school in general. Students will often openly share what learning activities, skills, and subjects they prefer. Ask questions that allow the students to speak freely about what they are experiencing without feeling they are being quizzed or that they are "talking about" their teachers.

These are some examples of questions you might pose:

- Describe the kinds of learning activities that are exciting for you.
- Describe the kinds of learning activities that do *not* excite you.
- What kinds of questions make you think?
- What subjects do you like? Why?
- What subjects do you *not* like? Why?

Make Sure Your Observations Are Comprehensive

It is not enough just to complete classroom observations, formal or informal. During visits, it is important to look for behaviors that indicate effective teaching and an environment conducive to learning. A number of indicators have been supported by strong research and generally have been listed on the teacher observation and evaluation documents adopted and provided by districts.

Some categories of those behaviors may include, but are not limited to, the following:

- effective management of instructional time
- effective management of student behavior
- effective instructional presentation
- effective monitoring of student performance

To ensure that teachers know what you will expect to observe during your classroom visits, take time at the beginning of the year and at several times during the year to review the observation documents with them. Be as explicit as possible in your discussion of your expectations.

Follow the district's prescribed evaluation procedures, and document what you see during the observation episodes.

INSTRUCTIONAL MENTORING: TRANSLATING HIGH EXPECTATIONS INTO HIGH PERFORMANCE

Once you've made your observations, then what do you do?

Note that you have a professional responsibility to provide feedback and guidance to teachers regarding what you observe during classroom visits and after the review of artifacts. The feedback and guidance allow you to advance the development of the staff and the achievement of students.

Recognize That You Probably Need Some Mentoring, Too

Whenever you need some advice, get someone you trust and respect to observe you mentoring your staff, particularly staff members you find to be "difficult." Carve enough time out of your day to debrief fully with this person, and take notes to which you can refer later. Role-play new skills and approaches with this trusted observer. Since you'll be able to use your new skills and approaches with more than one staff member, the time you put into this exercise will be well worth it.

Whether or not you have such a person available, you can always imagine what an ideal principal would think and feel about what you've observed in the classrooms. Imagine what that ideal principal would do, either to reinforce good performance or to rectify poor performance. Are there any disparities between that ideal principal's expectations and actions and your own? Figures 11.1 through 11.6 are worksheets that will help you sort out your reactions and actions, and create a plan to improve your own performance in relation to others and to yourself. If you do not have the time to work through all the worksheets, start at the place of your greatest need for development. Consider offering your staff a version of these worksheets, redesigned for them to engage in their own self-reflection.

Figure 11.1 Instructional leadership practices reflection activity

Directions: Review each of the following questions to help you reflect on the instructional leadership practices in your school. These questions are not comprehensive. They are not designed to make you feel guilty about what you may or may not be doing. These questions should stimulate thought about what you might consider doing this year to enhance your instructional leadership skills and facilitate improved teaching and learning in your school. Record your responses to each question.

1. Who creates the learning goals and how? Are they clear, understood, and accepted? If so, clear to whom, and understood and accepted by whom? How do you make sure this is true?

2. Do you protect academic time? How? Who helps you protect it?

3. How do you monitor what teachers are teaching?

4. Does your comprehensive school plan require the use of interim and multiple assessments to gauge student learning? What do you use and how often? How do you and the SPMT use the results?

5. Do you provide opportunities for dialogue and planning across teams, grades, and subjects? Are consensus, collaboration, and no-fault problem solving used? Are these sessions beneficial? How do you know?

(Continued)

Figure 11.1 (Continued)

6. Do you, the SPMT, SSST, and Parent Team share information (data, research, experiences) that leads others to adopt practices that advance student performance? How?
7. Do you challenge ineffective instructional practices? How are these practices identified, and by whom? What do you do to ensure such practices do not continue?
8. How do you protect your classroom observation time? How can you increase that time?
9. What methods or techniques do you use to determine what students are learning and what teachers are covering in their classrooms?
10. How do you use "meeting" (faculty, team, department, grade level, etc.) time in your school? What topics are covered? Are these meetings helpful in improving student achievement?

Figure 11.2 Suggested questions for principals' dialogue group

1. How do you and your team gather, use, and monitor data to make decisions about your students' achievement and social development levels, school culture, and school's public image?
2. How do you and your team engage the faculty and other critical educators in conversations about instructional practices and action research?
3. How do you and your team promote and provide ongoing, focused, and targeted professional development?
4. How do you and your team determine your school needs, articulate your school needs, and use planning processes and tools to meet your needs?
5. How do you and your team **invite** collaboration within the school **and** outside the school walls to ensure a continual state of growth in leadership?
6. What partnerships have you and your teams formed, want to form, and **need** to form to make SDP work for you and help to improve student achievement?
7. How do you define the term "empowered school community," and how can such a community work **for you**?

Figure 11.3 Self-management worksheet for principals: My ideal principal's expectations and actions about performance management

What to Monitor and Mentor	Monitoring: My Ideal Principal's Expectations	Mentoring: My Ideal Principal's Actions to Manage Change
Students' academic learning	*[generate a list for each cell in this worksheet]*	
Students' development along the six pathways		
Students' behavior		
Staff's academic learning		
Staff's development along the six pathways		
Staff's behavior		
Parents' academic learning		
Parents' development along the six pathways		
Parents' behavior		
District peers' academic learning		
District peers' development along the six pathways		
District peers' behavior		
District officers' academic learning		
District officers' development along the six pathways		
District officers' behavior		
Community partners' academic learning		
Community partners' development along the six pathways		
Community partners' behavior		
Ideal principal's own academic learning		
Ideal principal's own development along the six pathways		
Ideal principal's own behavior		

Figure 11.4 Self-management worksheet for principals: What supports my ideal principal's expectations and actions about performance management

From the Lists Generated for Figure 11.3 Select Expectations That, So Far, Remain Unmet in My Work Environment	Monitoring: What Supports My Ideal Principal's Expectations			Mentoring: What Supports My Ideal Principal's Actions to Manage Change		
	Ideal Inner Thoughts About These Expectations	*Ideal* Feelings About These Expectations	*Ideal* Behaviors About These Expectations	*Ideal* Inner Thoughts About These Actions	*Ideal* Feelings About These Actions	*Ideal* Behaviors About These Actions
Students' academic learning						
Students' development along the six pathways						
Students' behavior						
Staff's academic learning						
Staff's development along the six pathways						
Staff's behavior						
Parents' academic learning						
Parents' development along the six pathways						
Parents' behavior						
District peers' academic learning						
District peers' development along the six pathways						
District peers' behavior						
District officers' academic learning						
District officers' development along the six pathways						
District officers' behavior						

(Continued)

147

Figure 11.4 (Continued)

From the Lists Generated for Figure 11.3, Select Expectations That, So Far, Remain Unmet in My Work Environment	Monitoring: What Supports My Ideal Principal's Expectations			Mentoring: What Supports My Ideal Principal's Actions to Manage Change		
	Ideal Inner Thoughts About These Expectations	*Ideal* Feelings About These Expectations	*Ideal* Behaviors About These Expectations	*Ideal* Inner Thoughts About These Actions	*Ideal* Feelings About These Actions	*Ideal* Behaviors About These Actions
Community partners' academic learning						
Community partners' development along the six pathways						
Community partners' behavior						
Ideal principal's own academic learning						
Ideal principal's own development along the six pathways						
Ideal principal's own behavior						

SOURCE: Trudy Raschkind Steinfeld and Ann Levett-Lowe. Copyright © 2004 by The Yale School Development Program, Yale Child Study Center. All rights reserved. Reprinted from *Dynamic Instructional Leadership to Support Student Learning and Development: The Field Guide to Comer Schools in Action*, by Edward T. Joyner, Michael Ben-Avie, and James P. Comer. Reproduction authorized only for the local school site that has purchased this book. www.corwinpress.com.

Figure 11.5 Self-management worksheet for principals: What supports my own current expectations and actions about performance management

Select the Same Expectations as for Figure 11.4	Monitoring: What Supports My Current Expectations			Mentoring: What Supports My Current Actions to Manage Change		
	My Actual Inner Thoughts About These Expectations	*My Actual* Feelings About These Expectations	*My Actual* Behaviors About These Expectations	*My Actual* Inner Thoughts About These Actions	*My Actual* Feelings About These Actions	*My Actual* Behaviors About These Actions
Students' academic learning						
Students' development along the six pathways						
Students' behavior						
Staff's academic learning						
Staff's development along the six pathways						
Staff's behavior						
Parents' academic learning						
Parents' development along the six pathways						
Parents' behavior						
District peers' academic learning						
District peers' development along the six pathways						
District peers' behavior						
District officers' behavior						

(Continued)

Figure 11.5 (Continued)

Select the Same Expectations as for Figure 11.4	Monitoring: What Supports My Current Expectations			Mentoring: What Supports My Current Actions to Manage Change		
	My Actual Inner Thoughts About These Expectations	*My Actual* Feelings About These Expectations	*My Actual* Behaviors About These Expectations	*My Actual* Inner Thoughts About These Actions	*My Actual* Feelings About These Actions	*My Actual* Behaviors About These Actions
District officers' academic learning						
District officers' development along the six pathways						
Community partners' academic learning						
Community partners' development along the six pathways						
Community partners' behavior						
My own academic learning						
My own development along the six pathways						
My own behavior						

Figure 11.6 Self-management worksheet for principals: Aligning my expectations and actions about performance management

Areas in Which I Notice the Greatest Discrepancies Between My Ideal Principal and Myself (a comparison of Figures 11.4 and 11.5)	My Ideal Principal's Expectations and Actions	My Current Expectations and Actions	What I Can Do to Make My Expectations and Actions More Ideal
Students' academic learning			
Students' development along the six pathways			
Students' behavior			
Staff's academic learning			
Staff's development along the six pathways			
Staff's behavior			
Parents' academic learning			
Parents' development along the six pathways			
Parents' behavior			
District peers' academic learning			
District peers' development along the six pathways			
District peers' behavior			
District officers' academic learning			
District officers' development along the six pathways			
District officers' behavior			
Community partners' behavior			

(Continued)

Figure 11.6 (Continued)

Areas in Which I Notice the Greatest Discrepancies Between My Ideal Principal and Myself (a comparison of Figures 11.4 and 11.5)	My Ideal Principal's Expectations and Actions	My Current Expectations and Actions	What I Can Do to Make My Expectations and Actions More Ideal
Community partners' academic learning			
Community partners' development along the six pathways			
My own academic learning			
My own development along the six pathways			
My own behavior			

Mentors and Potential Mentors	Areas of Expertise	Contact Information

Keep Track of Teachers' Needs and Progress

Have a checklist that includes what you expect of teachers in your building. Review this checklist with all staff members involved in the instructional process. Using a checklist allows you and the person being observed to know what is expected. Many districts provide such a document for principals to use with their instructional staff.

You must also know the skills on which teachers should focus and the behaviors that demonstrate effective teaching and promote positive student learning outcomes. During observations, use the checklist to note what you saw the teachers doing. You may also find it helpful to note what the students are doing in response to the teacher's actions.

For informal, brief visits, be sure to leave notes in the mailboxes of teachers you've visited, indicating something positive you saw in their instruction, their teaching techniques, and/or their rapport with the students. For anything that you saw that draws concern, you should have a personal conversation with that teacher (at an appropriate time). For example, if you were in the classroom for 15 minutes and the entire time, the teacher seemed to ignore a certain group of students, you may not choose to write that down because it's not an official observation. However, you do want to let the teacher know that you were concerned about that behavior. It is always important to know the due process rules established for personnel you supervise, and to honor those rules and procedures. Be prepared to document any incidents or behaviors that warrant official documentation.

Giving specific feedback about what you observed is most beneficial to the teacher. Doing so allows you to target specific behaviors for development or reinforcement. With this approach, a teacher and observer can see progress over time. Such feedback can also help identify possible staff development needs for individual teachers or the faculty as a whole.

Use Individual Conferences to Mentor Based on What You Learned

Principals can use meetings to mentor the staff and students. The appropriate use of individual conferences to discuss performance is always helpful. These sessions should focus on what the data show and on how to address emerging concerns. Positive observations should also be shared in these sessions.

Use Faculty Meetings for Group Mentoring

Faculty meetings and department/grade-level meetings with a similar format can yield good results, too. At these meetings, you can talk about data, action research, teaching, and learning. Now, it is so easy—especially when they're frustrated and you are too—to get off on tangents: "The central office is not supporting us!" or "How are we going to do the testing this time?" or "Who is going to do this piece, and who is going to take charge of this activity and hear these reports?" Make sure that your faculty meeting times are devoted to review of the available data about how kids are doing.

Share the effective strategies that you've seen in observations. Share what you learn in general from your monitoring, because if you don't share it, people won't understand why you're observing. In addition, sharing effective strategies is a way of publicly acknowledging teachers who are putting the students' outcomes first. Sharing also promotes peer discussion about and collaboration on effective teaching.

Hold Students and Teachers More Accountable for Their Own Improvement

Form committees of people who have a concern about instructional or operational issues. Create time for them to meet because that work is important, too (but don't let it dominate your faculty meeting time). This allows some issues to be addressed by those most affected by them and allows for fresh perspectives on addressing them.

To promote student and teacher accountability for their own performance, a principal should involve them in examining their own performance. As principal, I observed that when the student report cards were issued, everyone looked at the grades. Discussions about grades were held with teachers and students. We had our class meetings, and we said to the students, "Look—something's got to change here. There are too many Ds on this list. Look at the percentage of Ds!" We asked questions about why the numbers played out as they did—whether the numbers were positive or negative. Students shared suggestions on how they might improve their performance and how the staff might help them. Students must be responsible for their learning, too. And if we don't make them responsible, they may not develop any sense of ownership for their future performance.

In the same way, you can encourage the teachers to look at their own practices. What are the grades they issued saying? Discussions about grades issued are just one way to promote reflection on success rates and effective teaching techniques. Ask the same kinds of questions you pose to the students. The teachers can offer suggestions about improving the situation and make commitments to do so.

Establish Times for Grade-Level and/or Department Meetings

Establish set times when grade levels or departments are meeting other than faculty meeting time. If you work in a district with a collective-bargaining agreement, you have only a certain number of times that you can meet. Thus you have to use that time wisely. If you can meet at least once or twice per week or month, make sure that one time is for the entire faculty. Let the other time be for the various departments or grade levels.

Ensure that these meeting agendas focus on the data available and the opportunities the data present for improvement. Minutes of such meetings should be kept to remind all of what occurred. Such meeting times can also be used to meet identified staff development needs.

It is important that you attend these meetings. You can share information or just observe. If you can't be present, get together with the meeting leaders before and after the meeting. Read the notes and (1) respond to the people affected by each issue, and (2) respond in a timely manner to each issue raised at the meeting.

FINAL THOUGHTS

This chapter is in no way a complete picture of what a principal can do to manage performance—his or her own performance or the performance of others. Only a sample of ideas and strategies can be shared here. The principal's charge involves juggling tasks and priorities, supervising people and programs, and responding to a number of persons, while trying to advance student achievement. Nonetheless, the charge to create the best teaching and learning environment for all students and staff is one that deserves and demands all the skills the principal has to offer.

READ MORE ABOUT . . .

To read about SDP's peer mentoring program for less experienced teachers, see Chapter 12 in this volume, "Teachers Helping Teachers: A Process That Honors and Supports Teacher Development."

12

Teachers Helping Teachers

A Process That Honors and Supports Teacher Development

J. Patrick Howley and Dawn K. Kelley

Relationships are at the core of learning and development, yet in many schools, teachers' relationships with each other occur by chance and can be neutral or even negative. In SDP schools, however, teachers' relationships with each other are nurtured and guided to be as generative and productive as possible, both within and across grade levels. Developed and guided by SDP's national faculty, Teachers Helping Teachers (THT) provides professional development in education theory and practice, in nonjudgmental observation, and in paired mentoring. In this chapter, THT's director and a whole-school reform facilitator describe the process in general and its results in one New Jersey school.

This chapter answers the question, "Why is a program like Teachers Helping Teachers (THT) needed in schools?" THT is a professional development program designed for teachers, based on a natural extension of the developmental theory we apply to children. Just as children develop uniquely along each of the six pathways, so do adults. The pathways are physical, cognitive, psychological, language, social, and ethical.

In THT, we model the developmental process so that teachers experience support in their own professional growth. Each teacher may have different strengths and weaknesses and therefore different professional development needs. THT seeks to support teachers in ascertaining their own professional needs by engaging them in a process of self-reflection and self-assessment. THT also encourages teachers to develop skills, described in the models of teaching and competencies, that help them to become more effective teachers.

Box 12.1   The Six Models of Teaching (based on Arends, 2000)

In brief, the six models are the following:

1. Presentation. The primary goal is to provide information. It is sometimes referred to as an "advance organizer model," in which the teacher explicitly shows what will be learned and how it relates to knowledge previously taught. A logical order of meaning and use of learning materials is part of this model. The teacher ends the lesson with questions for checking, understanding, and extending the thinking of the students.

2. Direct Instruction. The primary goal is to develop skills. It is used when the skill needs to be taught step by step. After getting students ready to learn, the teacher explains and/or demonstrates the steps, provides some guided practice, and then gives feedback before giving the students more time for practicing the skill.

3. Concept Teaching. The primary goal is to develop higher-level thinking. The teacher provides examples of what a concept is as well as what it is not. Students learn that people communicate through concepts and that the academic disciplines are structured around concepts.

4. Cooperative Learning. The primary goal is to develop social and academic skills. Cooperative learning goes beyond academic content and skills by simultaneously helping students to accept diversity and learn social skills. Four general approaches are at the core of this model:

- Student Teams Achievement Divisions, through which the learners are mixed on teams in as diverse a way as possible
- The Jigsaw Approach, through which different teams study a topic together and then report out to other teams who are studying other topics
- Group Investigation, through which a team does more in-depth learning together
- The Structural Approach, one version of which is called "Think-Pair-Share"

5. Problem-Based Instruction. The primary goal is to provide opportunities and develop skills in problem solving. Students are presented with authentic and meaningful problem situations that serve as springboards for investigations and inquiry. Typically, a problem is presented that is real, socially important, and personally meaningful to students. In considering the problem, they will have to apply or gain knowledge from many academic subjects, do an authentic investigation, and—working with a number of other students—construct some product in the form of artifacts and exhibits.

6. Classroom Discussion. The primary goal is to develop the skill of inquiry. Discussion promotes involvement and engagement and encourages students to take responsibility for their own learning. The teacher is a facilitator, managing the environment and making it conducive to active discussion. The teacher provides a focus for the discussion and then monitors students' interactions. The teacher listens, asks questions, creates and enforces ground rules, and expresses his or her own ideas. The teacher also asks students to examine and reflect on their discussions and their own thought processes.

The THT process was developed by Dr. Edward T. Joyner and Patrick Howley of the School Development Program (SDP) and is based on Richard Arends's book, *Learning to Teach* (2000). We shall describe the elements of the program as we follow the implementation process of one school, Mott Elementary School, in Trenton, New Jersey.

WHAT IS THE TEACHERS HELPING TEACHERS PROCESS?

THT is designed to help teachers use best teaching practices to meet the learning needs of students. Based on the principles of child and adolescent development, the underlying premise of the program is that teaching will improve and student learning will be enhanced when teachers, in a climate of trust, take time together to reflect in depth on their teaching and on how children learn and develop. Teachers involved in THT develop the knowledge, skills, and attitudes to implement six basic instructional approaches, improve their competencies in teaching, conduct peer dialogues, and reflect on teaching practices with partners.

The essence and main purpose of THT is to improve teaching. The process involves reflecting on the teaching/learning process after being observed or observing others teach, and then engaging in dialogues about teaching and learning. Teachers give a gift of time to one another to explore what is working and what is not working, so that children are helped to develop more fully along the six developmental pathways. Because observations of teaching are usually evaluative or have a coaching component, the THT program works hard to shift that perception so that teachers fully realize that THT is encouraging private reflection and independent learning without judgment or criticism from each other or from staff.

INTRODUCING TEACHERS HELPING TEACHERS

Alexander Brown, the principal of Mott Elementary School, obviously knew that relationships and development are the core concepts that guide the work of SDP. On a crisp autumn afternoon in the fall of 2000, he listened intently to his teachers' concerns about implementing THT. He was hoping to involve the entire faculty, though we had earlier suggested that it might be better to start small with interested teachers, to avoid creating resistance. We could then gradually help teachers understand that THT is a process that can help them, not just add to their work. Many teachers are not used to closely examining their teaching. They also need a high degree of trust in their colleagues as they visit each other's classrooms and dialogue about children and effective teaching.

As Mr. Brown listened to teachers' concerns, he was not defensive, although we knew that he was determined to set up all three SDP teaching and learning initiatives: THT, Balanced Curriculum Process, and Essentials of Literacy. Still, he listened to the teachers and respected their objections. A few weeks later, Pat Howley at SDP heard from Dawn Kelley, the Comer facilitator, that 11 teachers (out of 18) had volunteered to do THT, and she wanted to set up a schedule of six workshops on Saturday mornings!

The teachers of Mott School are not uncommon in their initial hesitancy as well as in their willingness to grow. The challenge for principals and for SDP is to demonstrate that we understand, respect, and honor what teachers are facing today—increasing paperwork, less respect from the community and students, more demands and expectations on them, intense pressure to raise test scores, little support, and no clear path out of these dilemmas. At the same time, we want to encourage teachers to improve their teaching by opening themselves to new opportunities. The principles of THT directly address these concerns and support and enable growth. While THT is not a quick fix and cannot provide solutions to many of the problems we face in education, it does attempt to lend support to teachers and at the same time challenge them (in a safe environment) to consider and reflect on sound research, practices, and processes regarding effective instruction.

SDP encourages teachers to honor and respect their profession in general and themselves and their colleagues in particular. This is essential if teachers are to open up, examine their own teaching, compare it with a model, reflect, and then share insights. A school climate of trust, in which the individual needs and concerns of teachers can be discussed, is primary. THT staff tried to press for the Mott School teachers to stretch themselves, but not so much that they would strongly resist. In general, teachers are not used to a climate in which their teaching is closely examined. THT staff could feel the Mott School teachers' vulnerability, trepidation, and fear.

Let us emphasize that this experience is much like you find in any school. The role of THT is to help teachers develop a sense of community so that they can be more authentic with each other. THT trusts that, deep down, teachers are only trying to do what is right for the children. As Parker Palmer says in *The Courage to Teach* (1998),

> Many of us became teachers for reasons of the heart, animated by a passion for some subject and for helping people to learn. But many of us lose heart as the years of teaching go by. How can we take heart in teaching once more so that we can, as good teachers always do, give heart to our students? (p. 17)

The cognitive and the emotional, as well as the outer and the inner lives of teaching are equally important. THT does not want to address one at the expense of the other. It is not only the cognitive and affective needs of children that are important; it is also the cognitive and affective needs of the adults in the school. This has been a deliberate but delicate balance fostered by THT.

Saturday morning in the middle of November, coffee, orange juice, and bagels awaited the Mott School study group. Dawn and her teacher friend, Lynda, had arrived early and got all the food ready. Teachers came in a little bit apprehensive, and some had that "Why-did-I-sign-up-for-this-on-Saturday-morning?" look. Dawn started our first session with one of her icebreakers.

Dawn has vitality and energy, and her enthusiasm is contagious. Although she is younger than most of the group of teachers she works with, it was clear that they loved and respected her, and the reason is that she respected them! Although she has a gift for planning and organization, she also knows the teachers as individuals. She listened and backed off when the teachers objected to a plan, and yet, like her principal, she would come back with an alternative to accomplishing the plan. Lois, one of the veteran teachers, commented that THT would not have been possible without Dawn, because the staff trusted her.

And so, together, Dawn, Pat Howley, and Thelma Johnson, one of our SDP consultants, started slowly to examine all of the aspects of THT with the group. We set up distinct areas in the library for presentations and note taking, and a circle for our dialogue sessions. After Dawn's icebreaker, we moved over to the other side of the room for discussion and dialogue.

To help us get started, we asked teachers to think about and then discuss, "What energizes you most as you work with kids?" This led us also to discuss what drains our energy. The dialogue we had was a way for the teachers to develop trust in one another and to get to know both Thelma and Pat as well as Dawn. Our informal discussions encouraged people to ask questions about what we were going to do. It also allowed the SDP team to introduce the overview of THT in a way that did not overwhelm the teachers. More important, the teachers began to share their concerns about education, their school system, and their work with children and parents. We eventually suggested that we provide an overview of the main parts of THT that were directly connected to some of their concerns and questions.

The teachers at Mott School know the importance of their profession. They realize that most individuals can say that sometime in their life, a teacher has had a positive influence on them. Being a teacher is the most significant of all professions. Every day, teachers are responsible for educating the future. More and more, this bright and rewarding career is met by many social challenges. Conceptions of teaching reflect the values and social philosophy of society, and as these change, so too does society's view of its teachers. No crystal ball has all the answers for these changes. Schools today must accommodate a wide variety of learning and cultural differences. Teachers are required to have a repertoire of effective strategies so the needs of all students can be met, and they are accountable for their teaching practices and for what their students learn. The ultimate goal for teachers is to help students become independent and self-regulated learners. The teachers at Mott School know that teaching changes lives. But like hardworking teachers anywhere, they can become discouraged and wonder whether they are doing all they can.

THE ESSENCE OF THE THT PROCESS IS REFLECTION

An underlying belief of the THT program is that reflection promotes development. The challenge is how to create the conditions that encourage reflection. The answer for THT was the process of dialogue. What encourages a dialogue is trust. THT simultaneously promotes trust, dialogue, reflection, and development. In this climate, success in improving the teaching process leads to the next success. Of course, the students' learning process improves.

The energy that each person put into the dialogue at Mott School quickly led to deeper reflection. The word *dialogue* literally means "conversation." By extension, THT takes "speaking together" to imply "thinking together" as people listen carefully to each other. The Mott School teachers didn't always agree, but they always listened. To *reflect* means "to recollect or realize after thought; to seriously contemplate." There are two basic ways of engaging in reflection. One is to take quiet time to think and to plan. THT encourages teachers to keep journals to support reflective thinking. THT provides handouts that describe the journaling process and its benefits, and provides notebooks for that activity. Another way for teachers to reflect is through discussion and dialogue. This requires teachers to build trusting relationships, to open up to one another, and to listen to one another without judgment. This is what was so energizing for this small group of teachers at Mott School.

> The teachers at Mott School began to spend more time in the dialogue circle. They revealed to one another their thoughts and feelings about teaching and—more important—about their own teaching. One teacher remarked to Dawn, "This is our 'therapy group.'" As in therapy, where individuals talk about what troubles them in life, teachers shared more and more about what troubled them in their teaching. Trust had developed among them, and their talking began to eliminate the isolation that teachers experience as they try so hard to meet the needs of children in their classrooms.

> As they developed more comfort in the THT process, the teachers shared more about their frustrations, fears, and concerns. The dialogues they had with each other and with us were rich and meaningful.

ELEMENTS OF THE THT PROCESS

THT can be understood most easily as involving a "six, six, and six" process: six "doorways" of reflection, six models of teaching, and the six developmental pathways.

Six Doorways of Reflection

Teachers are encouraged to open six "doorways" of reflection:

1. Using the six developmental pathways, teachers explore relationships between learning and development.

2. Through observing each other, teachers explore classroom teaching.

3. By reading and analyzing models of teaching, teachers inquire into teaching theory.

4. Through open dialogue, teachers explore the culture of the school and community.

5. By integrating THT with SDP's Balanced Curriculum Process, teachers align and balance their curriculum and then support one another in implementation.

6. By using the Myers-Briggs Type Indicator® (MBTI®) and Archetypes, teachers seek to gain an understanding of their personal and professional selves.

Six Models of Teaching and the Six Developmental Pathways

Although reflection is at the heart of the THT program, THT does not disregard research on teaching and the opinions of experts. Rather, while encouraging teachers to be less dependent on experts' opinions and to develop trust in their own observations and instincts, THT also encourages teachers to practice and/or stretch and try out different approaches to teaching.

To support teachers' reflections about teaching, we used the Developmental Pathways Video Program (1999), developed collaboratively by Guilford County Schools and SDP and supported by the Rockefeller Foundation. The material from the manual for the video was transposed into a PowerPoint presentation and related handouts. In general, THT's approach encourages teachers to have meaningful conversations about teaching in relation to development. During sessions, they are actively engaged (in contrast to many inservice workshops held in schools).

To further support teachers' reflections, we introduce six different models of teaching as described by Richard Arends in his book, *Learning to Teach* (2000). (See Box 12.1.) Arends cites the work of Joyce and Weil (1996), who identified more than 20 major models. According to their definitions, a model is an overall plan or pattern for helping students learn specific kinds of knowledge, attitudes, or skills. Arends focuses on the basic models that all teachers should master, describing the overall flow and steps that a teacher will take when using each model. The six models of teaching constitute one of the key organizers used in THT. The models are grounded in research and enable teachers to compare the research against their own teaching practices.

USING THE MYERS-BRIGGS TYPE INDICATOR (MBTI) FOR PROFESSIONAL DEVELOPMENT

Building on the trust and interest in more personal discussions that had developed in the Mott School study group, THT staff introduced the MBTI near the end of the second year as a means of deepening reflection. First, the MBTI personality instrument was used to help the teachers understand themselves and each other better as they worked together. Second, they applied insights from the MBTI to focus on the four learning types of children, and the four types of value systems of teachers.

The teachers learned to understand children by looking at four general categories:

- children who have a hunger for competence
- children who have a hunger for a sense of self
- children who have a hunger for action
- children who have a hunger for decision making

They also learned that they could look at teachers through the filter of four basic value systems:

- teachers who tend to focus on mastery of skills in a well-structured and organized classroom
- teachers who tend to focus on the whole child in an innovative and flexible environment
- teachers who tend to focus on acquisition of knowledge through open discussion of theories and concepts
- teachers who tend to focus on a cooperative environment, learning social skills, and the process of learning

Most of the Mott School teachers recognized that although they were drawn toward one of the teaching descriptions more than the others, they had learned early in their development as teachers to integrate all four value systems. The teachers read with much interest the four descriptions of students and had intense dialogues on which children had these various hungers and why. Although in these dialogues, they had started opening the sixth "doorway" of reflection (teacher as person), they also began to open the fourth doorway (culture and community), the first (child development), and the third (teaching theory).

Pat Howley observed that after every Saturday morning session, he drove back home to Connecticut energized by the THT meetings. He sensed that the teachers felt the same way.

STAFF ROLES IN THE THT PROCESS

When THT was first developed, there was an implicit assumption that principals and Comer facilitators would have active supporting roles and that they would know what to do. They did know what to do. And yet, many times, they requested clarification to be sure they all had the same idea in mind. As a result of these questions, THT clarified each of the roles (see Box 12.2). The role definitions are meant only as a guideline and can easily be modified and adapted to meet the needs of a particular school or teacher. In addition, checklists and a Process Document Inventory (THT PDI), were created that would help participants to know specifically what should take place to ensure successful implementation. (See Figures 12.1 through 12.4.)

(Text continues on page 171)

Box 12.2   Staff Roles in THT

Role of the Principal

The principal as the educational leader should model the process of THT and set the tone in the school. The principal will

- share the vision as to why we are doing THT
- show how SDP and THT are related to our attempts to improve student achievement and test scores
- explain that there are multiple causes for low test scores; that we are trying to address as many as we can; and that parents, the central office, and society in general also have major roles to play in improving student achievement
- talk about the importance of using core curriculum content standards as a guide by

  describing to the faculty how this is an opportunity for personal and professional growth

  discussing the six developmental pathways and the need to address all the pathways in the classroom as well as in their own personal development

- connect THT to SDP's guiding principles and reassure teachers that this is not an evaluation process by

  communicating to the staff the importance and relevance of THT to the school vision, emphasizing that teachers are all professionals and have much to learn from one another

- describe how he or she will help teachers find the time to get together and reflect on the teaching/learning process

Role of the Comer Facilitator

The Comer facilitator plays a key role in demonstrating a clear commitment to the Comer model and the THT process. The facilitator will

- be proactive in dealing with conflicts and communication difficulties within the school and on the topic of THT
- maintain neutrality and independence within the school
- consult regularly with the director of THT and/or the implementation coordinator

Role of the Teacher

Teachers have six primary responsibilities as participants in THT. They will
- attend THT training
- identify a model of teaching on which to focus
- integrate the developmental pathways into lesson plans
- engage in an observation/reflection cycle with a partner
- visit the classrooms of their partners
- meet on a regular basis and use the doorways of reflection to guide their reflections

Figure 12.1 Principal's implementation checklist for Teachers Helping Teachers (THT), Yale School Development Program

Name of School	
District	
School Address	
Phone	Fax
E-mail	
Principal*	
Assistant Principal	
Comer Facilitator	

This checklist is designed to give you a practical and concrete list of desirable THT operational behaviors. The items clarify what constituent groups in the school need to do to ensure successful implementation of THT. As with any aspect of comprehensive school reform, it takes approximately three to five years for a school and/or district to create the appropriate structures, develop a plan, and significantly improve student achievement and social behaviors.

Directions: Read each item. Write the date(s) and check the items that have been accomplished. Use the items in the checklist to monitor ongoing program progress. Ideally, all items need to be accomplished.

Your main role is to ensure that teachers meet and dialogue together on a regular basis, reflecting together on children and teaching and learning. They should fill out the THT Monthly Report Form and hand it back to you so that you can send it to the director of THT. You also want to ensure that teachers are using the six developmental pathways, models of teaching, and/or competencies of effective teaching as frameworks to guide their reflective practices.

*See *THT Manual:* Guidelines for Implementation, Role of the Principal. Read Richard Arends's (2000) book, *Learning to Teach*. As instructional leader, the principal may assign certain tasks to others.

Date	Yes	No	Task
			1. Discuss THT with the leadership team (SPMT).
			2. Discuss THT with your Student and Staff Support Team (SSST).
			3. Discuss THT with the Parent Team (PT).
			4. Schedule a THT orientation and/or training (for teachers, Comer facilitator, principal, assistant principal, all applicable personnel).
			5. Explain and discuss importance of THT to faculty.
			6. Facilitate selection and assignment of participating THT pairs.
			7. Develop, facilitate, and monitor schedule for THT partners to exchange classroom observation visits and engage in peer dialogues.
			8. Schedule consultations and trainings by SDP/THT staff for the teacher pairs.
			9. Read the *THT Manual* and Richard Arends's book, *Learning to Teach* (2000).
			10. Maintain contact with THT director at the School Development Program.
			11. Each month, collect and send the THT Report Forms (filled out by the teachers) to THT director at the Yale School Development Program office.

Figure 12.2 Comer facilitator's implementation checklist for Teachers Helping Teachers (THT), Yale School Development Program

Name of School
District
School Address
Phone   Fax
E-mail
Principal
Assistant Principal
Comer Facilitator

This checklist provides a practical list of THT operational behaviors. The items clarify what constituent groups in the school need to do to ensure successful implementation of THT (three to five years).

Directions: Read each item. Write the date(s) and check the items that have been accomplished. Use the items in the checklist to monitor ongoing program progress. Ideally, all items need to be accomplished.

Your main role is to ensure that teachers meet for dialogue on a regular basis, reflecting together on children and on teaching and learning. You also want to ensure that teachers are using the six developmental pathways, models of teaching, and/or competencies of effective teaching as frameworks to guide their reflective practices.

*See *THT Manual:* Role of the Comer Facilitator. Also, read the "Role of the Teacher" section. Review and learn the Teaching Competencies. Learn the essentials of the six developmental pathways. Learn the models of teaching from Richard Arends's (2000) book, *Learning to Teach.*

Date	Yes	No	Task
			1. Give input into selection and development of THT partners.
			2. Visit THT participants and their classrooms to learn teaching styles and characteristics of students.
			3. Monitor and troubleshoot schedules for THT classroom visits and peer dialogues.
			4. Use the Six Developmental Pathways video series to train THT teachers and help them infuse the pathways into all aspects of their teaching and learning process.
			5. Teach one of the models of teaching.
			6. Read and use issues discussed in the *THT Manual* to ensure that teachers engage in meaningful peer dialogues that are based on reflections that will lead to transformation of their teaching practice.
			7. Study the Six Developmental Pathways and Teaching Competencies. Use these data as the framework for classroom observations and coaching.
			8. Ensure that teachers read and follow their own Implementation Checklists.
			9. Remind teachers to fill out and hand in a Monthly Report Form to the principal.

Figure 12.3 THT partners' implementation checklist for Teachers Helping Teachers (THT), Yale School Development Program.

Name of School
District
School Address
Phone   Fax
E-mail
Principal
Assistant Principal
Comer Facilitator

This checklist is designed to give you a practical and concrete list of desirable THT operational behaviors. The items clarify what constituent groups in the school need to do to ensure successful implementation of THT.

Directions: Read each item. Write the date(s) and check the items that have been accomplished. Use the items in the checklist to monitor ongoing program progress. Ideally, all items need to be accomplished.

Your main responsibility is to meet and dialogue with your partner on a regular basis, reflecting together on children and on teaching and learning. You also want to make sure that you use the six developmental pathways, models of teaching, and/or competencies of effective teaching as frameworks to guide your reflection. It is important that you do not see yourself as a coach for your partner, but more as a colleague who engages in a mutual learning process. (See the sections on Peer Dialogue in your *THT Manual*.)

See *THT Manual:* Role of the Teacher. As a participant, you need to be committed to self-reflection about the appropriateness of your delivery of instruction and the quality of student outcomes in your classroom. Read the *THT Manual* and use the concepts. Read Richard Arends's (2000) book, *Learning to Teach*. THT is designed around regular teaching-learning dialogues between partners. During the dialogues, any one of the doors of reflection may be discussed. Use the topics in the Observation/Reflection Cycle after classroom visits to enhance content of peer dialogues.

Date	Yes	No	Task
			1. Identify and use at least one model of teaching.
			2. Prepare lesson plans and create units of study that fully integrate the six developmental pathways (physical, cognitive, psychological, language, social, and ethical).
			3. Use the developmental pathways as a framework during partner dialogues about children.
			4. Use a model(s) of teaching and/or a teaching competency as a framework for partner dialogues.
			5. Use the Observation/Reflection Cycle during peer dialogues.
			6. Use at least one of the Doors of Reflection during peer dialogues.
			7. Read the *THT Manual*. Read Richard Arends's book, *Learning to Teach* (2000).
			8. Exchange classroom visits to get to know your partner and his or her students.
			9. Exchange regular (as often as feasible) classroom visits to observe and reflect on issues that affect the improvement of teaching and learning.
			10. Meet on a regular basis with your partner for reflection dialogues.
			11. Fill out the Monthly Report Form and hand it in to your principal.

Figure 12.4 Teachers Helping Teachers process documentation inventory

Quality Indicators	Not At All	Beginning	Partial	Full	Exemplary	Supporting Evidence
Principal						
The principal reads and uses the *THT Manual* and Richard Arends's book, *Learning to Teach* (2000).						
The principal discusses THT with the SPMT.						
The principal discusses THT with the SSST.						
The principal discusses THT with the Parent Team.						
The principal explains and discusses the importance of THT to faculty.						
The principal schedules a THT orientation and/or training for teachers, Comer facilitator, principal, assistant principal, and all applicable personnel.						
The principal facilitates selection and assignment of teachers who become THT partners.						
The principal develops, facilitates, and monitors the schedules for THT partner dialogues.						
The principal schedules consultation/training by SDP/THT staff.						
The principal collects and reads the THT monthly reports submitted by the teacher partners.						
Facilitators						
The facilitator reads and uses the *THT Manual* and Richard Arends's book, *Learning to Teach* (2000).						
The facilitator provides input about selection and development of THT partners.						
The facilitator observes and documents teachers' instructional styles.						
The facilitator observes and documents the learning styles and characteristics of students.						
The facilitator monitors and adjusts schedules for THT classroom visits.						
The facilitator plans and provides time for peer dialogues.						
The facilitator monitors and facilitates all strategies related to implementation of THT.						
The facilitator plans forums to share the ongoing use of the Implementation Checklist.						

(Continued)

Figure 12.4 (Continued)

Quality Indicators	Not At All	Beginning	Partial	Full	Exemplary	Supporting Evidence
The facilitator provides support for completing the teachers' monthly reports.						
The facilitator ensures the collection of reports for the principal.						
The facilitator conducts training sessions and presents the Six Developmental Pathways video series to help teachers integrate the pathways into all aspects of their teaching and learning processes.						
Teachers						
Teachers read and use the *THT Manual* and Richard Arends's book, *Learning to Teach* (2000).						
Teachers select and study a model of teaching that they think will improve their instruction.						
Teachers practice the selected model of teaching in at least one content area to enrich instructional strategies and boost student achievement.						
Teachers prepare lesson plans that integrate the six developmental pathways (physical, cognitive, psychological, language, social, and ethical).						
Teachers create units of study that integrate the six developmental pathways (physical, cognitive, psychological, language, social, and ethical).						
Teachers use the six developmental pathways during partner dialogues as a framework for discussing children's growth, development, and learning.						
Teachers use a model of teaching as a framework for partner dialogues.						
Teachers use the Observation/Reflection Cycle during partner dialogues (when applicable).						
Teachers use at least one of the Doors of Reflection during partner dialogues.						
Teachers exchange classroom visits to become familiar with their partners' teaching styles and their students' learning styles.						
Teachers exchange regular (as often as feasible) classroom visits to observe and reflect on issues that have an impact on the skill development needed to improve teaching and learning.						
Teachers meet at minimum once a month with their partners for reflection dialogues.						

Teachers complete a monthly report and submit it to their principal or facilitator.						
Staff Development						
The school strengthens the THT process by having teachers use the MBTI to examine learning types of children and teaching types of teachers.						
The principal strengthens the THT process by having THT partners meet and discuss how they will help each other implement any new initiative and/or learnings from workshops they attend.						

The *principal* supports the process through his or her actions. The principal models the process by fully participating in THT, being open to learning, and asking questions. This conveys to teachers that the principal is willing to expend time, energy, enthusiasm, and commitment to the project. The principal should provide the rationale and motivation for involvement of teachers in THT. The principal sets the tone not only this way but also by sending memos, discussing THT in teacher meetings, scheduling observations, and training. The principal should meet with the Comer facilitator and have regular phone discussions with the director of THT and the THT implementation coordinators who will visit their schools.

The *Comer facilitator* is not an evaluator. The facilitator assists in generating trust among and between the teachers so that they can come to him or her with feedback, questions, and problems in implementing THT.

Box 12.3 Phases of THT Implementation at Mott Elementary School

Phase I

In Phase I of THT, we examined the content and process of the program. Four-hour Saturday workshops were scheduled every other month. The focus of this training was to develop knowledge of the six instructional models and 10 competencies of effective teaching. The training also introduced participants to peer dialogue. The process involved observing, listening, participating in dialogue, and giving nonjudgmental feedback.

(Continued)

Box 12.3 (Continued)

Phase II

In Phase II of THT, Learning and Teaching Dialogue Teams were formed. In this process, we created a climate of trust conducive for risk taking. The facilitator helped to form teams that visited each other's classrooms. Our Yale consultant visited the pairs of teachers to answer questions and participate in the observation and dialogue. During the observation, the observer recorded what was said, who said it, and when it was said. Also, the observer recorded the behaviors of the students, materials used, interruptions, and movement through the room. (In the margins of the observation log, the observer noted his or her reflections on what was being observed.) The teachers exchanged perceptions, listed questions, and shared feelings with each other about the process. They infused the six pathways into lessons, and they discussed needs of students and challenges for themselves. After the classroom visits, time was scheduled for preobservation meetings, observations of teaching, and post-observation dialogues. The framework of the six developmental pathways guided the teachers as they reflected on and discussed teaching and children's learning.

Phases III and IV

In Phase III of THT, we focused on skill development. Individual teachers selected a model of teaching to guide their reflections and researched the model they chose. In this phase, the *THT Manual* provided a guide for pre- and post-observations and dialogues. The Observation-Reflection Cycle describes this process (see Figure 12.5).

When we went to a Phase IV and included all the teachers in the school, we started with the Myers-Briggs Type Indicator® (MBTI®). This activity helped everyone understand their differences in teaching and understand the way different students may learn. It had been well received by the small group of teachers that first participated in THT, and we felt that the MBTI would stimulate observation and reflection, both of which are essential to the THT process, so we introduced MBTI activity.

Two years into the THT process, Mr. Brown retired, and Elizabeth Ramirez became the new principal. As the transition took place at Mott School, Ms. Ramirez and Dawn Kelley created a trusting partnership. They asked to meet with the director of THT (Howley) and create a plan for involving the whole faculty in the process of reflection. They wanted to send a message that all teaching types would be respected and supported, so they requested to start THT with the MBTI. They wanted to create a no-fault environment as they identified personality and teaching type and teaching differences among the faculty. Elizabeth emphasized with the faculty that they were learning together. She took the lead: She created an environment for learning by her own involvement, and she explained to the staff the purpose and direction of the THT work. She has modeled it by being a full participant in the training, sitting with the staff, and participating in dialogues on teaching. She has demonstrated to the staff that it is okay to explore strengths and weaknesses we all have as teachers. She is living out the vision we had for the role of the principal in THT.

In implementing SDP, including THT, the *teacher's* role is to help form a new culture within the school. This change is subtle yet powerful. In THT, the culture change is the acceptance of the belief that teaching, like the professions of doctors and lawyers, for example, is a practice. It involves continually learning, growing, and changing. The practice is never mastered because the job is too complex, and because society is always changing. When we acknowledge this and embrace methods to continually improve, it will be a major change in educational culture. As a core group of teachers at Mott School began to meet on Saturday mornings and entered into a process of taking responsibility for the direction of the staff development sessions, a new culture emerged.

STRUCTURES FOR FLEXIBILITY

We have learned again and again that a program like THT will not work unless the principal is active in guiding the process. In addition, a Comer facilitator who has developed trust with the principal and with the faculty and has a clear understanding of the process assures that active participation by the teachers will take place.

When we first implemented THT, we did not have enough structure for the principal, facilitator, and teachers. As we listened and learned from their feedback and questions, we clarified their roles, created forms, and outlined the steps for successful implementation. We are grateful to all the schools that lived no-fault and collaboration and helped get this program started. We reached a point at which some teachers felt that our structure and forms were too constrictive. We then helped teachers to see that the structures were more like a map for implementation that could be used when they needed to find their way. We had created a process that was flexible enough to be tailored to each school. We envisioned it being adopted as is, or adapted and modified as needed. We created it so that in some schools, teachers at one grade level could pair off and visit each other's classrooms, or pair off across grade levels for dialogue sessions. We envisioned, as has happened at Mott School, teachers meeting in small groups by grade level. Some schools might focus the reflection process on the models of teaching, others might use the developmental pathways, and still others might use the MBTI to reflect on themselves, on students, and on teaching. The essence of the THT process is teachers' reflecting so that they become more aware of the critical issues of teaching and learning. We saw the need to clarify the roles so that in this structured but very flexible process, the key players would know what they needed to do to make it work (see Figure 12.5).

Figure 12.5 Observation/Reflection Cycle

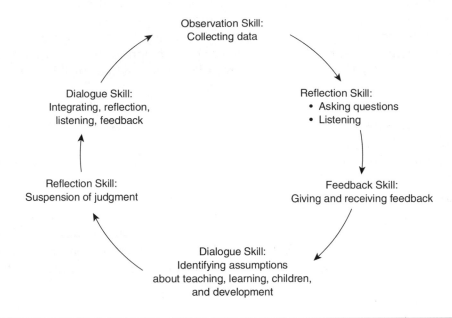

Mott School took the essence of THT and modified it to meet the challenges they were facing. Within the school, Dawn Kelley and her principal individualized and tailored certain components of the THT manual to meet the unique needs of partners or individual teachers. This is exactly what a program that is based on development should do.

THT IS INTEGRAL TO THE SDP PROCESS AT MOTT SCHOOL

Mott School has benefited directly by the implementation of THT. Teachers have learned a variety of teaching models to enhance student achievement. The six developmental pathways have been embedded as a framework for meeting the needs of students. Teachers have been encouraged to reflect on the school's goals, curriculum, teaching methods, and materials. THT has been a practical strategy for gathering data about teaching and learning. It has deepened staff understanding of SDP and teaching, and it has promoted no-fault, collaboration, and consensus in the classroom. What teachers know and can do is the most important influence on what students learn. Teachers at Mott School have done both private reflection and independent learning, as well as group reflection with their colleagues, without being judgmental of each other and in the absence of criticism from outside evaluators. The teachers have taken the time to think about what they do in their classrooms that makes a difference. They have explored how students are affected by their actions, and they've worked hard at improving their teaching. THT has been and continues to be an integral part of their SDP process.

REFERENCES AND SUGGESTED READINGS

Arends, R. (2000). *Learning to teach.* Boston: McGraw-Hill.

Fairhurst, A. M., & Fairhurst, L. L. (1995). *Effective teaching, effective learning.* Palo Alto, CA: Davies-Black.

Golay, K. (1982). *Learning patterns and temperament styles.* Santa Ana, CA: Manas-Systems.

Guilford County Schools. (1999). *Developmental pathways video series: Based on the Comer School Development Program.* Greensboro, NC: Author.

Joyce, B., & Weil, M. (1996). *Models of teaching* (5th ed.). Englewood Cliffs, NJ: Prentice Hall.

Keirsey, D., & Bates, M. (1984). *Please understand me.* Del Mar, CA: Prometheus Nemesis.

Lawrence, G. (1993). *People types and tiger stripes* (3rd ed.). Gainesville, FL: Center for Applications of Psychological Type.

Lawrence, G. (1997). *Looking at type and learning styles.* Gainesville, FL: Center for Applications of Psychological Type.

Murphy, E. (1992). *The developing child.* Gainesville, FL: Center for Applications of Psychological Type.

Palmer, P. (1998). *The courage to teach.* San Francisco: Jossey-Bass.

Scanlon, S. (1999–2000). *The Type Reporter, 75, 76, 77, 78* (Newsletter). Fairfax Station, VA: The Type Reporter.

READ MORE ABOUT . . .

To read more about the Myers-Briggs Type Indicator (MBTI), see "It's All About Effective Relationships: Frameworks for Understanding Ourselves and Others," Chapter 13 in *Six Pathways to Healthy Child Development and Academic Success: The Field Guide to Comer Schools in Action* in this series.

13

Turning Nonreaders Into Readers Through Essentials of Literacy

Fay E. Brown

SDP's Essentials of Literacy Process offers low-performing students a safe environment in which to learn how to read, employing a "six-station" approach to skill development and a high adult-to-student ratio. This ratio is achieved through the commitment of the principal, the involvement of community members, and university partnerships. It has a remarkable record of success with mainstream and special education students that goes far beyond literacy to produce measurable improvements in self-esteem, self-control, and engagement in the classroom. The process is described here, along with case vignettes.

Every child who enters school wants to be a successful student, sometimes despite behaviors that might suggest otherwise. Unfortunately, in some schools, many students encounter various difficult and challenging conditions that prevent them from achieving success, starting with the basic skill of learning to read. The future prospect for students who can't read is often quite dismal—through no fault of their own. This point was underscored in a report titled *The Reading Teacher* (1998), in which the author stated,

Learning to read and write is critical to a child's success in school and later in life. One of the best predictors of whether a child will function competently in school and go on to contribute actively in our increasingly literate society is the level to which the child progresses in reading and writing. (International Reading Association and the National Association for the Education of Young Children, p. 196)

Gary Phillips, acting commissioner of the National Center for Education Statistics, described the intensification of the gap between the reading skills of the highest- and lowest-performing students in a press release that accompanied the most recent report of the National Assessment of Educational Progress (NAEP) (2001). He said, "Over the past eight years, we have seen a gradual widening of the gap between the reading skills of the highest- and lowest-performing students. The best students are reading better, while the worst students are falling further behind" (2001, April 6). That same report revealed that 37 percent of fourth graders performed below basic level on the 2000 NAEP test.

Across the country, in many public schools, particularly in urban districts, a great number of principals and teachers are bemoaning the fact that too many of their students are entering and leaving third grade reading one to two levels below grade level. This problem, if not corrected, could be the first warning sign of a cadre of school dropouts. Herr and Cramer (1988) made that argument poignantly clear by stating that many students who "permanently absent themselves from formal education during the junior high and high school years, actually drop out of school psychologically during the elementary grades" (p. 253).

It may be argued that one of the contributing factors to this dropout phenomenon is that there are too many students in classrooms, particularly in urban schools. For example, the teacher-to-student ratio in most classrooms ranges from 1:24 to 1:30. This means that one teacher may be responsible for helping 24 to 30 students learn and develop, almost always without the benefit of an instructional aide. Given that students enter school at varying levels of preparedness and different levels of motivation, in classrooms with such teacher-to-student ratios, students can easily fall through the cracks or inevitably become treated as the forgotten ones.

To address this risk, some schools seek out and implement programs that are developmentally appropriate and sufficiently comprehensive to move children from the status of poor readers with bleak futures to proficient, skilled readers capable of achieving great successes. One such program is the School Development Program's (SDP) Essentials of Literacy Process (EOL), developed in 1993.

DEVELOPING LITERACY SKILLS FOR PROBLEM READERS

EOL is an intervention aimed primarily at developing literacy skills for students who have been identified by their teachers as "problem readers," that is, students reading significantly below grade level. The process is based on the premise that there are certain "essentials" or fundamentals of reading that must be incorporated into a successful reading program:

- Story Sense
- Vocabulary Development
- Book Immersion

- Story Writing and Publishing
- Letter-Sound Correspondence

Story Sense

Story Sense is reinforced at a story station where students, in groups of four, listen and respond to a story read to them by an adult facilitator. Students are given the opportunity to ask questions, make comments about certain portions of the story, and predict how the story will end. They are also encouraged to retell the story in their own words, using some of the new words learned from the story. Here too, students are encouraged to develop their critical thinking skills by agreeing or disagreeing with the writer's point of view, by suggesting changes for characters and settings in a story, and sometimes by personalizing a story to make it more relevant and meaningful. Story Sense is further reinforced at the listening station, where students listen to prerecorded stories as they follow along in their books. Listening to stories provides students with wondrous and vicarious experiences that they might never otherwise experience in the real world.

Vocabulary Development

Vocabulary Development is reinforced at a vocabulary station, where visual, auditory, and kinesthetic techniques are employed to motivate and encourage students to learn a number of new words each week. To develop their repertoire of words, students are given lists of the 1,200 most frequently used words in school texts. They are encouraged to use some of these words to develop sentences. Often, many of these words carry over into their writing (see the description of the writing station). Familiarity with the dictionary is encouraged to help the students further expand their vocabularies. At this station, students are also given incentives as a way of encouraging their continued efforts at developing their vocabularies.

Book Immersion

The idea of Book Immersion is promoted through the overall setup of the Reading Room and at various stations, particularly at the guided reading station. At this station, different strategies (e.g., oral reading, silent reading, read-alouds, and partner reading) are employed to guide students' reading and comprehension. Reading Room staff are encouraged to set up the room in a manner that has books displayed all around the room to facilitate students' easy access to a variety of books and to encourage browsing. Every day, students are also guided to take home a book to read with or to a parent or sibling to further develop their reading skills and to strengthen the home-school connection.

Story Writing and Publishing

Story Writing and Publishing is carried out at a writing station, where students are encouraged and helped to express their talent and creativity through various writing activities. At this station, students are taught the tenets of process writing. The facilitator works with students one-on-one to help sharpen their writing skills. Edited works are "published" at this station, and students have the opportunity to read individually selected stories to their classmates and often to other invited guests at a monthly or bimonthly "authors' tea." In Reading Rooms equipped with computers, students develop their word processing and other computer-related skills by using the computers as tools in the writing and publishing process.

Letter-Sound Correspondence

Letter-Sound Correspondence is promoted at the phonics station. The major premise for this station is that while students need assistance in unlocking initial consonants "to break the code," this learning should be guided by interesting and stimulating activities—not skill-and-drill methodologies like completing ditto sheets. In other words, students learn decoding skills in a fun way, using manipulatives, and sometimes they sample actual foods beginning with the particular letter-sound being taught, instead of simply completing activities in workbooks. They are also exposed to activities and games that teach them word building and analysis skills by employing the concepts of onsets and rimes.

The Reading Room

These fundamentals of literacy are demonstrated through instructional activities carried out within six learning stations set up in a teacher's classroom, referred to as "The Reading Room" (Brown & Murray, 1998, p. 4). The Reading Room is described as a classroom where

- Adults demonstrate the belief that all children can learn.
- Students read, write, listen, think, learn, and make good decisions for at least 90 minutes each day.
- Students who are experiencing difficulty with their reading skills learn to become good readers in a highly stimulating, nurturing environment.
- Students experience success on a daily basis and celebrate their successes at the end of each week.
- Members of the community assist a teacher in promoting students' mastery of the language arts, while helping to facilitate other aspects of their development.
- Child development theories and principles undergird the daily practices and activities.

EOL takes into consideration the individual variation of all the students who are selected for the program, and uses an eclectic approach to enhance the students' literacy skills. Over a daily two-hour period, students in groups of four rotate in a clockwise manner to the six stations (story, phonics, listening, guided reading, vocabulary, and writing) every 15 to 20 minutes (see Figure 13.1).

A trained adult, such as a teacher, paraprofessional, university student volunteer, or parent, facilitates the activities at each station. For every adult, there are only four students. This small ratio, combined with the various activities at the stations and a classroom climate that is nurturing and developmentally oriented, continues to yield positive outcomes for students.

POSITIVE OUTCOMES FOR STUDENTS

In 1996, the program was pilot tested in one elementary school in New Haven, Connecticut, with 24 third-grade students. These students were selected by their

Figure 13.1 Diagram of the Reading Room

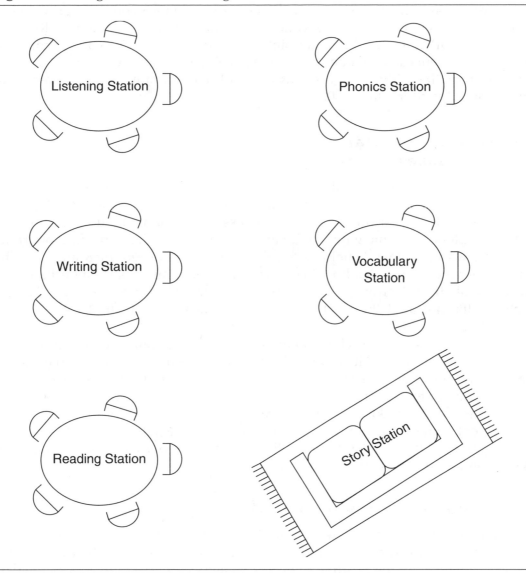

teachers from each of the three third-grade classrooms, and they were designated as the poorest readers from those classrooms. Third-grade students were reading at kindergarten or Grade 1 level. After approximately seven months of being in the Reading Room, all of those 24 students improved in their reading skills, with more than 50 percent of them reaching grade level in their reading proficiency (Brown, Maholmes, Murray, & Nathan, 1998).

At this writing, EOL is currently being implemented in 22 of the 26 elementary schools in New Haven. For the school year 1999–2000, data were obtained from each of these Reading Rooms to determine the progress students were making and also to diagnose weaknesses so that the needed assistance could be provided to particular students. Data were collected using the Developmental Reading Assessment (DRA) at two different points in the school year. DRA scores collected from these students at the end of second grade (May 1998) were used as the baseline data. Data for the midyear assessment were collected in January, and end-of-year data were collected in May 2000.

The Developmental Reading Assessment

The Developmental Reading Assessment (DRA) was developed by Joetta Beaver in collaboration with primary teachers, and published in 1997 by Celebration Press. This instrument is used to assess and document students' development as readers over time within a literature-based instructional reading program. The DRA was developed, field tested, and revised between 1988 and 1996 by primary teachers and Reading Recovery teachers from urban, suburban, and rural school districts from different regions of the United States and Canada. "The results indicated the teachers' overall satisfaction with the DRA" (Beaver, 1997, p. 7).

The DRA is used by teachers on an annual, semiannual, or quarterly basis to observe, record, and evaluate changes in students' reading levels. It is also used as a tool to create a meaningful plan to promote improvement in students' reading. The DRA assessment texts represent a range of difficulty on a scale from A to 44. Levels A through 2 represent kindergarten; 3 through 8 represent preprimer; 10 through 12 represent primer; 14 through 16 represent first grade; 18 through 28 represent second grade; 30 through 38 represent third grade; 40 represents fourth grade; and 44 represents fifth grade.

EOL Student Scores Increased

Students' DRA scores were summed, and the average or mean score was obtained for each Reading Room from the 22 schools for each of the three assessment points. Looking at all the Reading Rooms as an aggregate (see Figure 13.2), the data revealed that on the average, regular students had a baseline score of 13.3, which the DRA Locator Guide indicates as primer reading level. By January, students had a mean score of 17.5 on the DRA assessment, which indicates an end-of-first-grade to beginning-of-second-grade reading level. Scores on the May DRA assessment revealed that students were reading on a second-grade level, with a DRA mean score of 25.2. Across the schools, mean scores ranged from 18.6 (second grade) to 35.7 (third grade). Individual student scores across all the schools indicate a range from 4 (preprimer) to 40 (fourth grade). In other words, these DRA scores reveal that on the average, students made a year-and-a-half to two-years' growth in their reading during the 1999–2000 school year.

Special Education Students

Figure 13.2 also indicates data for special education students. Of the 548 students who were in the Reading Rooms, about 25 of them were special education students.

Figure 13.2 Average gains for Essentials of Literacy (EOL) students in regular and special education (N = 548) on the DRA

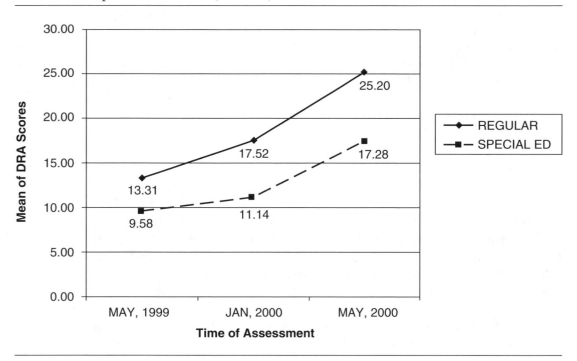

EOL was not designed for the special education population; however, several teachers find it a most beneficial program for these special needs students. One teacher had the following to say:

> This program has given us the perfect opportunity to put in place an inclusion program. Our special education teacher facilitates the writing station. Within our program, we include her three full-time special education students and five part-time special education students. For one of my part-time special education boys in particular, this inclusion has been incredibly valuable. He is so much more confident and able in reading and writing. In addition, perhaps partially because he now works within our classroom rather than leaving for resource services, he has become a truly productive, participating member of our classroom. Before EOL, he was so disruptive that we looked forward to the two hours he would be gone so that we could get our work done without constant interruption.

Figure 13.2 reveals that on average, the special education students in the Reading Rooms had a baseline DRA score of about 9.6, indicating the beginning of primer reading level. By January, there were slight improvements to a score of 11.1, indicating a midprimer reading level. May scores show significant improvement with a mean score of 17.3, indicating a first-grade reading level. In other words, these special education students made an average of two years' gain in their reading for school year 1999–2000.

SELECTED CASES

Lauri (pseudonym) attends school in another urban school district in which the school implements SDP, including EOL. The author visited the school to conduct a midyear assessment of the effectiveness of EOL. This assessment included a discussion with a group of staff persons. The group included the author, the principal, the school's psychologist, the Reading Room lead teacher, and three other facilitators from the Reading Room.

At one point in the discussion, the principal said to the psychologist, "Dr. Smith (pseudonym), I need to talk to you about testing Lauri for special education." The Reading Room lead teacher quickly said, "Oh no, Mrs. Johns (pseudonym), Lauri does not need special education services." The principal then said, "But we discussed this about a month ago, and you said that given Lauri's continuous poor behavior and very poor performance, you were sure that Lauri needed special education services." The teacher then said, "That was before Lauri was placed in the EOL reading program. Since Lauri has been in the reading program, she is no longer tardy in coming to school, her physical appearance has improved dramatically, her acting-out behaviors are few and far between, and her academic performance has improved significantly. It's as if she is a new child. She doesn't need special education." The principal was markedly impressed that such dramatic changes had occurred for Lauri. Lauri's story truly moved this author and served as a reminder that sometimes in order to see children perform to their highest potential, schools have to be willing to change some environments in which they place their students, and sometimes employ some nontraditional ways of teaching.

In another evaluative session in a different school district, this author asked the teachers in attendance to share some of their stories, both successes and challenges, so that we could all plan more effectively for the following school year. Two teachers from the same Reading Room told a story of three girls. They mentioned that these three girls "were the most difficult students" they had had during their years of teaching. They were constantly acting out, hardly ever stayed on task, and were incessantly impolite to teachers and students. One of the teachers mentioned that she had had those students since first grade and their behaviors continued in the same disruptive manner through to the third grade. They explained that over the years, they had tried everything they knew of to bring about some changes with the girls, but nothing seemed to work. They said they had tried detentions, suspensions, after-school programs, and early-morning programs, all to no avail. Then they said, "As far as we were concerned, these students were lost."

The teachers further explained that when their school decided to implement EOL, they put the three girls in the Reading Room. To their amazement, in just about a week, the teachers started noticing changes in the students. "They were rotating to the stations with everyone else, and the most mind-boggling phenomenon is that they were staying on task. In less than three weeks, we saw a change in these kids that we could not begin to describe. They were different. As the months progressed, they were completely different. We saw them behave in positive new ways, and we received work from them we did not know they were capable of producing." The phrase "They were lost" left an indelible impression with this author, who often wonders how many children are failing in schools every day because they are seen as "lost" and who may not be receiving the kind of intervention that could make the difference for them as EOL did for those three girls.

FACTORS CONTRIBUTING TO THE SUCCESSFUL IMPLEMENTATION OF EOL

The data above reveal some outstanding gains in reading for the students who were in the Reading Rooms in New Haven schools for the school year 1999–2000. However, it must be underscored that EOL is not a magic cure in and of itself. Like any other program, EOL is only as good or as powerful as the level to which it is implemented.

Core Staff

As described above, EOL is a comprehensive process that operates within a six-stations approach. With one adult facilitating each of the stations, it becomes a people-intensive process. Thus schools that are serious about implementing EOL need to have a core staff of four to six facilitators working in the Reading Room each day for those two hours while the program is in session. Because there are six stations, the ideal number of facilitators should be six. On days when one or two adults are absent, the Reading Room can still function efficiently with four adults by combining two stations (e.g., Listening and Story stations) or suspending those two stations for the day.

The Principal

Not only must there be commitment for adequate staffing of the Reading Room on a daily basis, there also must be a commitment on the part of the principal to work in conjunction with the Reading Room staff to have a highly functioning station.

This principal has to be a leader who promotes a shared vision for the school and who works collaboratively with the staff, parents, and other stakeholders to provide services that are in the best interest of the students. Personal observations of Reading Rooms and discussions with staff have revealed that, invariably, Reading Rooms tend to function more efficiently when the staff feels supported by the principal, in word and deed.

Parents and Community

It must be understood that when students at a particular grade level are reading significantly below grade level, it is not just a problem for the grade-level teachers, but for the entire school and its community—which includes parents. So, a successful EOL program demands the involvement of the principal and parents, and it strongly encourages the involvement of other community partners, especially students from local universities.

Successful Reading Rooms, therefore, require a team approach and a commitment from each member of the team. It takes people who believe in children and who are willing to work hard to help those children become proficient readers. The success in New Haven schools was derived not only from the committed hard work of the staff at individual schools but also from the very focused and organized efforts of staff at the central office level, particularly the Reading Department staff. Believing in the potential of the students, these individuals invested time and resources and worked tirelessly with individual school personnel and with SDP staff to ensure the success of the program.

Six Developmental Pathways

SDP emphasizes a developmental understanding as the core component to effective teaching and optimum functioning of schools and classrooms. This developmental understanding is at the heart of EOL.

During the training that is conducted by the Yale SDP staff for school personnel who are committed to implementing the program, these adults are reminded that the students with whom they will be working are not just "brains on sticks" and should not be treated as such. They should be treated as whole persons, with their different and varied needs. They are taught about the six developmental pathways (physical, language, social, psychological, ethical, cognitive) along which students grow, develop, and learn.

This developmental understanding is demonstrated in the Reading Room on a daily basis in the various ways in which the adults interact with the children. For example, if a student seems off task at a particular station, the adult cannot be so quick to assume laziness or some other negative explanation for the student's behavior. Instead, the adult considers alternatives, and by talking with the student, identifies the problem and suggests a solution that is in his or her best interest.

Students are in EOL because they are reading below grade level—some of them, two or more levels below grade level. It is therefore necessary for these students to be in an environment that they experience as safe and nonthreatening. Providing an environment that is permeated by a developmental understanding rather than a deficit understanding assures success for students that is sometimes revealed in data such as the DRA scores (see Figure 13.2). One of the tenets of the Reading Room that is reinforced as nonnegotiable is that "Every day at every station, every child *must* experience some success." The program is designed to promote such successes.

KEEPING LITERACY A PRIORITY

In this current educational and political climate, it would seem that ensuring that every child learns to read is a major priority. There needs to be follow-through, however, at every level to make this priority a reality.

When children get to third and sometimes fourth grade and are still reading at a kindergarten or first-grade level, it is safe to say that they are not experiencing academic success. Unsuccessful or frequent failure experiences are sometimes expressed in different acting-out behaviors in and out of school that place students at even further risk for bleak futures.

If these children are going to have a chance—a chance that each child deserves—to be successful, then every effort must be made to teach them how to read. EOL is one initiative that some schools have put in place to ensure that no child slips through the cracks, or as has become popular, to ensure that "no child is left behind."

REFERENCES

Beaver, J. (1997). *Developmental reading assessment resource guide.* Glenview, IL: Celebration.

Brown, F., Maholmes, V., Murray, E., & Nathan, L. (1998). Davis Street magnet school: Linking child development with literacy. *Journal of Education for Students Placed At Risk, 3*(1), 23–38.

Brown, F., & Murray, E. (1998). *Essentials of literacy: Implementation guide.* Unpublished manuscript, Yale School Development Program, Yale Child Study Center, New Haven, CT.

Clay, M. (1968). *The early detection of reading difficulties.* Porstmouth, NH: Heinemann.

Herr, E., & Cramer, S. (1988). *Career guidance and counseling through the life span: Systematic approaches* (3rd ed.). Boston: Scott, Foresman.

International Reading Association and the National Association for the Education of Young Children (IRA and NAEYC). (1998). Overview of learning to read and write: Developmentally appropriate practices for young children. (A joint position of the IRA and the NAEYC). *The Reading Teacher, 52,* 196–200.

National Assessment of Educational Progress (NAEP). (2001). *The nation's report card.* National Center for Education Statistics. Washington, DC: U.S. Department of Education, Institute of Education Sciences.

14

Student Learning in Math and Science

Youth Development Matters

Michael Ben-Avie

When schools fully implement the Comer Process, their students do better in math and science. Why? The answer is in the appropriate alignment of each grade's math and science curriculum with students' developmental competencies and needs. To create successful math and science learners, educators must find ways to strengthen students' ability to persevere at their tasks, cope with social challenges, feel effective while solving challenging academic problems, and develop trusting and supportive relationships with adults.

I t makes a great deal of sense that schools that fully implement the Comer Process see improvement in students' performance in math and science. For example, Ben-Avie et al. (2003), in "Social and Emotional Development in Relation to Math and Science Learning," describe the administration of the Behavior Assessment Schedule for Students (BASS) (Haynes, 1995) to a total of 831 urban, minority middle school students in School Development Program (SDP) schools. BASS is designed to measure students' self-reported thinking and beliefs about their social interactions and problems. The study also obtained students' achievement scores in mathematics. The strength of the relationship between students' social knowledge of themselves and others and their achievement in mathematics was found to be strong ($r = .80$; $p = .04$). In both situations success depends on (1) awareness of the challenge and an ideal outcome, (2) skills for mapping out a strategy to solve the problem, and (3) willingness to persist in and refine the strategy until a positive outcome is achieved.

THE LEARNING AND DEVELOPMENT INVENTORY

To help middle and high schools clarify whether students are not achieving in math and science due to youth development issues or math and science issues, we developed the Learning and Development Inventory (LDI). LDI defines youth development in terms of a student's cognitions, emotions, and behaviors. Within the school setting, youth development is understood as competencies in coping, belonging, future orientation, friendship, and seeking adult guidance. Student learning is understood as competencies in academic focus, academic persistence, student engagement, language skills, and problem solving in math and science.

Ben-Avie et al. (2003) describe studies using LDI that revealed important predictors of students' academic perseverance, which is defined as students' persistence in performing strategic behaviors that increase the likelihood of academic success, regardless of obstacles or distractions. In the order of their importance, these predictors were

- students' ability to quickly recover their healthiest sense of self during and after challenging social situations (coping)
- students' feelings of efficacy when solving challenging problems in mathematics and science (problem solving in math and science)
- students' tendency to trust adults and to develop supportive relationships with them (engagement with adults)

Raising the bar of academic standards is perhaps the least effective way to help students who are failing to learn math and science. Our studies have shown that successful problem solving in math and science is associated with academic perseverance, coping, and engagement with adults. Students' level of future orientation—the ability to conceive of one's own development—was also found to be associated with problem solving in math and science. Students who are stuck in the learning of math and science need a school community that takes youth development into account while providing rigorous academic content.

YOUTH DEVELOPMENT AND CURRICULUM

Middle and high schools ask us how to start addressing youth development in relation to student learning in math and science. We respond by explaining that school districts and schools are inundated with "add-on" programs designed to address students' social and emotional needs—not to mention math and science curricular programs. Schools may not recognize the source of stress for the students. During a data interpretation workshop, administrators had expressed unhappiness with the school's curriculum. After a lengthy dialogue, it dawned on the administrators that their unease had nothing to do with the curriculum. Rather, they were seeing too many students who were not persevering in learning. With guidance, the administrators began to see that the school day was stressful and unpredictable for the students.

In addition to the regular curriculum, the school had launched 10 separate educational initiatives. For example, several staff members, including the principal, were recently trained in a seminar that dealt with positive discipline. These staff members returned to the school and had morning meetings in every classroom. Staff members who did not participate in the training were ambivalent about these meetings, and the students were not behaving as expected at the meetings. When asked the objective of this initiative, one of the administrators replied, "To improve the students' interpersonal relations." To her surprise, the principal responded, "No." The objective, she said, was to improve student-teacher relations. Other initiatives in the school had almost identical objectives, but used different methods. The students were confused and not coping well.

The first step, then, to address youth development in relation to student learning is to take a look at all the add-on programs within the school. Incorporate the essence of the add-on programs into curricular units of the regular school day. In this way, you will be able to spark positive developmental experiences, those experiences that lead to an enhanced understanding of one's own developmental trajectory. They also have the effect of stretching students' future orientation and therefore motivate engagement in current schoolwork as a way of achieving future goals.

When students' developmental needs are balanced and aligned with math and science curricula, these curricula produce positive developmental experiences. The second step is to implement strategies in math and science courses that help students to plan and persist until they achieve short- and long-term goals for their future.

ENGAGEMENT WITH ADULTS

James P. Comer, M.D., has taught us that the quality of relationships impacts students' level of future orientation, which we have seen is associated with problem solving in math and science. In our research on youth development in relation to student learning in math and science, we found that students who had high-quality relationships with both peers and teachers tended to have the highest levels of future orientation. Taking youth development into account requires far more than the implementation of a "developmentally appropriate" math and science curriculum. We want to make the case to science and math educators that they will do their jobs more easily and better when youth development is part of their tool kit. And we want to make the case to youth developers that they will serve the students better when they themselves know more about teaching math and science in schools.

REFERENCES

Ben-Avie, M., Haynes, N. M., White, J., Ensign, J., Steinfeld, T. R., Sartin, L. D., & Squires, D. (2003). Youth development and student learning in math and science. In Norris Haynes, Michael Ben-Avie, & Jacque Ensign (Eds.), *How social and emotional development add up: Getting results in math and science education* (pp. 9–35). New York: Teachers College Press.

Haynes, N. M. (1995). *Behavior Assessment Schedule for Students.* New Haven, CT: Yale Child Study Center.

READ MORE ABOUT . . .

To read more about the Learning and Development Inventory, visit SDP's Web site (www.comerprocess.org). Click on "research and evaluation" on the left-hand side. Then click on "surveys."

15

Guidelines for University-School Collaborations

A Report of Experience

Francis Roberts

Fourteen guidelines for systemic implementation of the SDP model are presented by a former university partner of the Westbury Union Free School District. The guidelines will help school systems distinguish a Comer collaboration from other collaborations they have tried in the past and will increase the likelihood of highly effective partnerships.

During a long career, I have seen a lot of university-school collaborations, partnerships, projects, and joint ventures. I have been a participant and observer in many of these, some of which were similar to the Comer Process and some quite different. I also have a long familiarity with the Yale School Development Program (SDP), dating back to 1973, when I was at Yale on a research fellowship and had the pleasure of accompanying Dr. James P. Comer on a visit to the Martin Luther King School, one of the two initial "Comer Schools." From 1997 to 2002, I was the university coordinator of an intense Yale SDP collaboration with the nearby

Westbury School District, in New York. This initial period of the collaboration was supported by a major grant from the Rockefeller Foundation. The concepts that I discuss in this chapter reflect the central findings developed during this grant period. Here, then, are some of my reflections on what I have experienced, as well as observations on what I have learned from other university relationships with public schools.

To provide focus and provoke discussion, I offer these observations in a form I call "Guidelines for University-School Collaborations." In studying these points, it will be clear that some are based on collaborations quite different in intent from SDP. Awareness of these differences is important for any school district or university considering a Comer collaboration, since the initiation of any new partnership will be taking place against a backdrop of all of the participants' prior experiences, good or bad.

PARTNERSHIP GUIDELINES

1. Parties entering a Comer collaboration should consider carefully how this new relationship is the same as or different from other university-school interactions

For example, public schools often reach out to universities for consulting help or expert guidance or specific services. Schools may request a curriculum audit, an evaluation of the efficiency of the bus services, an audit of the finances, staff training in diagnosing the needs of special education children, or a hundred other specifics. These services are often sought from university specialists, and the expectation may be fulfilled by a process of consultation or expert visits.

Sometimes, schools or whole school systems seek comprehensive outside review. My first major experience in school-community projects was as a doctoral student and very junior member of the staff of the Harvard Center for Field Studies, which was contracted to do an independent comprehensive study of the Pawtucket School District, in Rhode Island. The intent in that study was to evaluate virtually every aspect of the educational program and to make recommendations for action. It was neither collaborative nor intended to be. Although that comprehensive study was helpful and resulted in many changes to the Pawtucket School System, I later learned how hugely different that "outside expert" approach was from the Comer Process.

Just as it is the case that school systems often look to universities for help, it also is common for universities to seek help from schools. During the seven years that I was superintendent of schools in a large university community, for example, it seemed that almost every week, some faculty member or department from the university approached our local schools seeking permission to use the schools for a research project. Although very sympathetic to the potential value of such research, I often had to refuse participation if the proposed activity seemed likely to interfere with the children's learning.

The two most common kinds of university-school collaboration are those emanating from the college admissions and placement offices and the requests from colleges for student teaching or other field placements. Each of these forms of cooperation is valuable and mutually advantageous. But their intent is not to support deep, systematic school improvement.

These examples, familiar to all of us, must be kept in mind as school leaders or college faculty begin discussions about initiating a formal collaboration with SDP and a nearby university. The extent, quality, and both positive and negative results of all prior experiences deeply influence the climate of opinion in which a Comer initiative is considered.

2. Early in the game, the parties should identify the key power players and opinion leaders in each setting and explore the prospective collaboration with them

It is, of course, vital to join with the official leaders of the collaborating parties, such as the superintendent, college administration, and parent and teacher leaders. But it is even more important in some ways to test the waters with the many other key players in each setting, people who significantly influence the climate of opinion or may be thought to have their pulse on the day-to-day activities and complications of the school or university.

Determining who these power players and prime opinion leaders really are is not as easy a task as it may seem. Often, the people who shape opinions in school and college settings are themselves low-profile figures who are not necessarily the first people who come to mind. To locate these key players requires multiple searches, subtle inquiry, and close listening. It is a step often overlooked. Not uncommonly, planners are met with enthusiasm and eagerness from persons in official positions, and the innovators may mistake this encouragement as support from behind the scenes. Bear in mind my earlier observations about the different interests of schools and universities and the likelihood that the school staff, principals, and parents have mixed feelings about prior "interventions" and school improvement programs.

3. Support of the collaboration by the "people in power" greatly facilitates acceptance

In our collaboration with the Westbury School District and Long Island University (LIU), one of the most important elements of support was the early and frequent expression of public support by the designated leaders of the two organizations, the Westbury School District and LIU.

From the beginning in Westbury, the collaboration had the public support of the superintendent of schools, the president of the Board of Education, and many of the key administrators. It is not to be expected that everyone will be "on board" at the start, although this is desirable, but support at the top is critical for many reasons. Perhaps the most important reason is that the top leadership sets the agenda for an organization, and if the collaboration is to have priority attention, it has to have that prominence. Endorsement from the top will tend to draw others in. In a comprehensive school system, it is to be expected that some schools will be more involved than others and that support at the top will help inspire support among those initially reluctant.

At LIU, one of the most important factors in getting the collaboration under way was the early and strong public support from the president of the university, Dr. David Steinberg. LIU is a huge, multicampus, private institution enrolling more than 28,000 undergraduate and graduate students. It would not necessarily be assumed that a university president in such a large organization would take close notice of a collaborative project of the kind envisioned. From the start, Dr. Steinberg gave the collaboration not only considerable public recognition but also personally hosted some of the initial planning sessions, including a crucial early dinner meeting attended by the entire Westbury Board of Education, the senior officers of LIU, and Dr. Edward Joyner and colleagues from Yale. In addition, from the very first discussions and explorations, the project had the fullest support of Dr. Jeffrey Kane in his role as dean of the School of Education. Dr. Kane, who is now university vice president, played a central role in the initial application to the Rockefeller Foundation, and he has supported the collaboration every step of the way.

4. Extra resources are essential at the beginning

It may be in some rare cases of university-school collaborations that just raw interest and energy are enough to get a program under way, but if that works, it is mainly because of good luck. In the case of the collaboration with the Westbury Schools, we saw how essential the start-up support was from the Rockefeller Foundation. We also saw how that support leveraged additional support. The Rockefeller Foundation found the idea attractive that SDP was interested in building a partnership with a large university away from New Haven and also with the participation of a full prekindergarten through Grade 12 school system. On the basis of an initial proposal, the foundation made a one-year grant. Without that generous support, the project would not have begun.

The grant provided for support for senior university faculty to participate, money for significant numbers of Westbury teachers and some college staff to begin introductory-level training at Yale, and related support for materials and other activities. The support of the foundation was matched by in-kind support and released time from both LIU and the school system. This initial support then made it possible for the parties to firm up plans and program designs for an additional two years of Rockefeller support.

5. An enduring university-school collaboration cannot be dependent on the start-up resources alone

In designing and appraising our new collaboration, we recognized that it could not meet our goal of an "institutionalized long-term partnership" if that long-term partnership depended excessively on continued outside funding, especially funding from only one main source. With this in mind, we tried to carefully allocate the expenditures from the Rockefeller Foundation in ways that would contribute to the long-term success of the collaboration. Hence the funds at this stage were spent mainly on training large numbers of participants, especially large numbers of teachers and as many of the administrators as possible. The key point here is that the start-up funding was not used for ongoing regular activities such as additional school staffing, since we recognized that if the collaboration in the early years became dependent for operational expenses on outside sources, there was the near certainty that work would end when the funds ran out.

To further reduce the dependence on a single source of outside funds, we decided in the second year on a "stretch-out strategy" in which the amount of money provided by Rockefeller would be spent gradually over a longer period, thus making the transition away from the special funding easier to accomplish. The initial plan after the first year of Rockefeller funding had been to use the added Rockefeller grant over the next two years, but by invoking the "stretch-out strategy," we sought approval to run the grant an added nine months, thus gradually scaling down the rate of expenditures. I think if this principle of "stretching out the funds" were applied more often in the early years, the classic problem of abandoning good work when the funds run out might occur less often.

6. Initial outside funding can leverage additional support

Once we had conceptualized our collaboration and were well under way, we began to use the basic concepts as a framework and vehicle for seeking additional funds from multiple sources. We wanted these funds for a variety of specific activities that would contribute to the development of the project, rather than simply support ongoing operational expenses. It was our idea that with a good base established and some strong relationships firmed up, we could then move the collaboration beyond the start-up phase and toward a permanent relationship between LIU and the school system. Within this framework, more specific projects could be carried out. Our success in this has been impressive.

For instance, the Comer model and the collaboration have been used by the grant writers in the school system as a basis for seeking federal and state grants. Several have been awarded, the most recent of which builds directly on the collaboration and includes specific support for activities to be supplied by Yale and by LIU. Similarly, LIU has used the collaboration's conceptual framework and its established partnership to seek other project support. Two grants merit special notice: They are from the Annenberg Foundation and the Verizon Foundation. Both the Verizon grant and the Annenberg grant flowed conceptually from the initial design supported by the Rockefeller Foundation.

The Annenberg Foundation grant was awarded first. This was used to create a major literacy and reading initiative in the Westbury schools. The Annenberg grant was of critical importance at the time we received it. We had gone through the early period of the collaboration and had the Comer Process and the SDP structures constructed, but even at that stage, people were beginning to complain that the project was "more form than content." In other words, many said they could see no impact on teaching and learning. The Annenberg project was directed by a senior member of the C. W. Post School of Education faculty, Dr. Joseph Sanacore, who planned and led an imaginative series of collaborative professional development activities focused on literacy. The work has received rave reviews from the foundation and praise from the staff in Westbury. With some added funding, Dr. Sanacore has continued this work.

Equally exciting has been a major grant from the Verizon Foundation to carry out a two-year master's degree program in pathbreaking applications of educational technologies. In this program, nearly two dozen Westbury teachers and administrators are completing a cutting-edge program that will provide the school district with a whole cadre of leaders in this important field. The program was created under the leadership of Dr. Bette Schneiderman and Dr. Michael Byrne, cochairs of the graduate department of educational technology.

There are many attractive features of the Verizon project. First, it places in the hands of Westbury teachers cutting-edge telecommunications skills and concepts, to which underfunded and marginalized schools rarely have access. Second, the program is designed to help the Westbury teachers gain online access to teachers in other schools worldwide and to a rich lode of other resources connected through LIU's Electric Educational Village, a resource that has received formal recognition and praise from the Smithsonian Institution.

Other grant applications are pending. From our initial experience, it is clear that funding agencies are attracted by the idea that a school district and a nearby university are not just looking for one-shot projects: They have become long-term partners in school development, and they are working within a clear, strong design and plan into which specific additional activities make significant and coherent contributions.

7. University-school collaborations should not depend on specific persons alone

Since the Westbury and LIU partnership with SDP got under way nearly five years ago, there have been changes "at the top" in all three places. The initial support in Westbury for the partnership came from the foresight and enthusiasm of then-superintendent of schools, Dr. Robert Pinckney. After he left Westbury, the superintendency was assumed by Dr. Constance Clark, who was recruited in part on the basis of her prior experience with the work of Dr. Comer. In fact, Clark's recruitment was one of the first "measurable" milestones of the collaboration. The board of education, in using its growing familiarity with the Yale program as a set of criteria, was able to find a new superintendent who knew the Comer Process.

At Yale, our primary partner was Dr. Jack Gillette. When Dr. Gillette became head of the Yale Teacher Preparation Program, Dr. Ann Levett-Lowe became our prime Yale partner. At C. W. Post, Dr. Jeffrey Kane was the dean of the School of Education for the first several years and was the principal university officer leading the project. Kane has now become the vice president for Academic Affairs for the entire multicampus LIU, but the current dean continues to offer strong support.

There are two implications from the above. First, it is crucial that the design of a collaboration assume the possibility, even the likelihood, that some of the key leaders will change as the work gets under way. This means that the design should focus on long-term efficacy, not on the particular person or personality of the founding leaders. Second, the collaboration needs to have "depth in the backfield"; that is, it needs to involve a considerable number of people, some of whom may be expected to assume larger leadership roles as the work advances. One example is personal: I am the prime university faculty member in the collaboration, and I plan to retire shortly. But a smooth transition seems likely since my role will be arranged in new ways and will be shared by other LIU faculty. Their roles will differ from mine, but the fact that most have been associated with the collaboration for some time will facilitate and broaden the leadership change.

8. Do not assume that school and university faculty and administrators understand each other's institutional cultures

Because most university collaborations with public schools tend to be based in schools of education, one might assume that most of the college faculty understand day-to-day life in public schools and are experienced in relating to that culture. Similarly, since all public school teachers and administrators have spent years in college environments, we might assume that they understand how colleges and universities work. The reality may differ.

One of the reasons that so many university connections with public schools do not amount to much is that university faculty sometimes project the notion that because they are at the university, they know what teachers and school leaders need to do to improve schools. This notion may seem like sheer arrogance on the part of university faculty, but that usually is not the intent. For example, when we began to explore possible ways in which professors might contribute to the collaboration, one or two eagerly suggested to me that they might come to the school system and give what they called, not surprisingly, "guest lectures." Their intent was both generous and well-meant, but I had to ease them onto another pathway, one in which they might join school partners in shared activities.

We found in our work that shifting some professorial colleagues from the model of lecturing to the schoolteachers was important and readily understood. But sometimes that shift was complicated by the ironic fact that this was exactly what many of the Westbury teachers also expected: The teachers' mental model, based on past experiences, was that college professors were "visiting experts" when they came to schools. Only by spending lots of time in the school district in many different activities—and especially by demonstrating partnership behaviors in meetings—did we gradually begin to overcome the handicapping impression that the university intended to dominate the collaboration.

Developing and sustaining collaborations is a continual learning process for all of the key participants. Just take the example of the differences in the school calendar between the university and the public schools. Universities tend to follow daily, weekly, and annual schedules that are very different from schools' schedules. The colleges have different times when they are on break, and they begin and end at different times, and so on. Thus when school partners try to reach their university partners, they often find connections difficult. Just the fact that most college faculty work at least part of their weeks in their home offices rather than at the campus takes some getting used to by school system partners.

On the other hand, many college faculty do not realize (or remember) that school-teachers are effectively locked into their class schedules for most of the day and cannot be easily reached. College professors often do not even know that it is rare for a schoolteacher to have direct access to a school telephone, except in the faculty room or school office, and that few teachers have messaging services at school. Thus even such simple tasks as arranging meetings or seeking information can be an ongoing challenge. On many occasions, rather than engaging in the frustrating business of telephone tag, I found it most workable simply to get in the car and drive to the school to make a personal connection, get information, or make arrangements. I knew, of course, that such face-to-face contact is really the best, anyway.

Once the school and the university begin to understand these differences in style and institutional culture, things get easier. And as more and more people make regular use of e-mail, cell phones, and personal digital assistants, the communication will become easier still. Here again, it will probably tend to be the university members who have access to the better means of communication.

Another aspect of the differing institutional cultures is the way in which power is allocated. At the school system level, administrators are often sensitive about a collaboration such as SDP, in which power is increasingly distributed among many. Public school systems are traditionally organized on a hierarchical basis, so teachers have to frequently check with their administrators and seek their approval; when bypassed, the administrators may be concerned. On the university side, where power is traditionally broadly distributed, college faculty may assume that school-teacher partners have similar latitude. On the other hand, some college faculty, impatient for action, may wonder why a principal, for example, does not just order something to be done. And in a few cases, we have seen somewhat amusing situations in which a school administrator has called a senior university officer to make a request that would better be directed to the specific professor who had responsibility to act. The college faculty members in such situations can be expected to bristle at such top-down approaches.

9. Learn the subtleties of the "Yale connection"

We all know the powerful energizing force and conceptual resource that Dr. Comer, Dr. Joyner, and the entire SDP provide. In many ways, this is what really distinguishes this collaboration from other school improvement programs. But making the fullest use of the "Yale connection" requires careful and continuing planning.

Having been familiar with SDP since 1973 and having a great respect for the work of many other Yale faculty, such as Dr. Seymour Sarason and Dr. Edward Zigler, I was thrilled at the possibility that LIU might establish a long-term working partnership with Yale. This enthusiasm was shared with most of my colleagues, but at first, not all. What I learned from quiet, coffee break discussions was that some colleagues were quite defensive about the proposed partnership. It seemed to some that we were falling into the "prestige trap" and that our own faculty had, in fact, deeper experience in working with public schools than did most faculty at Yale. It was pointed out, for example, that Yale did not have on its faculty even one professor of education. As we got to know our new partners, it became clear that the people at Yale had sought out the relationship with LIU and our School of Education precisely because we did have faculty competencies, deep public school experience, and strong local ties needed to complement the very different strengths of the Yale staff. We also found our new colleagues a delight to work with.

The Yale connection had a different initial impact in the Westbury School District. Whereas every college professor knows about Yale, that is hardly the case with many school faculty and parents. Here again, a period of relationship building and familiarity is needed. What greatly facilitated this were the intensive training weeks at Yale. We put a large portion of our initial grant support into getting parents, administrators, and lots of teachers to New Haven. The enthusiasm and motivation of those early weeks built an essential foundation. Even five years later, the sessions are often referred to as if they took place only weeks ago. And when we moved to the stage of arranging Comer Process training at the C. W. Post campus, led jointly by Yale and LIU, all of the partnership elements began to solidify. Dr. Comer's keynote speech on child development to a summer institute at our campus added important human ties to the Yale connection.

One additional comment on the subtleties of the Yale connection. We found it really important to decide when and how often to have field visits by our Yale consulting partners. This involved first getting to know the person who would be working with us and what his or her special contributions might be. We were greatly assisted by Dr. Jack Gillette's enormous planning, analytic, and organizational skills and the skillful way that he worked with all of us in school and community meetings. And when Dr. Gillette moved across campus at Yale, Dr. Ann Levett-Lowe became our prime consultant. Her rich and comprehensive experience as a school administrator and her senior role at SDP offered a level of credibility with all of us, and especially the Westbury school leadership, that has led to big gains in the program. The key, we found, has been to think carefully about when and how to make manifest the powerful energies and experience of all of our Yale partners.

10. Remember the Woody Allen principle

Woody Allen is widely reported as saying, "Ninety percent of life is just showing up." This has for me been a constant guideline from the moment our collaboration got under way several years ago. "Just showing up" is hardly the heart of the collaboration, but it is one of the most useful tools one could imagine. I have always kept an eye out for opportunities to "be in the district." This has led me to faculty meetings, breakfasts in the schools, attendance at parties, and assemblies and school board sessions. I have found it useful to have occasions when I would go from school to school, delivering routine items such as notices of upcoming meetings, just to allow myself to be available to my school colleagues for conversation and sharing ideas. I often walk about the schools in an informal way, with no specific agenda, just to pass the time of day with teachers and staff. I have found it of immense help to be seen frequently in the district and school offices so that those important staff at all levels, from secretary to assistant superintendent, recognize me as an insider, not an outsider. Having spent many years as a teacher, principal, and superintendent makes these informal visits easy and familiar for me, perhaps more so than for some of my university colleagues who do not have that background or personal style. But whether one is accustomed to it or not, it is a practice to be cultivated for any university staff who want to build and sustain a partnership with public schools.

11. The School Development Program must focus on the full prekindergarten–Grade 12 span

It is the widely held view in some educational circles that if the children get off to a good start in elementary school, later success is virtually assured. Our experience in working with a whole school district leads us to modify this view. There is no doubt that a poor start is a terrible handicap. But there are two other factors. First, it is increasingly well understood that the dominant force once kids reach the middle school and high school years is the teen culture, not the parent culture, and not the school. If, therefore, elementary students enter a middle or high school where the school is not mindful of the huge difference in the impact of the peer culture, many of the gains acquired in a Comer-oriented elementary school may be washed out or overridden. On the other hand, as SDP continues to gain experience working with middle and high school populations (including students, parents, teachers, and administrators), I believe it will be found that the early and middle-teen years may offer significant opportunities to repair or make up for bad elementary school experiences that many children have.

In exploring this added dimension, SDP will need to study carefully what changes in the model may be needed. For example, relatively later in the work in Westbury, we began to work more intensively at the middle and high school levels and were often brought up sharply by the differences between the departmentalized, highly decentralized secondary schools and the home-classroom-centered elementary schools. We also have begun to think harder about the schools' social psychology and group dynamics. In the high school years particularly, parent participation as in the standard SDP model may need to be radically modified to involve more students directly, and not merely by including a few students on a School Planning and Management Team (SPMT). To this end, we have begun to train the students in the high school in the Comer Process, for example.

12. More emphasis is needed on teaching and learning in the classroom

If I were to make one shift in emphasis in the design of the Yale School Development Program, it would be to focus it—from the beginning of a collaboration—more sharply on the school classrooms. I know that SDP staff are very much aware of this point and that much more is being done along this line. I am still not sure that this problem has been fully explored.

The SDP's design relies heavily on the formal structures, the SPMT, and its associated components. In organizational literature, these elements are referred to as parts of the "formal organization." All of us with long experience with school systems know that the system's effectiveness depends greatly on that formal organization working well, and SDP does work extremely well when faithfully carried out.

But I believe SDP will benefit from a more carefully planned extension into the classroom and into the domain of teaching and learning, which, beyond relationships, is the central function of the school and the payoff for the kids. This expanded emphasis requires some careful thought if SDP's prestige is not to be diluted by a short-run emphasis on educational efforts that are too narrow. Specifically, as one who served two decades as a school superintendent, I readily concede that schools are forced to face the current reality of excessive state and national testing of students. And, of course, the way to do this is to "test-prep," by aligning the curriculum of each grade in ways that conform to test patterns. I also know how important it is for the continued vitality of SDP to be able to demonstrate that the program is not only good for kids but also can compete with other reform programs in the testing game. But professionally, we know that the testing mania will not last forever and that it is not a formula for improving schools.

Rather than taking the defensive posture of structuring the teaching and learning component of SDP more toward meeting narrow, measured objectives through a compulsive, narrow curriculum design, it is my hope that SDP will reach out for wider professional experience in designing an expanded focus on teaching and learning. Models more akin to the long experience of the Bank Street College of Education and its developmental interaction, child-centered focus are far more compatible in the long run with the sound principles of SDP than is a more restrictive and obsolete model of graded instruction and tight curriculum alignment.

13. In developing the Comer model, more emphasis is needed on the community outside the schools

In the earlier stages of SDP, a central goal was, as Dr. Comer has suggested, to re-create within the school key elements missing outside. This remains an essential goal. But as we are becoming more and more aware, in certain crucial ways in many challenged communities, what goes on outside the schools has at least as powerful an impact as what goes on inside the school.

For example, our partner community has a very large proportion of adults who have no children in the public schools. Either these adults have enrolled their children in other-than-public schools or they have no children or their children have grown up. But in our state (New York), each public school system must each year submit its annual budget to a public vote. If the voters have little motivation to vote for the budget and instead are motivated to keep tax rates down, the school budget can be defeated, with the obvious harmful consequences. Thus there exists in this state, at least, a highly consequential link of steel between the community and the school program.

In some communities, the community link is nearly the same as the parent link, and one can expect positive support if that link is carefully cultivated. But in many of the more challenged school districts, there are, in addition to the large proportion of voters who have no children in the schools, a great many parents who are not comfortable participants in the voting process. In such settings, for example, we have many parents who do not speak English and many who are not even citizens. They either cannot or are less likely to participate in annual school budget votes, thus leaving the outcome of the vote to be determined by others.

It has been our experience that it is a mistake to assume that the adults in a community who do not have children in school are determined to vote against school budgets. But a part of SDP needs to focus on helping Comer school parents, teachers, and leaders to engage these adults in the political process. It is worthwhile, but hardly enough, to have a few representatives from the outside community on SPMTs. Comer leaders must go out actively to engage youth organizations, police, religious organizations, civic organizations, neighborhood groups, senior citizens, and those at recreational centers and in political clubs. Teaching political action is as important as teaching relationships.

14. It takes a whole university to partner effectively over time with public schools

This phrase, of course, has a familiar echo to all SDP partners. It occurred to me as I thought about the university parallel to the SDP reminder that "it takes a whole village to raise a child." As I have thought more about university-school collaborations that might mean the most to needy public schools, I realized that my focus has tended to be on what the professional School of Education offers: the greatest number of university faculty who have experience and expertise in precollegiate education. Among my colleagues are experts in curriculum in all fields and disciplines: specialists in learning technologies; school management and leadership; guidance and counseling; literacy, speech, and language; handicapping conditions, and so on. In the work with Westbury, faculty from all of these special university competencies have been called upon or expressed interest. But most universities have more to offer.

For example, we have on our campus an outstanding program in the arts and music. Kids in schools these days find the arts pressed to the sidelines in the struggle to boost achievement test scores. And music is almost the central interest of many teenagers. Might we find connections there, I wondered? With ease, I found a faculty member who soon began to connect with the music program in the Westbury high school; we hope to bring students to the campus to work with tools and techniques for creating and recording new music. We are beginning discussions with college faculty in the College of Arts and Sciences to explore connections in history, mathematics, biology, languages, and literature. Similarly, we have experts in the health sciences we hope to engage. And one of the most productive dimensions so far has been a collaboration with the Office of Career Services and the Admissions Office at the university, which has brought all of the ninth-grade students in Westbury to campus for a career day and all of the tenth graders to campus for a college day. We have also hosted board of education retreats on our campus and hosted the opening convocation of the entire school faculty and staff as they began a recent school year. We see these connections as just the start of multiple, enduring connections as we enlist the interests of our whole university.

READ MORE ABOUT . . .

In Chapter 16, "Implementation of Systemic Reform: Step by Step From Vision to Reality," Constance Clark shares her perspective on Westbury's transformation.

To read about SDP's initiative to impact classrooms, see "Comer-in-the-Classroom: Linking the Essential Elements of the Comer Process to Classroom Practices," Chapter 6 in this volume.

AUTHOR'S NOTE: This work was made possible in part through funding from the Rockefeller Foundation and the U.S. Department of Education.

16

Implementation of Systemic Reform

Step by Step From Vision to Reality

Constance R. Clark

The Westbury Union Free School District on Long Island has achieved statewide recognition for improvement since it adopted the SDP model. Its superintendent describes the model's implementation as occurring in six major steps, which she presents here. These steps will help guide other superintendents to determine their own routes, from their first vision of what is possible all the way to seeing SDP become a reality in their own districts.

Reforming school districts and schools in a systemic way is one of the most difficult challenges facing educators in the 21st century. My challenge as superintendent of the Westbury Union Free School District has been to transform the district so that schools redefine their cultures to reflect the developmental pathways of students, as outlined by Dr. James Comer. For any districtwide reform to be successful requires the commitment of the entire school staff and a different way of thinking and interacting. Prior to the implementation of the School Development Program (SDP), Westbury had experienced a decline in student performance and a major shift in the ethnic population. In this prekindergarten–Grade 12 district of 3,900 students, academic performance was a major concern of the board of education, district staff, and community. Implementing the SDP reform model promised a complete renewal and recommitment for the district.

As this recounting of my experiences will show, the initial stages and implementation of the process took dialogue and understanding, dialogue and collegial planning, dialogue and risk taking, followed by more dialogue and time. Terrance E. Deal and Kent D. Peterson (2003) speak of the challenge of changing the culture of organizations such as schools. The reason why this process is so difficult is that the culture is ingrained in people's patterns of behavior and thoughts, and institutional norms. SDP interrupts these patterns in order to create new ones that better serve the needs and outcomes of students. These new patterns are based on healthy relationships among all those in the community.

In Westbury, I was brought in because of my experience with SDP in Washington, D.C., where I had been deputy superintendent. Before he retired, the former superintendent in Westbury, Dr. Robert Pinckney, and the board had actually started the change process using the SDP model. They told me, "We want you to walk on water!" The board had the awareness that the district, as a whole, needed to change, and they wanted the change process to be guided by the SDP intervention to which they had already committed themselves. Thus SDP's systemic reform became the yardstick by which all activities would be measured.

It is important to note here that neither politics, adult issues, test scores, revised curriculum, nor an integration of best practices are at the center of the Comer Process. Rather, this model focuses on the child and what is right and best for the child, as understood through the framework of the developmental pathways. In Westbury, there were several positive elements at the inception of SDP three years ago. Paramount was the commitment of the board of education and their desire to provide the best education possible for all students. The board of education comprised long-term residents of the community who wanted to reverse the decline in student performance and results. They studied the Comer Process and saw its value in restructuring schools, rather than just trying to focus on test scores while all other factors remained the same. As superintendent and a resident of the community, I had the opportunity to live and demonstrate the Comer Process, serving as a model of collaboration in all my activities in and around the schools and community. Another positive mainstay was the school district's partnership with Long Island University's C. W. Post School of Education and, specifically, the support received from Jeffrey Kane, who was then dean of the School of Education and is now university vice president; Francis Roberts, who was university coordinator of the Yale SDP collaboration in Westbury; and other members of the university faculty. Throughout the implementation process, the university has continued as an active partner.

As the newly appointed superintendent, I was charged with paving a path to improved student performance. As a former administrator of the District of Columbia Public School District, charged with the responsibility of implementing SDP districtwide and facilitating the involvement of the major stakeholders, I knew SDP could be successful if the major stakeholders were involved in the process. Therefore, one of the first things I did was to activate the SDP districtwide steering committee. My challenge was also finding a way to establish success, given the new State of New York mandates and high-stakes testing required of the district. It was my vision that the constituents would understand the benefits to be derived from the collaboration and would embrace the Comer Process.

However, there was resistance and some noncommitment to the process in pockets across the district. My goal was to penetrate the resistance through team building and collaboration. I valued the buy-in of the professional staff and viewed that element as critical to the success of the process in Westbury. *My vision was success, not failure.*

STEP 1: CREATING AND CULTIVATING AN ENVIRONMENT FOR OPEN DIALOGUE AMONG STAKEHOLDERS

Edward T. Joyner, executive director of SDP, maintains that the Comer Process is a question of will. He says the process saves people who want to be helped and who engage in self-development, once they are given nonjudgmental feedback about their performance. Through reflecting on this statement, I came to appreciate the reason for the pockets of resistance in the district. The teachers were not yet convinced that substantial or systemic change could be realized. The teachers did not fully understand the Comer Process and its ultimate benefits. As one of the introductory steps, I met with the districtwide steering committee, which included members of the community and the district staff. Joyner and Gretchen Lofland (representing the Yale team), Roberts (representing C. W. Post), and members of the districtwide steering committee introduced the facts of SDP to the teachers. This meant living the process of the guiding principles each day within the culture of the district.

As I reflected on the steps taken to implement the process, ongoing staff orientation was critical in creating an understanding of the philosophical basis of the model. This step required more than an overview with a brief sharing of successful results of other schools, districts, and places; it required a thorough indoctrination of the process through daily experiences.

One barrier that I faced as the new superintendent was my own need to learn more about the district culture that had developed over more than a generation. This knowledge and understanding helped me to be sensitive to what others considered important. District staff and the districtwide steering committee and I identified strategies for overcoming the resistance to change in general.

I also realized that to develop trust, I needed to reach out to schools in order to learn more from the teachers about their feelings and their understanding of SDP. I conducted information-gathering sessions over lunch with the teachers that allowed us to dialogue about any number of concerns related to the process. Through these conversations, we learned more about each other. These conversations gave me an opportunity to gain support and to clarify the uniqueness and practicality of the Comer Process as the strategy we would use. The general feeling afterward was that this wasn't just another model that would pass away, but that we were all committed to staying the course.

STEP 2: LEARNING THROUGH ACTIVE PARTICIPATION AND STRATEGIC PLANNING

Prior to implementing the Comer Process in the district, there was not an overall strategy. To remedy this lack of facilitation and to improve coordination of long-term effort throughout the district, a district strategic plan was developed through the collaboration process. Before this, every school had worked in isolation, and they lacked common goals. By collaborating, we came to recognize the lack of coordination among district programs and the lack of alignment with state standards. Our new strategic plan became a stepping-stone to formalizing the curriculum and pedagogy. It also helped to formalize ongoing communication within and among the schools. The focus on strategic planning became an integral component in the implementation process in the district.

Although research shows the efforts in an educational arena to be loosely coupled, it became evident that changing any aspect of the district's procedures would lead to changing others. Dr. Comer explains that adults talk to adults in functional communities. When schools are not functioning, adults are not talking to each other and, therefore, not talking about students. Thus I made time for teachers and administrators to begin talking through the collaborative planning process and begin developing a common focus that could be of interest to every stakeholder.

Test scores of individual classes were obtained by the district office and shared with the teachers. Providing teachers time to discuss a relevant topic began the collaborative process. The focus was on data, individual classes, children, and root causes. The teachers and administrators began to engage in collaborative communication with each other. Staff meetings and superintendent's conference days were centered on the process and relevant topics of school improvement.

To achieve far-reaching success, the initial phase of implementation needed to include representatives of all of the partners. Parent meetings held at the board of education allowed yet another segment of the population to consider strategies for improving results. This was another starting point for finding success through the Comer Process. Through data analysis, all interested parties—teachers, parents, administrators, counselors, and others—began to communicate using the guiding principles of consensus, collaboration, and no-fault.

Dr. Comer underscores that it is the integration of the home and school that determines what takes place within a school. Parental involvement serves as a major component in this process. I believe in having parents as partners in the learning process. No matter how effective a school is, the parents are the first and most influential teachers of their children. When parents are working collaboratively in a school, they are influential with other parents. Our schools had a core of involved parents. Our challenge was to extend the circle to include more parents and to encourage them to engage in the life of the school. Our community also had willing community members; we needed to call them together and invite them to volunteer for programs and services for the children. The first steps here involved more meetings to learn about each other, about all our hopes and dreams for the children, and about the talents and abilities each of us could offer.

STEP 3: BUILDING CAPACITY THROUGH STRATEGIC PLANNING

Once the key players knew each other and understood the task we faced together, the next activity involved calling together representatives from each group to map out or plan what our immediate goals would be, and the logical activities or steps for achieving them. The product of several meetings was the strategic plan, which was reproduced and distributed to all concerned.

Professional development sessions were conducted by outside consultants and district staff for principals to ensure that they understood the direction and purpose of the strategic planning process. This open dialogue with principals ensured that we kept what was working, making sure that it transitioned into the strategic plan. Principals brainstormed as to how they could use the district plan to create local school plans. The entire planning process reflected SDP's approach.

Representatives from all the constituency groups worked together to set goals and activities for each building. Time for discussion was built into the work sessions to allow all concerned to ask questions and explore possibilities of anticipated changes in the district. This time for dialogue was crucial for those who previously had participated only in organizations in which there are only leaders and followers.

Historically, the principals had had good relationships with community members, parents, and teachers. This played a key role in the success of this process. It was important for the school community to understand the Comer Process so they could work to cultivate others' interest and participation in it. They needed to be assured that they would be supported as they learned about the SDP Process and implemented it in their schools.

All staff members were involved in Yale's national leadership academy sessions. These were conducted in the hope that those most interested would become leaders and provide training for other staff members at each school, thus creating an internal capacity for training other staff members.

STEP 4: CREATING COMMUNICATION CHANNELS THAT ENHANCE UNDERSTANDING

Open communication was established by organizing building teams, the district council, and the district steering committee. Once each School Planning and Management Team (SPMT) was formed, meetings were held to ensure everyone's involvement in the process. From these meetings grew the idea to have a district newsletter to report on Comer activities across the district. The *Comergram Newsletter* was created and published throughout the year to tie the constituents and efforts together. This newsletter allowed those still unsure of the possibilities of the Comer Process to learn about the achievements and efforts of those already involved and committed.

As acceptance of the process grew, individuals began to express that they needed more information about the process. Questions led the teams to understand that different people have different ways of engaging in change. Some are happy to engage in the process and learn about it by participating in a team that evolves over time. Others want information: to know the history and theory behind the process and predictions about the long-term steps that will be followed. Professional development was planned that responded to these different styles of engaging in the implementation of SDP.

STEP 5: IMPLEMENTING SYSTEMIC PROFESSIONAL DEVELOPMENT

The first week after the end of the school year was devoted to training. Representatives from the many groups came together to learn more about the Comer

Process. The training permitted time for the individuals to refine collaborative skills and team building. The training was held at C. W. Post campus sites, which reinforced the partnership between the district and university.

Another layer of training is focused on team leaders as an effort to build internal capacity. This takes place at Yale University. This intensive training focuses on the developmental pathways and helps participants to understand their relationships to teaching and learning and building functional schools. Over the past three years, principals and teachers have consistently participated in the Yale University academy and leadership training. Grants funded a district Comer facilitator, who serves as the in-district expert, guiding the principals in their daily work as part of a districtwide process.

As the participants have learned more about the initiative, more requests have been generated for training. Districtwide monthly meetings are held to monitor progress and problem solving about misunderstandings or obstacles that have been impeding forward movement. The participants are now actively seeking ways to increase communication in a formalized manner. The evolution of the districtwide steering committee now serves as the mechanism for charting district progress and success.

Strategies employed to enhance the model have included the following:

- Each school identified a Comer communicator to represent that school on the districtwide steering committee. The primary function of the committee is to address the issues relative to the implementation of SDP.
- Teams have been formulated. Schools submit names of their SPMT team members, and meeting dates for the year are established throughout the district.
- Continuous training sessions are held at the district office, the Yale Child Study Center, the C. W. Post campus, and local school sites.

STEP 6: EXPANDING THE PROCESS THROUGH REFLECTION AND REFINEMENT

To continue the momentum, the administrators were encouraged to participate in the Principals' Academy at Yale during the summer. Here, the principals had the opportunity to discuss the implementation of the process with others. Similarities and differences of implementation and strengths and weaknesses of implementation phases were shared. Time was allocated for brainstorming possible solutions to situations and for sharing successes and successful strategies. Ongoing training has been transferred to each local site for further refinement of the process.

When the principal and staff of each building were aware of the overall purpose of living the Comer Process, SDP's Staff, Parent, and Student School Climate Surveys (Emmons, Haynes, & Comer, 2002) were administered to determine the degree to which the faculty felt they were heard and their opinions respected in each building. Each school's SPMT addressed the findings of the surveys.

A LIVING COMER DISTRICT

The SDP model was adopted by the board of education prior to 1999. Over the ensuing four years, the implementation process has allowed a steady change in how the staff and administrators engage in systemic work, which is now based on the developmental pathways and collaborative decision making. Apprehension and suspicion have turned into conversations about how we can serve our students differently and maximize the educational process in our schools. Westbury has made significant changes and is still evolving with one goal in mind: to improve the quality of education for all students.

By the spring of 2003, when SDP had been in full implementation for three years, Westbury exceeded the New York State English Language Arts performance index at the fourth-grade level, and the fourth-grade scores exceeded the state standard. The middle school was ranked first in the state for having the highest gains in mathematics and was ranked 16th in the state for gains in English/Language Arts. Of the high school cohort, 75 percent passed the Regents Examination.

The experience of implementing the SDP model has been an enriching experience and has further reinforced the need for open communication and sustained professional development of all stakeholders. Westbury is making the mark. Our district is clearly child centered and collaborative. However, our next challenge is to further our work by refining programs to focus on the developmental pathways. Westbury is a living Comer district.

REFERENCES

Deal, T. E., & Peterson, K. D. (2003). *Shaping school culture: The heart of leadership.* San Francisco: Jossey-Bass.

Emmons, C. L., Haynes, N., & Comer, J. P. (2002). *School Climate Survey* (Rev. ed.). New Haven, CT: Comer School Development Program.

17

Assessing
Systemic Reform

*How Do You Know
That the Comer Process Is Making a
Difference in Your School or District?*

Christine L. Emmons

Program assessment and modification are core components of the Comer Process. In this chapter, the reader will learn how to design an assessment plan, collect the relevant data, interpret the results, and use them in meaningful ways to guide program change and improvement.

ACCOUNTABILITY AND
DATA-DRIVEN ASSESSMENT

In this age of accountability, when superintendents and principals are required to show that students are making adequate academic progress, it is important that administrators demonstrate that the programs selected for school change are effective in bringing about the desired results. The tradition in education is that new programs are tried, then discarded after a few months or a couple of years, or whenever the funds run out, without due consideration being given to the effectiveness of the program. In most cases, there has been no systematic assessment of the effectiveness of the program. The decision to keep or discard a program therefore tends to be made more for political reasons than on the basis of effectiveness. If consistent progress in student achievement and social skills is to be made, administrators must turn to reliable, consistently reported data for evidence that will support their program planning.

At the same time that we have seen increased accountability requirements, we have also seen reduced funding. The budget crises that exist in the majority of states have resulted in reduced funds to school systems, making it imperative that the funds spent on programs produce maximum returns and move the school system in its chosen direction. The conflicting demands of "more for less" raise the anxieties of administrators, teachers, parents, and, yes, students. When programs are implemented and discarded willy-nilly, even greater stress results. Change is difficult and stressful, and when there is a constant parade of programs marching through the school, in one door and out the next, teachers and principals may become change-proof, or simply indifferent. They may sit on the sidelines and watch the parade go by, saying to themselves as each program appears in the doorway, "This too shall pass." If superintendents want to bring about targeted and lasting improvement, programs must be selected and retained based on proven effectiveness.

The purpose of this chapter therefore is to help administrators

- understand the relationship between evaluation and implementation in the School Development Program (SDP)
- develop a comprehensive program evaluation plan for assessing the implementation and effectiveness of SDP and all other programs adopted by the district or any of its schools
- design strategies for sharing and using the results of the evaluation for the improvement of teaching, learning, and the environment in the schools

Within the Comer Process, assessment coupled with modification is one of the basic nine elements. If a school or district is implementing the Comer Process, then an assessment plan is as important as an implementation plan. As a matter of fact, the assessment plan is a part of the implementation plan. There have been several instances in my workshop on this subject when participants have asked, "How do we know that it is SDP and not something else that is making a difference in our school?" A good assessment plan will help you to answer that question, which will be discussed in greater detail later in this chapter.

Having an assessment plan is virtually useless if the results are not shared and used for improvement. It is like going for your yearly physical examination and not paying any attention to the results. You would not know the status of your health, what to keep doing, and what to change. This chapter will end with suggestions for sharing and using the results.

WHAT THE RESEARCH SAYS

We begin with a summary of the results of research done on SDP by independent evaluators, displayed in Box 17.1. This serves both as evidence that SDP can bring about positive school change and improved student outcomes and also as motivation for the development and implementation of a program evaluation plan, so that schools and districts can track their own progress. The rest of the chapter takes the form of a workshop and requires your active participation. The sections will mirror the information and activities shared in the workshop. The next section contains information and activities that will help you prepare for the development of the assessment plan.

Box 17.1   The School Development Program Has Been Proven Effective

Comprehensive in scope, the School Development Program (SDP) is also comprehensive in impact, (a) improving the effectiveness of school organization, (b) empowering teachers and increasing their sense of efficacy, (c) providing support for change, (d) reorienting schools on the well-being and healthy development of children as the central purpose of schooling, (e) improving school climate, and (f) improving student achievement, attitudes, and behavior.

School Organization

A major outcome of the implementation of the Comer Process, usually the first outcome, is improved school organization (Wong, Oberman, Mintrop, & Gamson, 1996). SDP schools are better organized to deal with the tasks that they must perform and the issues that they have to address. The implementation of the Comer Process also results in greater collaboration among teachers and among all stakeholders (Millsap et al., 1997; Payne, 1994; Turnbull, Fiester, & Wodatch, 1997). School staff, parents, community members, district office staff, and the school board work with greater cohesion to achieve the goals of the school. Increase in parent involvement (Cook et al., 1999; Millsap et al., 1997; Noblit et al., 1998; Payne, 1994; Turnbull et al. 1997; Wong et al., 1996) is another documented outcome of SDP. In addition, school-parent linkages are strengthened (Wong et al., 1996), making it easier for parents and teachers to work together for the well-being of children. The Comer Process also helps to foster closer relationships between parents and the district as a whole (Wong et al., 1996).

School Empowerment

School empowerment is another major area of SDP impact. The Comer Process contributes to staff members' feelings of empowerment and ownership (Noblit et al., 1998; Stringfield et al., 1995). There is reduced teacher isolation (Turnbull et al., 1997), greater teacher involvement in decision making (Millsap et al., 1997; Payne, 1994), and increased teacher satisfaction and efficacy (Cook, Murphy, & Hunt, 2000; Noblit et al., 1998). The Comer Process also helps to create a sense of shared purpose among staff in the school (Noblit et al., 1998; Turnbull et al., 1997). The literature indicates that organizations in which staff members have a sense of ownership and common purpose and in which they feel empowered to make changes are the ones most likely to achieve and sustain success.

(Continued)

Box 17.1 (Continued)

Support for Change

The Comer Process not only gives school staff members the feeling that they can create change but also supplies them with the technology to bring about change, to borrow a phrase from Noblit et al. They also wrote, "Even though the SDP is a change in itself, it works to manage change, giving the school and its community a belief that they can control their school's destiny" (Noblit et al., 1998, p. 153). The SDP structure clearly provides support for change (Noblit et al., 1998; Payne, 1994; Turnbull et al., 1997; Wong et al., 1996). The three teams, guided by the three principles, perform the three operations in a spiral of continual renewal. Because it is "a process and not a program," SDP allows for continued renewal and improvement, and "the 'Comer Principles' are a constant touchstone for adult behavior" (Turnbull et al., 1997, p. 5).

The SDP also contributes to better communication and an improved flow of information (Payne, 1994; Turnbull et al., 1997). Because communication is the circulation system of change and information its life force, a healthy communication system facilitating the easy flow of information is critical for the success of the reform process.

Child Focus

Comer schools show an increased focus on the well-being of children, placing the child at the center of the education process (Payne, 1994; Turnbull et al., 1997; Wong et al., 1996). These schools develop enhanced social service support for students and families (Millsap et al., 1997; Payne, 1994). Children are viewed not as isolated individuals, but as members of family groups.

School Climate

Many studies report that SDP schools show improved social climate, manifested by better relationships and greater feelings of safety (Cook et al., 2000; Millsap et al., 1997; Noblit et al., 1998; Payne, 1994; Turnbull et al., 1997). The improved social climate is demonstrated by improved parent-teacher relationships; improved relationships among students, among staff members, and between students and teachers or other adults in the school; and increased teacher attachment to their schools.

In addition to changes in the social climate, the Comer Process may impact the academic climate as well. Comer teachers sometimes see the quality of their teaching practices improve more rapidly than do their colleagues in non-SDP schools (Cook et al., 2000). Comer students view their teachers as becoming increasingly more concerned with learning and trying harder and harder to get students to achieve. They see their classmates as ever more accepting of school values, and they view the schools as honoring academic achievement more and more (Cook et al., 2000). Greater attention is paid to instructional issues (Noblit et al., 1998).

Student Achievement, Attitudes, and Behavior

Through an extensive meta-analysis of the research on 29 widely implemented comprehensive school reform programs, Borman, Hewes, Overman, & Brown (2003) found that SDP is one of three school reform models proven to increase student achievement. Other researchers found that SDP had a positive impact on student attitudes toward education and improved overall student behavior at school (Cook et al., 2000; Wong et al., 1996). In an experimental study, it was found that students at SDP schools reported better anger control, greater disapproval of misbehavior, and less acting-out behavior (in and out of school) than their counterparts in control schools (Cook et al., 2000).

Conclusion

SDP is an operating system not only for bringing about change but also for managing and sustaining change. The difficulty with creating and maintaining change is the tendency for things to slide back into their original positions. How do you sustain what you have achieved as you keep moving forward, particularly given the constantly changing political and policy arenas? SDP is the answer.

PREPARING FOR THE ASSESSMENT PLAN

Relationship Between Implementation and Assessment

I conduct workshops on the topic, "How do you know that the School Development Program is making a difference in your school or district?" During those workshops, I ask participants where they see the relationship between implementation and research manifested in the Comer Process. Someone usually comes up with the answer: It is embedded in the assessment and modification element. That is correct. If you are implementing SDP faithfully, you must also be assessing its implementation and effectiveness. To go into greater detail, let us look at two questions and some sample answers given by workshop participants. Add your own ideas on the blank lines below.

Question 1. In what ways can research influence implementation?

Research can

- identify strengths and needs
- drive staff development
- be a rational basis for decision making
- demonstrate trends
- help to set goals

- let you know whether you achieve your goals

- _____

- _____

- _____

Question 2. How can implementation influence research?

Understanding the implementation process can

- help you identify questions for research
- help you change the direction of your research
- help with reflection on the process of implementation, especially if you're doing focus groups or interviews, or even examining data from surveys

- _____

- _____

- _____

Expected Outcomes

As mentioned above, an understanding of the implementation process can help with the identification of research questions. A program should be evaluated based on how well it is being implemented and on the extent to which it is accomplishing the expected outcomes. If you buy a broom, you do not expect to fly with it. You expect it to help you clean your house, but only the proper use of the broom will give you a well-swept floor. In the same way, before attempting to find out whether SDP is making a difference in your school or district, first answer the question: What difference do you expect SDP to make in your school or district?

Assessment Activity 17.1:
Take a Virtual Tour Through Your School

Follow Figure 17.1 and take a virtual tour of your school as it is today. If you are a central office administrator, choose any school in your district. Begin at the doorway, and when you get to the midpoint at the top of the diagram where it says, "Three Years Later," pause a moment, and in your mind, jump ahead three years in time. Now, continue onward with your tour, visualizing the changes in the school after three years of SDP implementation.

Reflection

- What changes did you see take place during your virtual tour?
- Read the sample reflections below about what workshop participants have seen on their virtual tours. How are your experiences similar and how are they different?

Figure 17.1   Virtual tour through your school

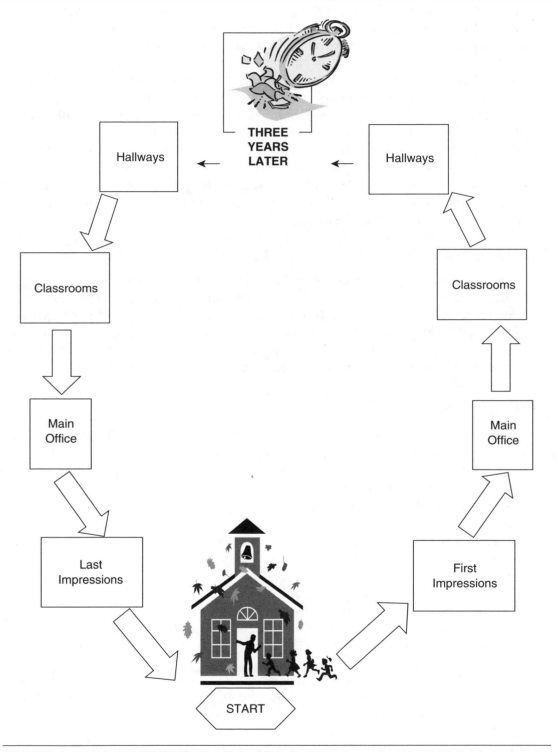

Sample Reflection 1

The first time, I saw a lot of children in the hall, challenged children who had been held over more than once. I also saw where teachers were planning, but planning for failure, not for success. The second time (three years later), I saw the school-based support team having a very important role in assisting these challenged children by really bringing resources to the classroom teachers: actually going in, observing these children in all educational settings, and making recommendations. [I saw teachers'] closeness with the parents in helping these children, to find out what is wrong—not necessarily going straight for referral, but using alternative methods. I also saw teachers planning for success and not feeling fear of assessment tools. [I saw the research results being used]—not just [staff] getting the papers and looking at them, but actually using them to plan for whole classroom as well as small-group or individual instruction.

Sample Reflection 2

In the preview, I saw the faces of children who looked like they were being controlled. There was an emphasis on control and management and discipline. Whereas in the latter viewing, teachers in general are seizing on the uniqueness of kids and seizing on the multiple intelligences and seizing on the diverse learning styles that these children have, and so all kinds of creative things are happening, rather than an emphasis on control.

SDP Effects

A summary of comments shows that after three years of SDP implementation, workshop participants expected to see the following:

- meaningful work taking place
- strong instruction
- improved discipline
- greater parental involvement
- greater collaboration
- improved school climate
- positive psychosocial adjustments
- students being responsible for their learning
- students being well disciplined and in good control of themselves
- high academic achievement

Figure 17.2 displays the model of SDP effects that contains the changes we expect to occur in phases over a period of about five years. We expect that the organizational structure of the school will be modified to incorporate the nine elements of the Comer Process. We expect that when you have full implementation of the model, the School Planning and Management Team (SPMT), Student Staff Support Team (SSST), and Parent Team (PT) will be working well using the guiding principles, instituting the three operations, and targeting child development. We expect that school climate, relationships, and parent involvement will improve. Strategies will be designed that help children mature along the six pathways. This should ultimately be demonstrated in such indicators as higher academic achievement and positive social skills.

Figure 17.2   Model of SDP effects

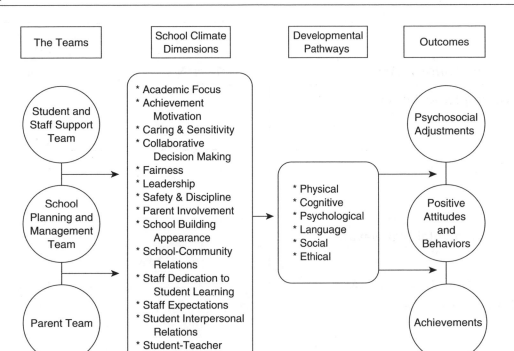

Assessment Activity 17.2: Tracking Down SDP Expected Outcomes in Your Comprehensive School Plan

Now that we have identified the expected outcomes, examine your comprehensive school plan or school improvement plan. Does it contain improvement and assessment activities for all of the expected outcomes? Use Table 17.1 as a checklist, writing in additional outcomes or activities that are or should be in your comprehensive school plan.

THE ASSESSMENT PLAN

Elements of an Assessment Plan

The program evaluation plan proposed here is designed to help you determine the extent to which the activities in your comprehensive school plan are being implemented and the goals achieved. It will allow you to view SDP from a variety of different angles. The intention is to make it easy for you to plan and carry out the assessment. Because the results will be used to guide decisions about changes or modifications to your comprehensive school plan, they should be easy to understand, share, and use.

Table 17.1   Expected outcome areas activity sheet

Expected Outcome Areas	Improvement Activities in CSP (Yes or No)	Assessment Activities (Yes or No)
SDP implementation		
School climate		
Developmental pathways		
Student attitudes		
Student behavior		
Student achievement		
Parent involvement		

The assessment plan includes three major elements:

- your research questions
- the methods you will use to seek answers to your questions, including:
  Who will participate?
  What instruments can you use to measure the important areas in which you are interested?
  When will you collect the data?
- the presentation of the results

Research Questions

The first step in an assessment plan is to develop the questions to which you want answers. As you draw up the questions, keep in mind the difference that you expect SDP to make in your school—in other words, the goals that you hope to achieve by implementing SDP and other programs or activities you have chosen. What are the critical questions you have regarding the implementation and effectiveness of SDP in your school or district?

Criteria for Research Questions

Here are five criteria that can help you determine whether the research question should be included in your assessment plan:

- The question addresses one or more of your goals for the implementation of SDP.
- The activity is in your comprehensive school plan.
- You and/or school staff can answer the question with available resources or help from the district.
- The answer to the question gives information about SDP implementation and outcomes at your school.
- There is interest in the answer or need for the data.

Here are sample questions that meet those criteria:

- What is the level of SDP implementation in the school, and to what extent is it changing over time?
- Is the climate in my school improving over time?
- Has student behavior improved?
- Is student achievement improving?
- To what extent are the developmental pathways being implemented in the classroom?

There should always be a question regarding the extent or quality of the implementation of any program that you have adopted, otherwise any claims that you make regarding its effectiveness or lack thereof will be called into question. To ensure empirical evidence of implementation, your first research question should therefore be: "Are we implementing the program, and if so, how much and how well?"

Assessment Activity 17.3:
Writing Your Research Questions

Using the Research Questions Activity Sheet in Table 17.2, write at least one research question for each expected outcome. Add other outcomes and research questions in the blank spaces provided. Use the criteria listed on the previous page as a guide for evaluating your research questions. Examples are given.

Table 17.2   Research questions activity sheet

Expected Outcomes	Research Questions
SDP implementation	1. What is the extent of SDP implementation in the school, and how is it changing over time? 2.
School climate	1. Is school climate improving? 2.
Developmental pathways	1. Are students' social skills increasing? 2.
Student attitudes	1. Have student attitudes toward learning improved? 2.
Student behavior	1. Has student behavior improved? 2.
Student achievement	1. Has student academic achievement increased? 2.
Parent involvement	1. Has parent involvement increased? 2.

Designing the Assessment Plan

Research design refers to the procedures used to

- identify the variables of interest in the research question
- decide who should participate and how you would group the participants
- identify ways of measuring the variables and collecting the data
- decide when to collect the data
- decide how to analyze and present the data

One can also describe research design as a series of four questions:

1. WHAT do you want to measure?

2. WHO are the people from or about whom the information will be gathered?

3. HOW are the variables going to be measured?

4. WHEN will the data be collected?

The decision that is made at each step depends on the answer to the previous question. For example, you need to know what you want to measure before you can decide from or about whom you will get the information. Each of these four questions is dealt with at greater length in the following sections.

Variables (What)

Identify what you want to measure. The "what" is the variable or variables of interest, and they should be specified in the research questions. Thus in the sample question, "What is the extent of SDP implementation in the school, and how is it changing over time?" the variables of interest are "SDP implementation" and "time." Table 17.3 illustrates the variables that correspond to the research questions in Table 17.2.

Having identified the variables, you are ready to define and describe each one. For example, what do you mean by "SDP implementation"? What do you mean by "school climate"? What do you mean by "student behavior"? Write down these definitions, discuss them with staff, review them, and then write your final definitions, using Table 17.3 for reference. After you have finished defining your variables, you are ready to decide where or from whom you will obtain your data.

Participants (Who)

The participants are the people from or about whom the information will be gathered. In making that decision, consider the most useful source of information. Continuing the example above, the people most likely to know about SDP implementation in the school are the people who are in the school on a regular basis. These would be the school building staff and the team members, who might include parents, students, and community members.

Once you have broadly identified the key informants, you must decide whether you will collect information from all of them or from a representative sample only. (If you will not be collecting data from the entire group of relevant informants, at

Table 17.3 Variables to be measured for each research question

Research Questions	Variables	Possible Definition of Variable (Sample only)
1. What is the extent of SDP implementation in the school, and how is it changing over time?	SDP implementation	The functioning and effectiveness of the nine elements of the Comer Process
2. Is school climate improving?	School climate	Quality of relationships among students, staff, and parents
3. Are students' social skills increasing?	Students' social skills	Appropriateness of behavior; ability to negotiate relationships
4. Have student attitudes toward learning improved?	Student attitudes toward learning	How students feel about school and learning
5. Has student behavior improved?	Student behavior	The manner in which students conduct themselves on the school premises
6. Has student academic achievement increased?	Student academic achievement	Scores on standardized tests in academic subject areas
7. Has parent involvement increased?	Parent involvement	Number of parents attending functions, volunteering in school governance

least make sure that meaningful subgroups of respondents are adequately represented.) In either case, consider collecting information that will allow a more in depth analysis of the data, for example, responses by men versus women, by instructional versus noninstructional staff, and/or by ethnic groups. If you want to make these comparisons, it is important to consider the issues early on so that you may request the relevant demographic information at the time of data collection. After identifying and defining the variables and deciding who the participants will be, the next step is to decide how the variables will be measured.

Measures (How)

How you measure your variables determines the manner in which you collect the data. There are many ways in which any variable can be measured. Some options are surveys, interviews, focus groups, observations, and tests, depending on the "what" and the "who."

Continuing with our implementation example, we may measure SDP implementation using the School Implementation Questionnaire–Abbreviated (SIQA) (Emmons, Haynes, Comer, Cook, & Joyner, 1999) because it was developed to survey the perceptions of school building staff and team members on the implementation of SDP in schools. Another measure is the Process Documentation Inventory (PDI) that SDP designed as an in-depth reflection tool for teams, particularly the SPMT, the SSST, and the PT. Box 17.2 contains a brief description of both the SIQA and PDI.

Box 17.2   School Implementation Questionnaire and Process Documentation Inventory

SIQA: School Implementation Questionnaire–Abbreviated

The School Implementation Questionnaire–Abbreviated (SIQA) is designed to gauge the extent to which schools are implementing the structures and principles of the School Development Program (SDP). The SIQA is used as a tool to document the process of SDP implementation and to examine the relationship between the extent and quality of implementation and related factors, such as school climate, student attendance, and student achievement.

Staff and team members rate their perceptions of the implementation of specific program components on a five-point Likert scale. Respondents are asked to indicate the extent to which specific SDP components exist in the school. The response choices range from "Not at all" to "A great deal" for some choices, and from "Never" to "Always" or "Completely" for others. The SIQA addresses nine major themes: Comprehensive School Plan (CSP) Effectiveness; School Planning and Management Team (SPMT) Effectiveness; SPMT Practice of SDP Guiding Principles; Student and Staff Support Team (SSST) Effectiveness; SSST Practice of SDP Guiding Principles; Parent Team (PT) Effectiveness; Parent Team Practice of SDP Guiding Principles; Inclusiveness; and Curriculum Developmental Focus.

PDI: Process Documentation Inventory

The SDP Quality Standards Process Documentation Inventory (PDI) was developed to assist schools with the process of replicating the Comer Process. The PDI is a self-diagnostic tool designed to assess both the level and quality of SDP implementation. The PDI is organized according to the five phases of

---

(Continued)

Box 17.2 (Continued)

the SDP Implementation Life Cycle, with rubrics describing the activities that should be taking place at each phase. At selected times during the year, team members (SPMT, SSST, and PT) rate the level of implementation of each of these activities (labeled "quality indicators"): "Not at all," "Beginning," "Partial," "Full," and "Exemplary," with supporting documentation. The team then uses the ratings to modify their program.

The Comer facilitator for the school or district may visit the classrooms and attend meetings to observe the functioning of SDP. An observation protocol may be used for such visits. It is also possible to use the SDP Implementation Life Cycle (Joyner, 2004) to determine the implementation phase of the school. Selecting still another example, we can look at the school climate question in Table 17.2, "Is school climate improving?" To assess school climate, you may use the SDP School Climate Survey (Emmons, Haynes, & Comer, 2002), which covers the dimensions listed in Figure 17.2. This instrument measures relationships among students, staff, and parents. Box 17.3 contains a brief description of the climate surveys.

Box 17.3 The SDP School Climate Survey

There are four versions of the SDP School Climate Survey: (1) the Elementary and Middle School Student Climate Survey, (2) the High School Student Climate Survey, (3) the Parent School Climate Survey, and (4) the Staff School Climate Survey. All four were recently revised (Emmons et al., 2002).

Elementary and Middle School Student Revised Version

The Elementary and Middle School Student Revised Version consists of 37 statements about school conditions, for example, "Teachers at my school help us children with our problems." Students respond on a three-point scale, according to how much they agree with the statement. The scale is labeled "Agree," "Not sure," and "Disagree." The questions on the elementary and middle school version cover the areas of fairness, safety and discipline, parent involvement, sharing of resources, student interpersonal relations, and student-teacher relations.

High School Student Revised Version

This version consists of 42 descriptive statements about prevailing school conditions, for example, "Teachers at my school help students with their problems." Students respond on a five-point Likert scale ranging from "Strongly agree" to "Strongly disagree," depending on how well they think the statement describes their school. The High School Student Revised Version includes items that cover the following aspects of school climate: safety and discipline, parent involvement, sharing of resources, school building, student interpersonal relations, and student-teacher relations.

Parent Revised Version

The Parent Revised Version consists of 41 descriptive statements about prevailing school conditions, for example, "At my child's school, parents have a great deal of confidence in the school staff." Parents respond on a five-point Likert scale ranging from "Strongly agree" to "Strongly disagree," depending on how well they think the statement describes their child's school. The parent version covers the following areas of school climate: academic focus, achievement motivation, principal caring and sensitivity, collaborative decision making, parent involvement, school building, school community relations, and student-teacher relations.

Staff Revised Version

The Staff Revised Version consists of 54 descriptive statements about prevailing school conditions, for example, "At this school, teachers find ways to motivate their students to learn." Staff members respond on a five-point Likert scale ranging from "Strongly agree" to "Strongly disagree" depending on how well they think the statement describes their school. The Staff Version covers the following school climate areas: achievement motivation, collaborative decision making, equity and fairness, leadership, safety and discipline, school building, school/parent/community relations, staff dedication to student learning, and staff expectations.

Timelines (When)

"When" refers to the times and frequency of data collection for each variable. Issues to consider when deciding on the time and frequency of data collection include:

- The type of data to be collected, for example, achievement, behavior, average daily attendance, parent involvement, or attitudes and opinions. If the district produces the data, when are the statistics available and how useful are they? Some districts use the attendance information for one day of the year, perhaps October 15, as the average yearly attendance for the school. Other districts use the average attendance of students throughout the entire school year as the average yearly attendance figure. The second measure is better than the first because it gives a more accurate picture of student attendance.

- The activities that are taking place at the school or district during proposed data collection. For example, are students in the final week of preparing for exams?
- The manner in which data collection will affect the flow of activities in the school. For example, would it be better to distribute surveys during the first or last period?

Ideally, you should collect the first set of data before you begin implementation of SDP, or as close to the beginning as possible. Having data prior to implementation allows you to have a picture of what your school or district is like before the intervention begins. This is called *baseline data*, because it is the base from which you begin. You need to have empirical data on what the school was like before you began implementation, so that you know what changes take place after implementation begins and as it deepens.

For optimal comparison purposes, the data should be collected around the same time every year (or month) and in the same manner. Variability in the time and manner in which data are collected affects the uniformity of the data and calls into question the comparisons across the years.

Putting the Assessment Plan Together

Now, it's time to put all the pieces together. You can use Figure 17.3 or 17.4, adding your own questions and/or additional variables, measures, and times of data collection.

SHARING AND USING THE RESULTS

In terms of analyzing the data and sharing the results, think of who will be the audience for these results. The results should be shared with all staff, with parents, and with students as the primary stakeholders. Some schools display the more positive results on the bulletin board. Others put them in newsletters or include them in district and state reports. Some schools even include the results in their accreditation review materials.

Presenting the Data

Presentation of the results is important. Graphs show the information in an interesting, easily understandable, and meaningful format, as Figures 17.5 through 17.11 demonstrate. In the section that follows, we will use the graphs to look at

- implementation (Figures 17.5 and 17.6)
- changes in school climate (Figures 17.7–17.10)
- achievement trends over time (Figures 17.11–17.12)

(Text continues on page 239)

Figure 17.3 Putting the pieces together

Question	Data to Be Collected (What)	Data Source (Who)	Measuring Tool (How)	What Time and How Often (When)
1. What is the extent of SDP implementation in the school, and how is it changing over time?	SDP implementation	Staff, team members, some parents	SIQA	Yearly in February/March
2. Is school climate improving?	School climate	Students, staff, parents	SDP climate surveys	Yearly in February/March
3. Are students' social skills increasing?	Students' social skills			
4. Have student attitudes toward learning improved?	Student attitudes toward learning			
5. Has student behavior improved?	Student behavior			
6. Has student academic achievement increased?	Student academic achievement			
7. Has parent involvement increased?	Parent involvement			

Figure 17.4 Assessment worksheet

Question	What	Who	How	When

Figure 17.5 School Development Program: Variation in implementation across schools, 2002

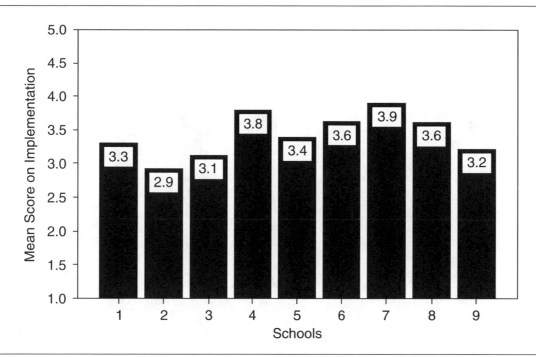

Figure 17.6 Change in SDP implementation, 2001–2002, School A

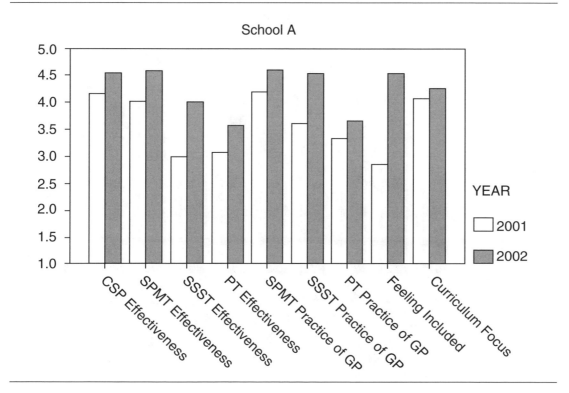

Figure 17.7 Staff school climate perceptions: Mean scores by school, 2001 and 2003

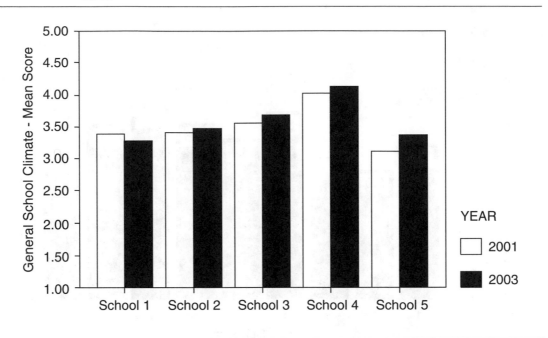

Figure 17.8 Staff perceptions on school climate variables: School 5, Mean Scores, 2001 and 2003

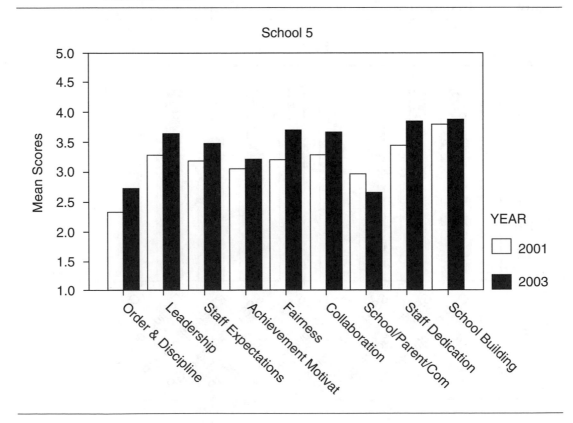

Figure 17.9 Staff perceptions on order and discipline, by school, 2001 and 2003

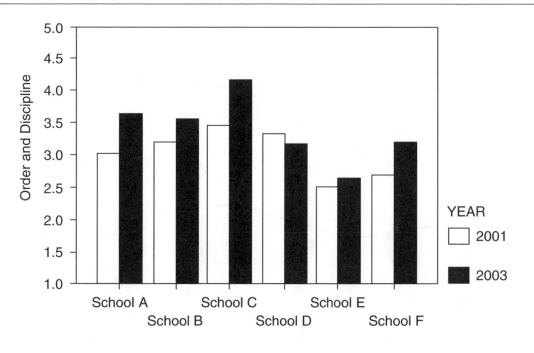

Figure 17.10 Staff perceptions on order and discipline, by school, 2001, 2002, and 2003

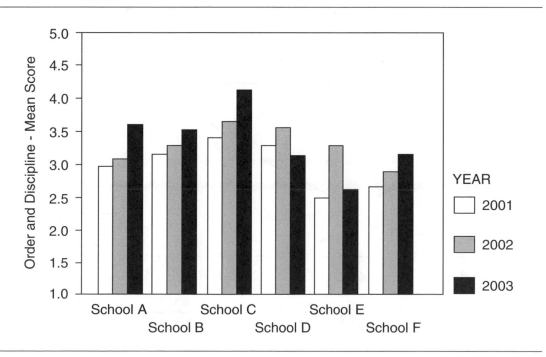

Figure 17.11 Grade 4 mathematics: Students meeting or exceeding state standards

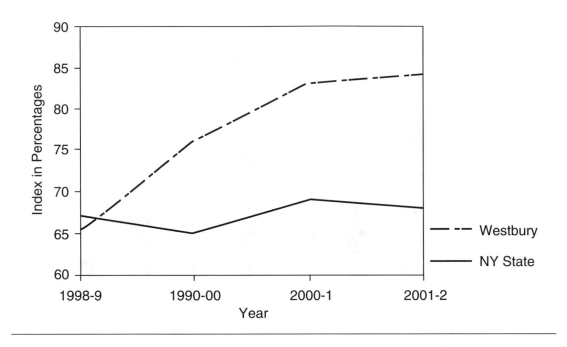

Figure 17.12 Grade 8 English language arts: Students meeting or exceeding state standards

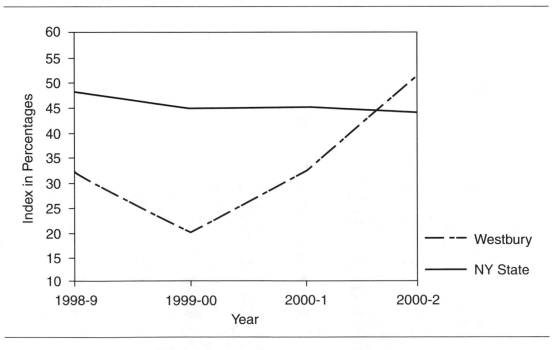

Figure 17.5 shows the mean score for nine schools on SDP implementation, using SIQA as the measure. At a glance, you can see that there is considerable variation in implementation across schools in the district. Figure 17.6 shows changes for one school in nine areas of implementation over the period of one year. This chart indicates improvement in all areas, but especially in SSST effectiveness, SSST practice of the guiding principles, and staff members' feelings of being included.

Figures 17.7 and 17.8 illustrate changes in school climate over two years. Figure 17.7 shows changes in general school climate for all schools in the district. Figure 17.8 shows changes for School 5 on each of the school climate variables, using the SDP School Climate Survey, staff version. Figures 17.9 and 17.10 show changes on only the Order and Discipline variable, but in Figure 17.9, information is given for only 2001 and 2003. Figure 17.10 gives the same information but for all three years.

When we examine Figure 17.9, we see that all schools except School D improved from 2001 to 2003. When we examine Figure 17.10, we see that all schools improved in Order and Discipline in 2002 but declined in Schools D and E in 2003. This information should prompt an examination of what happened with those two schools from 2002 to 2003 that may have had an impact on Order and Discipline. The next step would be to decide what should be done to improve conditions in those two schools. If the survey was not administered in 2002, we would not have had that information. This is one reason I recommend that SIQA and the School Climate Survey be administered every year for the first five years of implementation, and then every two to three years thereafter. Consistent high quality requires constant monitoring.

Figures 17.11 and 17.12 demonstrate achievement trends over time. Figure 17.11 shows that while the percentage of Grade 4 students that met or exceeded New York State standards in math remained about the same from 1998–1999 to 2001–2002, there was a huge increase in the percentage of Westbury students meeting or exceeding those standards. Figure 17.12 shows that while there was a slight decline in the percentage of Grade 8 students meeting or exceeding New York State standards in English Language Arts, there was a huge increase in the percentage of Westbury students overall meeting or exceeding those standards.

Using the Data

To wrap up this section, let's talk about how you can use your data collection results to improve the school. What group of people, do you think, might use these results to bring about improvement? While input from all stakeholders should be sought, of course, the SPMT would be primarily responsible.

Several worthwhile uses for the results have been suggested by workshop participants, including

- planning
- staff development and inservice workshops
- identifying urgent needs and problems that need immediate attention
- studying how you interact with people
- looking at and building on strengths
- helping people stay the course
- improving the image of the school in the community

Consistent with the action research approach, we invite you to suggest any other ways in which the results can be used to help schools.

REFERENCES

Borman, G. D., Hewes, G. M., Overman, L. T., & Brown, S. (2003). Comprehensive school reform and achievement: A meta-analysis. *Review of Educational Research, 73,* 125–230.

Comer, J. P., Haynes, N. M., Joyner, E. T., & Ben-Avie, M. (1996). (Eds.). *Rallying the whole village: The Comer Process for change in education.* New York: Teachers College Press.

Cook, T. D., Habib, F. H., Phillips, M., Settersten, R. A., Shagle, S. C., & Degirmencioglu, S. M. (1999). Comer's School Development Program in Prince George's County, Maryland: A theory-based evaluation. *American Educational Research Journal, 36*(3), 543–597.

Cook, T. D., Murphy, R. F., & Hunt, H. D. (2000). Comer's School Development Program in Chicago: A theory-based evaluation. *American Educational Research Journal, 37*(2), 535–597.

Emmons, C. L., Haynes, N., & Comer, J. P. (2002). *School Climate Survey* (Rev. ed.). New Haven, CT: Comer School Development Program.

Emmons, C. L., Haynes, N., Comer, J. P., Cook, T., & Joyner, E. T. (1999). *School Implementation Questionnaire—Abbreviated.* New Haven, CT: Comer School Development Program.

Joyner, E. T. (2004). The School Development Program Implementation Life Cycle: A guide for planned change. In E. T. Joyner, M. Ben-Avie, & J. P. Comer (Eds.), *Transforming school leadership and management to support student learning and development.* Thousand Oaks, CA: Corwin Press.

Millsap, M. A., Chase, A., Obeidallah, D., Perez-Smith, A., Brigham, N., & Johnson, K. (with Cook, T., & Hunt, D.). (1997). *Evaluation of Detroit's Comer School and Families Initiative* (2nd-year progress report). Cambridge, MA: Abt Associates.

Millsap, M. A., Chase, A., Obeidallah, D., Perez-Smith, A., Brigham, N., & Johnson, K. (with Cook, T., & Hunt, D.). (2000). *Evaluation of Detroit's Comer School and Families Initiative* (Final report). Cambridge, MA: Abt Associates.

Noblit, G. W., Malloy, W. W., & Malloy, C. E. (2001). (Eds.). *The kids got smarter.* Cresskill, NJ: Hampton Press.

Noblit, G., Malloy, C., Malloy, W., Villenas, S., Groves, P., Jennings, M., Patterson, J., & Rayle, J. (1998) *Creating successful urban schools: The School Development Program and school improvement* (Report submitted to the Rockefeller Foundation). Chapel Hill, NC: University of North Carolina at Chapel Hill.

Payne, C. (1994). *The Comer School Development Process in Chicago: An interim report* (For the John D. and Catherine T. MacArthur Foundation). Evanston, IL: Northwestern University.

School Development Program. (2000). *The School Development Program Quality Process Documentation Inventory.* New Haven, CT: Yale Child Study Center.

Stringfield, S., Millsap, M. A., Yoder, N., Brigham, N., Nesselrodt, P., Schaffer, E., Karweit, N., Dolan, L., Levin, M., & Smith, L. (with Gamse, B., Puma, M., Rosenblum, S., Herman, R., Bedinger, S., Randall, B., & Stevens, R.). (1995). *Urban and suburban/rural special strategies for educating disadvantaged children: Third year report.* Washington, DC: Office of Planning, U.S. Department of Education.

Turnbull, B., Fiester, L., & Wodatch, J. (1997). *"A process is not a program": An early look at the Comer Process in Community School District 13* (A report to the Rockefeller Foundation). Washington, DC: Policy Studies Associates.

Wong, P. L., Oberman, I., Mintrop, H., & Gamson, D. (McLaughlin, M. W., Project Director). (1996). *Evaluation of the San Francisco Bay Area School Reform Portfolio: Summary report.* Palo Alto, CA: Stanford University.

AUTHOR'S NOTE: This research was funded by a grant from the United States Department of Education, Office of Educational Research and Innovation.

18

The Best Education for All Our Children

Edward T. Joyner

Academic success for all children requires adults to move past deficit perspectives about children and to embrace developmental perspectives. The SDP's emphasis on the six developmental pathways ensures that all children and adults can grow and thrive to the best of each individual's ability.

Most children in our society are treated better than children have been treated in any society in the history of the world. But despite that, we as adults need to keep pressing on. Too many of our children are at risk of failing—not only in school but throughout their lives—because they have been born into disadvantaged circumstances that leave them unchallenged, alienated, or worse. We have a responsibility to these children and, through them, to our society as a whole. To fulfill this responsibility, it is critically important for us to provide all our children with the best education, both in and out of schools. Education is, after all, the foundation of equality and the foundation of a free society.

GETTING PAST "DEFICIT" PERSPECTIVES ABOUT CHILDREN

There have been a number of theories and explanations as to why low-income youth lag behind their more advantaged peers in achievement. Many of these explanations view problems within the children, their families, and/or their communities as the causes of limited success in school. Others suggest that the nature of schooling itself does not adequately address the needs of poor children. Among the most prominent of these theories are the following:

- *The deficit explanation:* Underachievement of low-income and African American children is a consequence of their having been reared in homes and families that inadequately socialize them for success in schools.

- *The cultural-ecological explanation:* Institutions that educate these children devalue their cultures and essentially try to force them to assume roles and adopt values that are at odds with their beliefs, values, and ways.

- *The community ecology explanation:* Political, economic, and social forces in the community create a climate in which it is difficult to influence young people to view schooling as a means to better their lives.

- *The genetic explanation:* Children of color are intellectually inferior due to genetic factors.

- *The interactionist explanation:* Individuals who teach these students have low expectations of them because of their subordinate status in the larger society. Consequently, the students learn less, expect less from themselves, and get locked into a downward spiral of low self-esteem and low school achievement.

At the School Development Program (SDP), we have different explanations. We believe that academic failure results when children who are underdeveloped or differently developed do not receive developmentally appropriate education, in effect, exposing them to educational malpractice.

Operating with a deficit perspective, the community sends a message to schools, and schools relay the message to the students: "If you don't score high on a test, we're going to punish you." Instead of telling children, "We're going to develop you. We're going to help you compensate for your unearned disadvantages," the children hear, "We're going to punish you and label you, and we're going to label the people who work with you. And we're going to make sure that you continue to label yourselves. And then when you have children, you can label them." Thus the district picks on the principal, the principal picks on the teachers, and the teachers badger the kids.

GETTING PAST "TEACHER-PROOF" SCHOOL REFORMS

One of the most exhausting things about the deficit perspective is that it labels not only children but also school staff. There are so many attitudes about what teachers and administrators can't do that some school reforms are purposely designed to be "teacher-proof" and "district-proof." The reformers come into a school and tell the staff, "You must do this, this, this, this, and this, and don't change a thing." These paint-by-the-number reforms tend to be applied to low-performing schools and districts on the assumption that "these people don't know what to do, so we must tell them."

But as a society, we have not treated public school educators with the respect that such a calling deserves. We have not provided prospective teachers with the length, breadth, and depth of content and experience that they need to teach well. And we have given third-class resources to many poor rural and urban school districts while demanding that the educators who work there produce first-class results. The children, parents, and educators who labor under such circumstances are heroic, but they must receive adequate support lest we become a nation of haves and have-nots.

MOVING TO A DEVELOPMENTAL PERSPECTIVE ABOUT CHILDREN

Part of the answer lies in two major efforts: to help Americans understand human development and to translate this understanding into action.

If wealthy children had to weather some of the misfortunes that a lot of at-risk kids have weathered, then they'd probably perform at the same lower level. Likewise, some young people may score at the highest level on standardized tests, but if they aren't well developed socially, if they don't make good ethical decisions, then all of that intellectual potential will go to waste because they'll never get a chance to use it, never be in a position where it will pay off for them.

In our culture as a whole, even though we need more academic support for our students, the problem is not test performance. The problem is antisocial behavior. So, how do we help troubled children develop ethics and positive habits that support society and lead to personal and economic success? How do we get them to recognize all their choices and to select only those that lead to a healthy future? In the past, many of these children have been shunted aside. But SDP's attitude is this: *Individual programs are negotiable, but individual children are not.*

HELPING ADULTS GROW AND THRIVE

Most educators come into the school system for righteous reasons, and yet many have tremendous doubts about themselves. Some are less well prepared than they need to be. As such, they are imperfect models for the children, and they know it. They want to do better, and yet they feel that to go out and develop new skills will take more energy than they have. To these teachers, SDP says: You can take heart and have courage as you reach for your personal best. You can be patient with yourself too, as long as you are trying. Keep on reading, work with a mentor, and take advantage of as many opportunities as you can to improve. Improving as a professional is a skill, like any other. And all skills get easier with practice.

Working on weaknesses is the height of professionalism. You know that you're operating on a high level when you can say, "I'm not satisfied just because I did this particular technique well. I want to get better at it. You know, if I got an 8 on the last exhibit, I want to get a 9 on the next one, or a 10. And even with perfection—I want to get better to make it more consistent."

SDP offers the structures, operations, and the process through which educators, support staff, parents, and the larger community can collaborate in a mutually supportive relationship to help *adults and children* grow in each of the developmental pathways. More important, it provides a set of guiding principles or rules of engagement. The structures are meaningless if leaders from the various stakeholder groups fail to embrace them. These principles must be kept at the conscious level as participants address the challenges of collaboration. Faithful application of these principles, and taking the high ground on every issue, will create the trust needed for team learning and long-term success.

Working in this way is so delicate that it can be undermined by leaders and followers who place selfish interests above the goal of creating the best possible environment for teaching, learning, and development. When the waters are troubled by unhealthy expressions of anger, hidden agendas, finger-pointing, and harsh language, it is difficult to provide safe passage for children. This does not mean that constructive criticism is unwelcome; it is always welcome as long as it is accompanied by a helpful heart.

Thus instead of being teacher-proof, the developmental approach of SDP is, in fact, teacher- and parent- and administrator-proved, -improved, and -approved. We sit down together and figure out where a district or a school needs to go, and we work to help people build the bridges to get there by creating a society in which everybody is learning on a regular basis.

In our way of working, there's no penalty for failure as long as that failure comes while you are actively trying to find a better way. Like scientists, we recognize that failure is a way to eliminate unworkable strategies: "Okay, that didn't work, and we don't have to try it again. But what have we learned from trying it? Now, let's build that learning into the next thing we try." And the SDP model of the six developmental pathways creates a huge field from which to harvest ideas for that next try.

This constant interest in better ways to accomplish growth and development generates an atmosphere in SDP schools that you can feel from the moment you walk in the door. And that interest, that excitement, that experimentation, and that expectation of good things create an upbeat mood with a contagious set of behaviors. Adults in SDP schools consistently show these behaviors, and the kids and the community pick them up automatically. We like to say, "Values are caught not taught," and the values that are caught in our schools propel students toward success.

HELPING EVERY CHILD MAKE THE GRADE

Our society needs the next generation to be good parents, good workers, and good leaders—to provide medical care, to make critical decisions about the military and politics, to advance the culture. Who is to say where the discoverer of a cure for cancer or the next great peacemaker in the world may be living? Looking at history, we know that such a creative genius can be born into any circumstance. So, the first order of business is to make sure that good schools are everywhere.

Our second order of business is to make sure that we have personal relationships with all our children. Right now, the social distance between many adults and adolescents is so great that their peer groups are far more powerful than they should be. Educators must realize that each child is important because he or she is unique. When we open our eyes and hearts to who each child really is, right now, we create a priceless environment of caring and support. Both children and their teachers flourish in schools with that kind of environment.

Think about the Native American beliefs that every living thing has a right to be here and to grow to its fullest potential, that we're all interrelated. Clearly, we need to believe that all our children are worthy of our best efforts, whether they become street sweepers or surgeons.

The kind of collaboration necessary to achieve this will require that we work through the anxiety, confusion, and chaos that is part of any struggle by a diverse group of people who are moving toward change. But when the goal is clear, and when people have the will to work together and the structure that makes their work possible, then diversity becomes a strength.

In SDP schools, disparate groups walk together every day, and they do not get weary in their journey. Their goal is so highly prized that self-interest is subsumed by the group's interest. And that group interest—that prized goal—is a healthy and productive future for all our children.

Index

NOTE: Page numbers in *italic* type refer to figures, tables, or boxes.

**CORWIN
PRESS**

The Corwin Press logo—a raven striding across an open book—represents the union of courage and learning. Corwin Press is committed to improving education for all learners by publishing books and other professional development resources for those serving the field of K–12 education. By providing practical, hands-on materials, Corwin Press continues to carry out the promise of its motto: **"Helping Educators Do Their Work Better."**